Restoring Cursed Earth

Restoring Cursed Earth

Appraising Environmental Policy Reforms in Eastern Europe and Russia

EDITED BY MATTHEW R. AUER

ROWMAN & LITTLEFIELD PUBLISHERS, INC.
Lanham • Boulder • New York • Toronto • Oxford

ROWMAN & LITTLEFIELD PUBLISHERS, INC.

Published in the United States of America
by Rowman & Littlefield Publishers, Inc.
A wholly owned subsidiary of The Rowman & Littlefield Publishing Group, Inc.
4501 Forbes Boulevard, Suite 200, Lanham, MD 20706
www.rowmanlittlefield.com

P.O. Box 317, Oxford OX2 9RU, United Kingdom

Copyright © 2004 by Rowman & Littlefield Publishers, Inc.

British Library Cataloguing in Publication Information Available

Library of Congress Cataloging-in-Publication Data

Restoring cursed earth : appraising environmental policy reforms in Eastern Europe and
  Russia / [edited by] Matthew R. Auer.
    p. cm.
  Includes bibliographical references and index.
  ISBN 0-7425-2915-0 (alk. paper)
    1. Environmental policy—Europe, Eastern. 2. Environmental policy—Russia
(Federation) I. Auer, Matthew R., 1966–.

GE190.E852R47 2004
363.7'056'0647–dc22   2004041758

Printed in the United States of America

⊖™ The paper used in this publication meets the minimum requirements of American
National Standard for Information Sciences—Permanence of Paper for Printed Library
Materials, ANSI/NISO Z39.48-1992.

Contents

Contents

Acknowledgments

Appraising environmental policy reforms in the post-Communist Eastern bloc is a project for a large team of researchers, and while the five contributors to *Restoring Cursed Earth* were equal to the task, they could not have completed their work without ample help from others.

Eszter Tompos, for example, provided invaluable research assistance for the chapter on Hungary, and Maria Reff helped master the list of works cited for that chapter.

Natalja Kohv and Petr Stepanek provided hard-to-find information for the chapter on the Czech Republic

Anto Raukas's assistance in helping develop the chapter on Estonia is gratefully acknowledged. No one is more knowledgeable than Anto about the people and organizations responsible for that nation's environmental rehabilitation. Helle Kuuk's knowledge and insights on the Estonian environmental context were no less vital.

Henry Hale and David Ransel provided helpful comments on earlier drafts of the chapter on Russia.

Barbara Jancar Webster's insights on environmental institutions in Central and Eastern Europe and Russia were helpful to me well before the first word of the introduction was drafted.

Later drafts of each chapter were strengthened by excellent recommendations from five anonymous referees. Their help notwithstanding, all omissions or errors of fact or opinion are the responsibility of the contributors or myself.

Matt Hammon's help was key in bringing the book to Rowman & Littlefield as well as in guiding later stages of the book's development. Thank you also to

Kirstyn Leuner and Jeska Horgan-Kobelski at Rowman & Littlefield and Julie May at Indiana University for assistance with text formatting.

I am grateful for grant support from Indiana University's Dean of Faculties and Research and University Graduate School.

Last but not least, I thank Anne Auer for putting in more than her fair share of child care hours during all stages of development of *Restoring Cursed Earth*.

Chapter 1

Lessons from Leaders and Laggards: Appraising Environmental Reforms in Central and Eastern Europe and Russia

Matthew R. Auer

When the iron curtain lifted over Central and Eastern Europe (CEE), a grimy curtain still separated East from West. The region's polluted air and water caught Westerners' attention then, and for somewhat different reasons, people both within and outside CEE and Russia are mindful of the former Eastern bloc's environmental problems, today. It is this continuing, broad-based, transatlantic interest in the region's environment that commends a book on the topic, and not merely because it is important or rightful to appraise the relative successes and shortcomings of environmental policies that affect the health of more than 270 million people and the well-being of millions of acres of natural habitat.

Since 1989, governmental and nongovernmental actors in CEE and Russia as well as influential external actors have endeavored to heal the Eastern bloc's environmental wounds and bolster governments' capacities to tackle current and future environmental problems. *Restoring Cursed Earth* strives to answer three related questions about this decade and a half of environmental reform efforts, namely: What are the accomplishments and shortcomings of these reforms? To what extent have external actors helped or hindered environmental reforms in CEE and Russia? Does accession of CEE countries to the European Union (EU) promise better environmental conditions in CEE and in Europe, generally?

The Environment in Central and Eastern Europe and Russia: Why It Still Matters

In 1991, *National Geographic* magazine displayed on its cover two soot-stained boys posing not far from one of Romania's great environmental eyesores—a carbon black factory in the town of Copşa Mică (Thompson, 1991: 36-69). From that story, many learned for the first time about the public health privations of peoples living in heavily industrialized regions of Central and Eastern Europe and the former Soviet Union (FSU).

In fact, the environmental story in these regions was more complex than the popular media first depicted it. Regarding Poland, for example, Magnus Andersson writes (1999: v),

> In many countries Poland has the reputation of being the "dirty man of Europe." There are certainly many "hot spots" in Poland but this is not the whole truth about the Polish environment. . . . there are huge areas of unspoiled nature in Poland such as the Bieszczady mountains in the south, the Baltic coastline in the north, and the so-called Green Lungs in the northeast.

Nevertheless, it was the photographs of environmentally damaged landscapes and peoples that awakened public interest in former Eastern bloc environmental affairs. Only the hardest heart could not be moved by the grim images and testimonials of those who worked in or lived downwind from the regions' giant steel foundries, smelters, coal mines, and power plants. The Eastern bloc's environmental problems had the same galvanizing effect on the public conscience as does any major natural disaster.

In the early 1990s, public aid agencies and international environmental nongovernmental organizations (NGOs) responded to the environmental health crises in CEE and FSU with financial assistance and technical expertise. But these actors also had a broader view than did the media about the overall environmental situation, recognizing that former Eastern bloc countries boasted large areas of intact wilderness and critical habitats for plants and animals found nowhere else in continental Europe. Hence, for example, the World Bank took an early interest in stanching pollution in the Danube River Basin and the World Wildlife Fund spearheaded conservation efforts in the Carpathian Mountains.

Today, self-interest, more so than compassion or recognition of the Eastern bloc's unique environmental attributes, keeps outsiders attentive to environmental goings-on in CEE and in Russia. To some extent, self-interest has always motivated Western participation in the region's cleanup. The United States' and European Union's debate with Ukraine about the future of the remaining nuclear power plant at Chernobyl and similar discussions between the West and Lithuania over atomic reactors in Ignalina began in the early 1990s and continue as this book goes to press. Of course, Western European countries are eager to avert another Chernobyl-like disaster—the 1986 accident mortgaged the health of thousands of Ukrainians and Belarusians and perhaps thousands more who are yet unborn. But from the beginning, the West's interest in shuttering Chernobyl and Ignalina was not merely about the health of people living right beside the plants, but of citizens living hundreds of miles downwind, in Germany, Sweden, Norway, and beyond (Darst, 2001).

As contributors to this volume attest, the environment continues to take center stage in bilateral and multilateral discussions between CEE and FSU countries and their neighbors, and self-interest explains why that is so. For example, Austria grumbles about a Czech nuclear power plant that lacks adequate containment structures (chapter 2). Finns shrug disappointedly at the latest setback to Estonian plans to remediate that country's highly polluting oil shale fired power stations, whose copious dust and sulfur emissions potentially threaten Finland's forests (chapter 5).

But environmental self-interest extends beyond bilateral relations, playing a major role in the drama of European Union enlargement. Environmental conditions in CEE countries affect the EU enlargement process, and while it is unlikely to be the *only* factor that determines whether a candidate joins or is left behind, environmental factors are consequential. Once CEE countries join the EU, the CEE's environment—clean or dirty—is an official part of the Union's environment. It is expedient for the EU to compel CEE countries to reform domestic environmental laws and policies, and in some cases, make painful economic trade-offs and adjustments today, rather than inherit countries in a messy state of transition tomorrow.

It is not as though CEE countries have been left to fend for themselves in redressing their environmental ills and in building up new domestic environmental institutions. The EU has made billions of euros available to facilitate candidate countries' adoption of EU environmental regulatory standards and to undertake programmatic reforms. The promises and pitfalls of EU-sponsored aid are considered at length in the chapters on the Czech Republic (chapter 2) and Hungary (chapter 3) whereas the consequences of aid from other external actors are key concerns in the chapters on Estonia (chapter 5) and Russia (chapter 6).

The preaccession instrument known as Poland and Hungary Assistance for the Restructuring of the Economy (PHARE), which provides assistance for institution-building and investments, disbursed nearly €1 billion between 1990 and 2002 in the environmental area. Since 2000, another €1.04 billion has been available annually for financing of major transport and environmental infrastructure projects through the EU's Instrument for Structural Policies for Pre-Accession (ISPA) (EEA, 2002e: 7). The EU concedes that its financial assistance will amount to only a fraction of countries' investment needs, and those needs are substantial (EEA, 2002e: 12). The European Commission estimated that for the ten CEE candidate countries, between €80 and 100 billion were required to conform with EU environmental legislation—equivalent to an average of around 2 to 3 percent of annual GDP for each accession country for several years to come. For some countries, the level of needed investments as a proportion of GDP is much higher; in Bulgaria, for example, it is 11 percent (EEA, 2000d: 7).

Active versus Passive Pollution Reduction

The flood of sad stories about polluted towns and ailing children that poured forth from CEE and Russia in the early 1990s has slowed down considerably in recent years. This is not merely because those stories have been told already; it is due to slowly improving environmental conditions in many parts of the former Eastern bloc. How has this environmental recovery come to pass? Alternative explanations include: the West's provision of generous foreign aid for environmental protection; the implementation of effective, domestic environmental policy reforms; private investment in environmental protection; economic and industrial recession; or some combination of all these factors. Opinions vary from strong praise for policy-driven environmental successes in CEE (Lalasz and Greengrass, 2002) to those who attribute only a small fraction of environmental gains to policy reforms and programs (Andersen, 2002).

What is not disputed is that pollution pressures on the air and waterways of CEE countries and of Russia diminished during the 1990s. Improvements in air quality were the most obvious. Consider, for example, the steep decline in the region's emissions of major air pollutants, such as sulfur dioxide, nitrogen oxide, and carbon dioxide. Figure 1.1 shows pollution trends for countries in the region that emit large quantities of sulfur dioxide on an absolute basis.

FIGURE 1.1
Transition Economies with Relatively Large
Sulfur Dioxide Emissions (1990-2000)

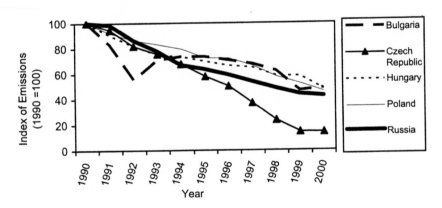

Source: European Environment Agency, 2002a.

FIGURE 1.2
Transition Economies with Relatively Small
Sulfur Dioxide Emissions (1990-2000)

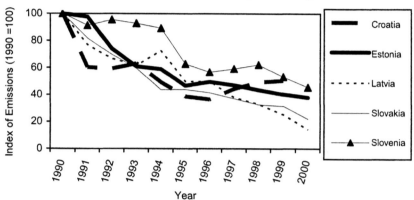

Year

Source: European Environment Agency, 2002a.

As was true of the large emitters, CEE countries with relatively smaller absolute levels of sulfur dioxide emissions cut these discharges by half or more by the end of the 1990s (figure 1.2).

Determining whether and to what extent declining pollution emissions resulted from intentional policy design or merely by default is to tease out "active" and "passive" forces for environmental change, respectively. Determining which factors were more consequential is a complex endeavor (Pavlínek and Pickles, 2000: 246). It is not a primary aim of this book to find, with mathematical precision, the more important set of causal variables. However, contributors to this volume are keenly interested in clarifying and illuminating the effects of the *active* forces for environmental change in the region, in particular.

Active, intentional efforts to reduce pollution and repair the environment, we contend, are manifestations of institutions at work. We adopt Douglass North's conception of institutions as a starting point for our project, namely that they

> are the rules of the game in a society, or more formally, are the humanly devised constraints that shape interaction. In consequence they structure incentives in human exchange, whether political, social or economic. (1990: 3)

Embedded in planned efforts to protect the environment are rules, conventions, and the incentives that are shaped by these rules and conventions. Consider, for example, a homeowner's decision to recycle aluminum cans from her household rubbish. A deposit law on beverage containers may inspire her to collect and sell back empty cans, in which case both rules and incentives motivate her behavior. Alternatively, a provision for mandatory recycling may compel her to recycle. Rules and incentives are at play, again: the homeowner wishes to avoid being fined for contravening the recycling law, and hence she complies. A third scenario finds the homeowner recycling because she deems it better for the environment. In this case, formal rules and incentives are less important than are informal conventions—in this case, conforming to social norms. In *Restoring Cursed Earth*, we explore a wide variety of institutions for environmental protection, ranging from those grounded in formal laws and regulations to market-oriented rules to informal codes of conduct.

The bulk of evidence suggests that post-Communist era institutions for environmental protection in CEE and Russia—many of which got off the ground in the early 1990s—did not affect environmental quality until later in the decade. During the first half of the decade, exogenous economic forces, including falling incomes, declining rates of consumption, and the collapse of heavy industry were more important determinants of environmental quality than were policies designed to rein in pollution emissions or protect natural habitats.

Relief from environmental stress in the early 1990s would appear to have been the bright lining to an otherwise gloomy period of economic disruption and social turmoil. But the downward sloping pollution trends demand closer inspection: While many types of pollution emissions declined in absolute terms during the early part of the decade, in relative terms, certain types of emissions actually *increased*. To illustrate, in the early transition years, in the Czech Republic, Slovakia, and Hungary, pollution discharges per unit industrial output rose for certain classes of air pollutants. In the Czech Republic, gross industrial output contracted by 32 percent between 1989 and 1992; however, emissions of particulate matter, sulfur dioxide, and nitrogen oxide decreased by no more than 26 percent during that same period (Pavlínek and Pickles, 2000: 316 passim). Many CEE enterprises used increasing amounts of energy per unit output during the early 1990s, but this problem was masked by the collapse of goods production, and especially that of pollution-prone heavy industrial goods (and hence, absolute levels of pollution emissions decreased).

In the second half the 1990s, some CEE countries appeared to master the puzzle of stimulating economic growth without increasing pollution intensity levels, allaying worries that once economic growth picked up, pollution levels would continue where they had left off during the Communist era. In the highly industrialized Upper Silesian region of Poland, for example, emissions of particulates reached record levels in 1991, and fell over the next two years in tandem with the region's economic collapse. But the trend lines diverged in the 1993-1997 period. Industrial production perked up in the region, rising nearly 50 percent from the recessionary lows of the early 1990s; during the same period, emissions of particulates fell more than 15 percent (Hughes and Lovei, 1999).

Similarly in Estonia, emissions of lead fell by more than 60 percent between 1991 and 1993, contemporaneous with the steep recessions in that nation's transport, oil shale combustion, and cement industries. But lead emissions continued to fall almost by half over the next five years, even as the economy recovered (Estonian Environment Information Centre, 2001: 35). In this case, the earmarks of intentional, institutional design are readily apparent. The government resolved to reduce lead in petrol, in step with political commitments made by European ministers at the Third Environment for Europe Conference in Sofia, Bulgaria, in 1995. There, ministers pledged to phase out leaded gasoline by 2005. Estonia had reduced its reliance on leaded petrol from nearly 100 percent in the early 1990s to around 10 percent in 1998 (Estonian Environment Information Centre, 2001: 35).

Even more surprising to environmentalists, Estonia's carbon dioxide emissions, which fell precipitously between 1991 and 1993, did not resume their climb when the economy recovered in the later 1990s. Over the 1990-1998 period, CO_2 emissions were cut in half (figure 1.3).

The institutional determinants of Estonia's environmental performance were more complex in this latter case. In part, lower CO_2 emissions were second and third order consequences of economic policy reforms adopted in the 1990s. For example, investor-friendly tax laws encouraged large inflows of foreign direct investment, and with it, more energy efficient equipment that replaced old capital stock. The service sector, and especially tourism, became a more important part of the economy as did relatively less-polluting light industries.

But CO_2 emissions reduction in other sectors resulted from a combination of deliberate action and unintended consequences. Consider primary energy production in Estonia, one of that country's key exports. Beginning in 1989, prices were liberalized for carbon-intensive fuels such as oil, oil shale, and natural gas, encouraging large domestic consumers of these fuels to become more energy efficient. Technology-driven changes helped reduce final energy

FIGURE 1.3

National Income and Carbon Emissions Trends in Estonia, 1990-1998

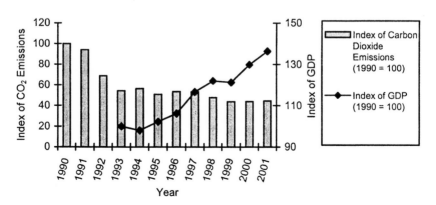

Source: Statistikaamet, 2003.

consumption in Estonia by 370 percent between 1991 and 1999. But even more important drivers were declining energy consumption due to the general collapse of industrial production in the first half of the decade combined with decreased household consumption, and a steep drop-off in export-oriented production of oil shale and oil shale generated electricity (Kraav, 2000). Hence, at least part of Estonia's environmental recovery occurred by default, namely by a sharp economic slowdown in its vital, export-oriented, oil shale industries. It is conceivable that a strong economic recovery in the heavily polluting oil shale sector could eventually set back progress in the cleanup of Estonia's air, waterways, and soils.

Poland's environmental revival also reflects a mix of intentional policies and progress by passive happenstance, though by its environmental ministry's estimation, the contribution of the former significantly outweighs the latter. Polish authorities assert that reduced discharges of untreated sewage, declining emissions of various air pollutants and other environmental improvements in the 1990s "were connected with recession in the economy only in small part." More significant were implementation of its National Environmental Policy by central and local administrators, new laws and regulations, and the introduction of market-oriented pollution control tools (UN, 1997). Some experts would agree: John Clark and Daniel Cole (1998: 6-7), for example, stress the rule of law, the strength of the economy, and the vitality of civil society as key determinants of successful environmental outcomes in Poland during the 1990s. But as Pavlínek and Pickles observe (2000: 247), in Poland as well as in the Czech Republic, Slovakia, and Hungary, relatively low absolute levels of pollution and high economic growth were fueled by the service, trade, and tourism sectors while heavy industries remained depressed.

Primary, pollution-intensive industries remain something of a wild card for future environmental quality in CEE and in Russia: if and when the business climate for sectors such as mining, steel, and industrial chemicals improve, it is conceivable that old environmentally unfriendly ghosts will haunt the region, again. Local pockets of severe, industrial pollution persist in some countries, especially in the southern tier and in non-Baltic republics of the former Soviet Union, where many primary industries are protected by the state, enforcement is spotty, and environmental upgrades are costly. Nevertheless, the record suggests that environmental legal and policy reforms *have* promoted environmental protection in the economically stronger CEE countries, even if these reforms are not directly responsible for every healthy environmental trend.

The magnitude of the benefits wrought by institutional reforms in countries like Poland, the Czech Republic, Hungary, Slovenia, and Estonia is apparent when compared with the disappointing results from poorer CEE countries that have either lacked the political will or the financial and technological wherewithal to protect the environment. Ukraine, Bulgaria, and Russia offer poignant examples of environmental privation resulting from institutional poverty.

The Donetsk-Kharkov region is Ukraine's industrial belt much as Upper Silesia is home to Poland's largest cluster of heavy industries. Even after the collapse of the Soviet Union, absolute levels of air pollution continued to rise in Donetsk-Kharkov until 1993, falling to Soviet-era levels by the mid-1990s. The region endured a steep economic recession during this period, but pollution emissions actually increased per unit economic output as the nation's leaders postponed plans to modernize several pollution-intensive enterprises. Meanwhile, the share of out-of-order and heavily depreciated equipment in factories grew through the mid-1990s due to shortages in operations and maintenance funds and a scarcity of trained workers to take care of environment-oriented tasks (Hughes and Lovei, 1999: 16).

The decline in industrial output also outpaced the decline of pollution emissions in Bulgaria. In fact, during the 1990s, Bulgarian export-oriented industries relying on antiquated equipment and few or no pollution controls held on to old markets in Western Europe, and in some cases, penetrated new markets. This was accomplished by the steep devaluation of the Bulgarian currency, increasing the competitiveness of Bulgarian exports on a price basis (Pavlínek and Pickles, 2000: 247). With the economy in a tailspin through the mid-1990s and growing only in the low single digits at century's end, the government was reluctant to enforce environmental regulations, and especially loath to regulate pollution from large factories producing goods for export. One result was that by the late 1990s, on a per capita basis, Bulgaria's sulfur dioxide emissions exceeded that of other large CEE countries by more than 100 percent (UNECE, 2001a: 182).

Reliance on out-of-order equipment was even more pronounced in Russia, and its environmentally pernicious effects were reinforced by authorities unwilling to make hard choices. The state overindulged enterprises that failed to pay taxes and provided generous transfers to failing industries even as official, direct subsidies were slashed (OECD, 1999: 35). Privatization of industries often resulted in the movement of state assets to enterprise managers and workers who had more incentive to maintain production and high employment than to increase efficiency and improve bottom line results. In these circumstances, industries had few incentives to become more energy efficient or to invest in environmental technologies. Reduced pollution emissions during the period were of the passive variety, almost entirely the result of economic decline rather than purposeful environmental decision making. Regarding air pollution, of the slow-reforming countries like Russia, the intensity of emissions fluctuated within a range of 10 percent on either side of the 1991 baseline, indicating no meaningful improvement in pollution discharges per unit economic output (Hughes and Lovei, 1999: 14; OECD, 1999: 44).

The Persistence of Communist-Era Institutions

Institutions—the rules that shape and constrain human interactions—can be either formal and explicit or informal and tacit. Contributors in this volume testify to the region's governments replacing old institutions, both formal and informal, with new and mostly formal ones. Contributors also expound on the resilience of the old institutions, particularly the informal ones.

Several chapters, including those on Hungary (chapter 3) and Russia (chapter 6) examine the permanence of old, environmentally unfriendly customs and practices from the Communist era. But the durability of Communist-era informal institutions is perhaps no better illustrated than in Romania's forestry sector (chapter 4).

Many informal institutions with direct or indirect effects on the Romanian environment originated in the Ceausescu regime as Communist Party functionaries, civil servants, and ordinary citizens alike participated in complex networks of illicit exchange, often just to make ends meet. Old ways of doing business die hard in Romania, where bribery, embezzlement, and graft are pervasive. Romania ranked 83rd in Transparency International's 2003 corruption perception index[1] out of 133 countries, placing it among nations with relatively high levels of perceived corruption. In the index, Romania ranked slightly lower (i.e., was perceived to be less corrupt) than Albania, Moldova, Macedonia, and Serbia and Montenegro, but more corrupt than eleven other CEE countries (Transparency International, 2003).[2]

In the 1990s, in counties throughout Romania, the forest service either participated directly in corrupt activities, such as illegal logging, or had knowledge of such activities. The highest ranking officers in the forest administration were embroiled in public scandals, including trading forestland in environmentally sensitive areas to commercial developers as well as collecting salaries from the state and from private forestry enterprises, simultaneously (chapter 4). These corrupt practices harkened back to the Communist era when supervisors and workers misused their office to bribe counterparts in allied industries or other sectors—a time-honored tradition in an economy plagued by chronic shortages of goods, and especially, consumer goods.

Institutionalists might conclude from the Romanian forestry case that informal institutions are resistant to changes demanded by new, formal institutions. As North contends (1990: 6),

> Although formal rules may change overnight as the result of political or judicial decisions, informal constraints embodied in customs, traditions, and codes of conduct are much more impervious to deliberate policies.

But it is not simply that informal institutions trumped official, reform-oriented rules in Romania. In addition, Romania's first generation of post-Communist politicians and lawmakers were guilty of perpetuating *formal* Communist-era institutions that abetted corrupt acts. Lawmakers authorized a single, state agency's monopoly over forest conservation, exploitation, and auditing functions—a formula from the 1980s—in an attempt to protect publicly owned forests from the chaos of decentralized forest management. In the process, Romania's forest service took advantage of glaring conflicts of interest, tempting line workers, supervisors, and chief officers to commit corrupt acts, with consequences not only for Romania's forests but for the reputations of civil servants and the integrity of the country's fragile democracy.

Natural resource management in post-Communist Romania was undermined by the persistence of formal, fundamentally unaltered, Communist-era rules as well as long-enduring informal rules. But bad environmental outcomes are not a forgone conclusion when pre-1989 institutions, whether formal or informal, persist in CEE and Russia. Some Communist-era institutions shaped good environmental outcomes in the years after the fall of the Berlin Wall. That may surprise readers who have been led to believe that no law or policy invented under Communism could produce environmentally friendly results.

In sharp contrast to the Romanian forestry case, where the institutional hangover from the Ceausescu era set back environmental reforms, Poland provides examples of Communist-era rules and procedures that were instrumental for institution-building after independence.

Many of Poland's recent environmental reforms were elaborations or refinements of older, formal norms for environmental protection rather than replacements of these institutions. Poland's 1980 Statute on the Protection and Shaping of the Environment is the basis for many of that country's sturdiest environmental institutions, including its system of environmental fees, its national environmental quality standards, and its pollution permitting system (Andersson, 1999: 180; Clark and Cole, 1998: 6). Fees and fines, for example, had been in existence since the 1960s; the 1980 Statute expanded their use. Nevertheless, these charges and penalties were set too low. Only in the 1990s did they rise high enough to gain notice by industrialists. Charges and fines increased by more than 1,000 percent in real terms during the 1990s (Andersson, 1999: 182).

Similarly, Poland launched wastewater treatment projects throughout the country in the 1980s, though many of these activities languished for lack of funds and low political interest. The rapid pace of sewage treatment plant construction in the 1990s—roughly 1,000 plants were under construction in the mid-1990s with some 350 to 400 coming on-line each year (Nowicki, 1997: 198)—resulted from the revival of old policies and not from the initiation of new policies.

Poland made slower progress protecting the environment in those areas where there was no institutional reference point from the 1970s or 1980s. To illustrate, during the Communist era, there were few formal rules governing liability for persons or property damaged by pollution. Since the state owned most of the resources capable of generating major risks to people or their property, in theory, the state would address any environmental liability complaint. In practice, victims of pollution damage had few options for obtaining compensation.

But the problem was not automatically solved by the demise of Communism in Poland. With no rules in place, the Polish government developed from scratch procedures for negotiating liability for past pollution—a priority concern for prospective foreign investors. In the early years after Communism, the government relied on an ad hoc, case-by-case approach to determine liability, which proved bureaucratic and inefficient (Bell and Kolaja, 1994: 116-119). Polish lawmakers also struck down formal rules from the previous regime that might have helped attract foreign investment to help clean up past pollution. The Joint Venture Law of 1991 eliminated special tax incentives for such investments (Pavlínek and Pickles, 2000: 253). New reforms were initiated in 1992 to regularize and streamline the environmental review of prospective privatization transactions; the new system eventually earned praise from both foreign investors and observers of Poland's privatization efforts (Auer et al., 2001: 16).

Where some of Poland's positive environmental successes stem from formal, Communist-era institutional processes, many of Estonia's environmental accomplishments can be traced to enduring *informal* institutions. Auer (chapter 5) contends that cultural and language ties between Estonians and Finns afforded Estonia special advantages over its Baltic neighbors in environmental institution-building. All of the Baltic States were major beneficiaries of environment-oriented foreign aid during the 1990s, but technical assistance from Finland to Estonia was especially generous and consequential. Linkages between midlevel environmental officials in Finland and the Estonian Soviet Socialist Republic were already established in the 1980s. Before the Soviet collapse, Finnish officials and technical professionals were already familiar with the problem setting in Estonia, including Estonian counterparts' technical needs. Having the human infrastructure for cooperation in place before the 1990s allowed projects of mutual interest, such as the Tallinn sewerage retrofit, to be identified relatively early in the transition period, and help persuade major creditors, such as the European Bank for Reconstruction and Development (EBRD), to move Estonia to the top of the list for environment-related loans. The Tallinn sewerage project found Finns and Estonians working side by side on everything from re-engineering the plant to building a self-sustaining public water company. (The latter was eventually bought by a group of private investors.) Emissions of biochemical oxygen demand (BOD) from the plant fell approximately 95 percent between 1991 and 1998; discharges of nitrogen and phosphorus also declined sharply over the decade (Auer and Raukas, 2002).

In part, EBRD and its bilateral donor partners were optimistic about the Tallinn sewerage upgrade because they were impressed by Estonian authorities' preparation for the activity and by pledges by Tallinn (in cooperation with its advisers from Helsinki Waterworks) to launch the first self-managed, self-financed water company in a former Soviet republic—an enterprise that was to operate independent of state or municipal subsidies (EBRD, 1994). The contract with EBRD was made possible once Tallinn municipal authorities agreed to institute user fees to pay for the new project—a policy that was implemented in the mid-1990s (Interview, Brian Hill, Chief Operations Officer, Tallinna Vesi, Tallinn, Estonia, July 30, 2001). In this case, institutions for environmental protection functioned well, as actors with clearly-defined institutional roles and authorities performed those roles and invoked those authorities. Key ingredients of success included elected officials who authorized higher user fees and environmental authorities who agreed to relinquish their day-to-day management of the new water enterprise.

Environmental Authorities as Institutional Actors

After the announcement of the Tallinn project, many other municipalities throughout CEE and Russia began overhauling their own water/sewer systems, often with the help of external credit.[3] But in other arenas of environmental protection, successful outcomes were harder to achieve. Underachievement in areas as varied as environmental monitoring and data management, drafting and authorization of environmental regulations, and implementation of market-based environmental mechanisms are explained by the lackluster performance of weak public environmental organizations operating in problematic institutional settings. In some instances, the organizations themselves failed to develop institutional rules and procedures to bring order, routine, and continuity to their work. In other instances, rules and procedures enforced by other powerful actors marginalized newly created environmental authorities. Examples of both types of institutional shortcomings are considered below.

With the establishment of state offices for environmental protection in many CEE countries, some environmentalists declared victory too early. While it is true that governments in virtually all CEE countries moved forward quickly to create environmental ministries or their equivalent, many of these agencies were understaffed during the 1990s, were poorly financed, or were recurrent losers in head-to-head battles with more powerful ministries (Fagin and Jehlička, 1998: 123-124; Millard, 1998: 156-160; Pavlínek and Pickles, 2000: 200; Baker and Baumgartl, 1998: 193-194). It was one thing to have official organizations in place promoting environmental protection and quite another for these agencies to implement and enforce environmental rules and procedures.

New environmental authorities were challenged by the need to design and institute well-defined procedures to ensure consistent, high quality work outputs. In some instances, the quality and dependability of work tended to rely on the competence of particular personalities in the organization; the departure of said individuals invariably created organizational crises. The tribulations of creating environmental information systems in Romania is a case in point. That country's main environmental agency, the Ministry of Water Resources and Environmental Protection, is charged with collecting, analyzing, and disseminating environmental monitoring data. But according to the United Nations Economic Commission for Europe (UNECE), the ministry is highly dependent on the work of outside professionals who produce environmental information on a contractual basis and who enjoy few public financial guarantees. "Consequently," the UNECE declares (2001b: 53),

> permanent and coherent data production is very dependent on *persons* in the administration as well as in the research institutes concerned. The reliance on persons rather than on formal organizational principles increases institutional vulnerability in general and the fragility of the data and information management system in particular. (emphasis in original)

At the local level in Romania, environmental data management is more fragile still. "Local authorities also have an environmental information duty, but they do not know how to go about it (for lack of means, of trained personnel, of clear procedures and responsibilities, etc.)" (UNECE, 2001b: 53).

In some cases, translating formal authority into real authority is constrained by inadequacies in environmental laws. In Hungary (chapter 3), for example, a landmark framework law on environmental protection was greeted with much fanfare on its enactment in 1995. But at the end of the decade, many issue-specific laws and regulations had not been promulgated. The absence of more detailed rules forced regulators to "make it up" as they performed their various enforcement duties and it tempted regulated actors to push the limits of acceptable behavior, since these limits were not actually legally defined.

A nearly opposite problem emerged in the Czech Republic. In the early years of the transition, critics accused the government of enacting too many environmental statutes, too hastily. Moreover, many of the new laws were essentially copies of Western European statutes and were not always relevant to Czech environmental and institutional contexts. As Pavlínek and Pickles argue (2000: 197; 200), several core statutes were amended within a few years, bolstering critics' complaints about the hurried pace of the first round of environmental lawmaking.

Auer and Legro in this volume (chapter 2) also find that despite the Czech Republic's mostly successful transposition of EU environmental laws, environmental protection is not well integrated into other sectoral policies and it tends to be played off economic priorities. Those seeking to invoke the nation's new environmental statutes usually lose in disputes involving high profile economic development projects, such as the construction of the Temelin nuclear power station. In the Czech case, but also in other CEE countries and in Russia, agricultural, transportation, and commerce-oriented ministries with environmental functions often do not recognize themselves as organizations with environmental duties nor as participants in environmental institutions.

Bulgaria more so than either Hungary or the Czech Republic created official organs for environmental protection without implementing rules to ensure honest and effective public management. As in the Czech Republic, Bulgarian environmental laws suffered from a combination of rushed enactment followed by frequent revision. Environmental standards were set too low, were poorly enforced, and judges qualified to adjudicate technical environmental cases were scarce (Baker and Baumgartl, 1998: 191-192). But Bulgaria's failure to develop a "rule of law" was more conspicuous because public officials had no reference points for accountability. There were few laws governing the conduct and responsibilities of public administrators, giving government officials vast de facto discretion over regulated actors, including when and whether to enforce environmental rules. According to Baker and Baumgartl (1998: 193):

> This has made it easy for political parties to gain control of the civil service, as witnessed by the fact that changes of government have been accompanied by changes at all levels of public administration. . . . Furthermore, the failure to depoliticize Bulgaria's system of public administration means that this and the rule of law are seen by the public as instruments of political control.

The professionalization of public service was slowed down by party politics in Slovakia too. There were four governments between 1990 and 1992, and three alone in 1994; each made sweeping changes to staffs and organizational structures in the environmental bureaucracy (Huba, 1997: 263). Political and administrative entropy were greater still in Romania: between 1990 and 2000, there were ten Ministers of Environment (UNECE, 2001b: 52).

By decade's end, most of the wealthier CEE countries had enacted norms for a professional civil service, thereby making public actors more accountable to ordinary citizens. Some of the reforms included job guarantees that effectively reduced civil servants' susceptibility to graft and arbitrary political decision making (OECD, 1999: 63). As described in this volume by Novac and Auer (chapter 4), these types of reforms came relatively late to Romania. In the forestry sector, they were adopted only after a decade of paralyzing corruption in the state forest service.

But even in the more institutionally advanced countries in CEE like Poland and the Czech Republic, where public agencies are relatively transparent and accountable to the public, politics often triumphs over formal institutional rules and procedures, and officials with environmental responsibilities seem to be especially vulnerable in this regard. Part way through Poland's transition, a former Minister of Environment complained that ministries such as agriculture, health, and social welfare did not "pay enough attention" to environmental issues and that individuals in those organizations who were charged with environmental policy responsibilities were "not active in fulfillment" of said duties and tended to suborn environmental considerations to the primary mission of the ministry (Nowicki, 1997: 208).

It is perhaps unsurprising that state offices other than national- and local-level environmental agencies in CEE and in Russia were relatively unenthusiastic about the environment, since environmental protection was a low priority for most presidents and prime ministers. To illustrate, former Communists and Nationalists who came into power in Slovakia in 1992 made no secret of their disdain for environmentalism. In playing on voters' anxieties about rising unemployment and the loss of social security guaranties, antireform politicians touted Communist-era "accomplishments" as symbols of progress, including "the major monuments of Communist industrialization and gigantomany" (Podoba, 1998: 136-138; see also, Pavlínek and Pickles, 2000: 189). The Czech government under Prime Minister Václav Klaus also adopted a "go slow" approach to environmental reforms, though this strategy was motivated more by antiregulatory zeal than any Communist-era nostalgia. Of Klaus's attitudes to the environment, Pavlínek and Pickles contend (2000: 200):

> Klaus consistently challenged the importance of environmental protection and management during the transformation, and undermined efforts to deal with the legacy of environmental devastation. He saw environmental protection as a secondary problem that should be dealt with only after economic transformation of the country had been "successfully" completed and then only through economic levers. He also repeatedly refused to accept the concept of a state environmental policy because it included the principle of sustainable development. For Klaus, sustainable development was a Western invention that was not relevant for the Czech Republic.

The lowly status of environmental protection was reflected in the small budgets and staffs at the Czech environmental ministry. In some cases, apathy about environmental reforms and understaffing of environmental agencies proved counterproductive to the rule of law and public accountability that Klaus claimed to hold dear. To illustrate, it was discovered that decisions about projects receiving money from the country's largest environmental fund were at the discretion of a single state employee (Pavlínek and Pickles, 2000: 200).

Newly elected leaders in CEE countries and heads of environmental agencies were also persuaded that free market forces might preclude the need for large regulatory bureaucracies found in countries like the United States and in Western Europe. In these instances, the aim was to create institutions without organizations. Western aid agencies encouraged the use of economic incentives to promote environmental protection in CEE. Many of the economic tools in place in the region are standard regulatory instruments used in advanced industrialized countries, including charges on pollution emissions and fee-based systems for certain environmental services, such as water delivery and sewerage. Others were more innovative and uncommon even in the West, including emissions trading and auctions for pollution permits (OECD, 1999: 112).

In some countries, pollution fees and fines proved to be important sources of revenue for governmental operations, including environmental functions. Countries like Poland used fee revenue to capitalize national environmental funds, and hence fees were recycled back to society in the form of grants for environment-oriented projects (OECD, 1999: 133).

However, as tools for constraining behavior—the essence of well-functioning institutional arrangements à la North—pollution charges and fines have not been especially effective in CEE or in Russia.[4] The OECD found (1999: 109):

> Pollution charges and non-compliance fees have not created strong incentives for pollution abatement or reduction. Even in the countries with the highest charges, like Poland, rates have been several times below the cost of pollution control equipment, suggesting that polluters find it cheaper to pay the charges.

Countries that avidly used penalty and fee systems discovered that economic incentives for environmentally friendly behavior did not function properly in the absence of a real, active, regulatory presence. To illustrate, Lithuania set fines for noncompliance at high rates—a seemingly well-conceived policy to discourage would-be violators. Nevertheless, permit violations remained high during much of the 1990s because environmental agencies were strapped for adequate monitoring and enforcement resources (OECD, 1999: 109). Many CEE politicians, enchanted by the perceived power of economic policies to solve complex environmental problems, inevitably shortchanged these policies by failing to provide for the organizational needs of regulators.

Environmental Interest Groups and Institutional Change

The interplay between institutional rules and organizational performance affected not only official organizational actors in CEE and in Russia, such as environmental ministries and inspectorates, but also nonstate actors, such as NGOs. NGOs discovered that old, reliable strategies for galvanizing public opinion and forcing political change all but ceased to be effective in the years after the collapse of Communism. NGOs and environmentalists that remained prominent actors in public affairs were resourceful enough to adapt to new political conditions and employ new strategies. Some of these organizations were adept at institutional change. But for the majority of environmental NGOs, the transition process was wrenching as public interest in environmental problems waned and as organizations struggled with chronic human and financial resource constraints.

Pressing economic problems tended to overshadow other concerns that had seemed vital in the previous decade, such as environmental protection. Deep economic recessions, the collapse of large industrial enterprises, rising unemployment, and the cessation of guaranteed pensions and various government transfers quickly superceded worries about pollution, threats to biodiversity, or environmentally dubious construction projects.

Debates over the restitution of private property distracted many government agencies at national, provincial, and local levels. Environmental aspects of these debates tended to be eclipsed by the broader, more emotive question of entitlement to the resources in question. In Estonia, for example, the fate of an environmentally contaminated airfield near the town of Tartu provoked a long-lasting quarrel between government officials and private claimants. But the debate had little to do with environmental risks at the site. Mostly, citizens were angry about authorities' indecision over who would receive title to the land and under what circumstances (Interview, Anto Raukas, Institute of Geology, Tallinn Technical University, Tallinn, Estonia, 31 July 2001).

In other parts of CEE and the former Soviet Union, the continuing drama of national self-determination all but extinguished public interest in environmental protection. Citizens' curiosity in controversial issues, like the fate of the Temelin nuclear power station in Czechoslovakia, faded during the "Velvet Divorce" between the Czech Republic and Slovakia. Environmental issues also tumbled down the list of public concerns in former Yugoslavia as Serbia waged ruinous wars with former Yugoslav republics, and eventually, with its own autonomous region of Kosovo. Conflicts between two major ethnic groups in Macedonia kept environmental policy reforms in check in that nation.

The Baltic States were spared violent interethnic conflict, but nevertheless, tensions over citizenship and language rules took center stage in the transition years, especially in Latvia and Estonia. Environmental concerns brought together Russian speakers and ethnic Estonians in a powerful national political movement in the late 1980s. But it ceased to be a unifying force in the 1990s. If anything, environmental concerns divided the populations, as ethnic Russians were conspicuously employed in pollution-intensive industries such as oil shale energy and chemicals. These industries were doubly cursed during the transition period, as their output contracted sharply during the economic downturn and they were the target of elevated environmental enforcement. In Estonia's pollution-intensive northeast, where more than three-quarters of the population are ethnic Russians, citizens who rallied to calls for pollution reduction in the 1980s worried much more about job security and declining incomes in the 1990s.

Environmental movements also lost fervor in the 1990s because they ceased to be one of the main fora for opposition politics. Under totalitarianism, environmental grievances were one of only a few that the ruling class would tolerate, and complaints had to be aired with caution. But environmental activists lost their comparative advantage after the collapse of Communism. Soon thereafter, in many CEE countries and in the former Soviet Union, a process of sorting out took place between "real" environmentalists and individuals who had used environmentalism to push other agendas, and in some cases, to promote themselves. On the one hand, environmental movements were weakened as the most prominent political voices in the organizations left, sometimes becoming lawmakers or political appointees but ceasing to be effective advocates for environmental reform. Those who remained committed to environmental activism tended to have less entrée to networks of powerful political actors or they sought to distance environmental issues from the rough and tumble of party politics.

In Poland, for example, activists hesitated to push for environment-oriented reforms in the platforms of political parties during the early 1990s (Gliński, 1998: 138-139). In Estonia, the Estonian Green Movement split into two separate organizations following the collapse of the Soviet Union, one overtly political, the other committed to environmental protection but forswearing formal political activity (Auer, 1998: 671). Neither organization proved as effective as its undivided predecessor in capturing the public imagination nor in advancing members' interests.

Environmental loyalists—those whose first allegiance was to environmental protection rather than to political opportunity—nevertheless realized that displaced anger at Communism provided much of the fuel for popular environmentalism in the late 1980s. Hence, the more perceptive environmentalists understood early on in the post-Communist period that public interest in environmental affairs would fade. Reigniting that interest became the primary endeavor for many NGOs in the 1990s and in the early twenty-first century.

In this collection (chapter 6), Abrams and Auer argue that, in part, Russian NGOs have been ineffective at rejuvenating public concern for the environment, and not merely because ordinary citizens are preoccupied with other problems. Another force holding popular environmentalism in check is environmentalists' skepticism about ordinary citizens' abilities to understand and appreciate complex environmental problems and the trade-offs involving environmental quality. Trust is in short supply in Russia: it is lacking not only between NGOs and the state, but among the various environmental organizations and between NGOs and society at large. Moreover, international NGOs like the World Wildlife Fund, foreign governments, and private foundations such as Soros have been key sources of moral and financial support for Russian civic associations—so much so that citizens doubt whether NGOs are fighting for the interests of ordinary Russians.

Indeed, funding from external actors was instrumental to the survival of many civic groups in CEE and in the former Soviet Union during the early 1990s. But NGOs in the stronger economies in CEE became more self-reliant later in the decade. By 1998, domestic funding exceeded foreign funding for environmental NGOs in Poland, Hungary, and the Czech Republic; that year, only 5 percent of total NGO funding in Poland came from external sources (OECD, 1999: 87). Civic organizations in southern tier countries like Albania, Bulgaria, and Macedonia continued to depend heavily on foreign sponsors late into the decade (OECD, 1999: 87), as was the case for Russian NGOs.

Since the demise of Communism, a recurrent problem for Western backers of Russian NGOs is deciding whom, among the many Russian petitioners for aid, to underwrite. The choice is complicated by the sheer number of civic associations in Russia. The OECD estimated that there were 1,000 to 1,500 environmental NGOs in Russia in the late 1990s though this count did not include organizations that promote environmental causes in the context of other issue areas (e.g., women rights; conservation of cultural landmarks) nor did it include unregistered organizations.[5] Many of these organizations were very small—in Russia, half had fewer than twenty-five members (OECD, 1999: 85) with most operating at the local level. Indeed, only 3 percent of NGOs in Russia focused on national-level issues and concerns (OECD, 1999: 85).

In principle, external actors' sponsorship of local NGOs might be particularly sensible: presumably, locally based organizations are more knowledgeable about local problem contexts and have a relatively large interest in solving these problems. But reproducing the results of even the most successful local NGO activities proved difficult in Russia because these organizations were often reluctant to collaborate with other NGOs, even for the purpose of sharing information. The problem is rooted partly in NGOs' insularity and the narrowness of their areas of interest. But it is also due to a lack of trust and to competition among NGOs for scarce external sources of funds.

Not only does poor networking affect Russian NGOs' capacities to replicate or adapt successful projects and avoid repeating disappointing ones, but also weak networks handicap environmental advocates because NGOs lack a collective voice. This problem is not confined to Russia; for example, reluctance to share information and to collaborate curbs the effectiveness of civic groups in Lithuania (UNECE, 1999a: 21) and to a smaller extent, in Poland (Gliński, 1998).

Polish NGOs, however, have proven relatively more adept than their counterparts in Lithuania or Russia at becoming "professional" organizations. The professionalization process has been one of responding and adapting to changing social and political conditions so as to remain relevant in public affairs. Strategies used in the late 1980s to promote organizational interests, such as direct confrontation and spontaneous protests, have given way to routinized forms of political action. The latter include participation in governmental advisory bodies; lobbying of lawmakers; and collecting, synthesizing, and disseminating environmental information.

Polish NGOs' increasing effectiveness as policy advocates is abetted by larger institutional changes, and in particular, the maturation of democratic values in society at large and the firming up of the rule of law. Environmental NGOs might languish were it not for the state's willingness to abide by public information provisions stipulated in Polish law. These laws are conspicuously lacking in southern tier countries like Romania (UNECE, 2001b: 52) where NGOs, not coincidentally, are less effective advocates for policy reforms.[6] In Latvia, the problem has less to do with accessing environmental information, per se. Rather, the procedures one must follow to obtain that information are not always clear. To illustrate, some NGOs complain that the government fails to spell-out procedural rules for inviting private opinions on major development projects nor does it publicize dates for hearings on such projects (UNECE, 1999b: 58; 60).

Rights to access environmental information and laws that nurture public participation have increased NGOs' powers and persuasiveness in Hungary, according to Bell (chapter 3), and Hungarian environmentalists have been relatively more keen on cooperating with one another and leveraging each other's strengths, so as to advance policy reforms.

Bell cites the profit motive and the skill revolution as key institutional drivers in the professionalization of Hungarian NGOs and for-profit environmental service companies. Hungarian environmental management professionals are helping clients save money through pollution prevention and clean production programs. NGOs and for-profit organizations in the Czech Republic perform similar services and are one of the reasons that Czech companies lead their CEE counterparts in attaining ISO 14000 certification (ISO, 2001: 9).[7] One hundred Czech companies received ISO certification by 2000; only seven other countries in the world had as many certified companies (ISO, 2001: 9).

It is not the case that the only effective NGOs are the ones confined to relatively wealthy and politically stable CEE countries. Nongovernmental organizations have been important participants in law drafting and consulting activities in some of the region's poorest nations. For example, the Albanian Society for the Protection of Birds and Mammals both initiated and drafted that nation's nature protection law. Bulgaria's National Parliament has consulted with NGOs in amending Bulgaria's national environmental protection act (OECD, 1999: 94). Abrams and Auer (chapter 6) report that some Russian NGOs have been effective as environmental educators and trainers—contentions that are corroborated elsewhere (e.g., OECD, 1999: 89).

But in these poorer quarters of the region, successful nongovernmental actors are more often the exception than the rule. Leaders of the few effective NGOs tend to demonstrate great tenacity and courage in regions where free speech and other political rights are not well protected. This would describe, for example, an effective lobbying effort sponsored by NGOs in 1996 in Kostroma oblast (Russia) against the construction of a nuclear power plant. The proposed project was eventually the subject of a referendum. The vote, and the campaign that preceded it, were made possible by a constitutional provision allowing popular referenda as well as a framework law permitting ballots on environmental issues (OECD, 1999: 98).[8] But these legal rights remained untested until the Kostroma case, and the ability of NGOs to make their case, or even to ensure their own safety, remained uncertain for much of the campaign. NGOs' safety-related concerns were not unwarranted considering the high-profile prosecutions of Russian environmental activists and journalists taking place around the same time (chapter 6).

The Kostroma case reveals that environmental legal protections can be upheld even in the most fragile democracies in the region. Strong state endorsement of these protections would be fully expected by citizens of a stable democracy. But especially in Russia and in CEE countries emerging from violent internal conflicts, the invocation of environmentally oriented political rights, and political rights generally, are momentous developments.

European Drivers of Environmental Reforms

Contributors to *Restoring Cursed Earth* find numerous instances where CEE governments are sincere in their efforts to administer domestic environmental laws and regulations. But assume for analytical purposes that there are governments in the region that lack enthusiasm for environmental protection. It is nevertheless incumbent for most of these governments to at least *appear* to implement recently passed environmental rules. To betray anything less than vigorous implementation could jeopardize these nations' plans to join the European Union.

Ten CEE countries (Bulgaria, Czech Republic, Estonia, Hungary, Latvia, Lithuania, Poland, Romania, Slovakia, and Slovenia) entered negotiations with the European Union in the 1990s to "converge economically, politically, socially, and culturally" with other EU member states (EEA, 2002b). Negotiations were concluded in December 2002 for eight of those countries—Czech Republic, Estonia, Hungary, Latvia, Lithuania, Poland, Slovakia, and Slovenia (EEA, 2002c).

Among the key steps in the accession process are the signing and coming into force of Europe Agreements between the EU and each candidate. These agreements address trade issues, political dialogue, and the process of "approximating" national legislation to that of the EU. The approximation process obliges each candidate to adopt the entire body of European Union Directives, resolutions, treaties, and related legislation into the national legal framework. Negotiations between countries and the EU determine the conditions under which the applicants will adopt, implement, and enforce the thirty-one chapters of the *acquis communitaire* (the body of EU legislation which candidates must adopt to become EU members), including an environmental chapter (chapter 22). Each chapter is negotiated separately. Through 2002, most of the accession countries had their environmental chapters "closed" (EEA, 2002d: 66-68), signifying that the candidate country and the EU reached agreement on the terms under which the candidate will adopt, implement, and enforce EU legislation, including EU legislation passed during the negotiation period (EEA, 2002e: 25). Closed chapters also specify the conditions for extensions to achieve compliance or "transition periods." All CEE candidate countries whose chapters were closed in 2002 received extensions to comply with various directives (EEA, 2002e). Accession countries are obliged to continue the approximation process, including implementation, after joining the EU. Still, the EU's final decision whether or not to grant accession depends more on the development of a credible Implementation Programme than on actual implementation and enforcement. The eight candidate countries with closed environmental chapters will probably be invited by the EU's two principal legislative bodies—the Council of the European Union (composed of European ministers) and the European Parliament—to join the EU in 2004.[9] But several years will pass before conclusive appraisals are made about the relative successes and shortcomings of new members' implementation efforts.

The complete transposition and implementation of all EU environmental norms into national legal and regulatory systems are monumental undertakings, but indications of earnest efforts to implement new laws are already evident in many CEE countries. Consider, for example, the Baltic States' efforts to conform with the EU's Wildlife and Habitat Directives (Nikodemusa, 2002). Moreover, CEE countries' tenacious bargaining with Brussels to extend compliance deadlines for certain directives suggests a high level of seriousness about the implementation process. Some countries performed careful cost-benefit analyses to determine investment needs and schedules for implementation. If these were merely empty gestures to appear resolute about implementation, these efforts were elaborate, time-consuming, and expensive for the applicant countries.

However sincere are CEE governments about not only transposing EU laws but also implementing and enforcing them, an important unknown is the degree to which these norms will be internalized by society at large.

The impetus for many of the most important environmental laws in advanced industrialized nations comes from the grassroots level. In the United States, the earliest advocates for many of the nation's environmental statutes were not environmental agencies; indeed, such authorities did not exist or they were subsidiary bodies in agencies with nonenvironmental missions. Pressure for stringent laws governing clean air and clean water in the United States came from the bottom up, with environmental organizations and motivated citizens in the vanguard (Kraft and Furlong, 2004: 317; Rosenbaum, 1998: 58-59; 61). In the case of CEE countries' transposition of EU legislation, not only is the reform process top-down, but the reforms themselves were invented by actors and organizations outside CEE. It remains to be seen whether CEE political elites can persuade ordinary citizens about the universal exigency of European legal norms. Moreover, pro-EU advocates must convince skeptics that "acquis" does not signify *acquiesce* so much as it means *acquire*. Many worry about ceding too much authority to Brussels, having so recently endured Moscow's distant but nevertheless real control.

Internalization of EU legislation is, as Tom Garvey affirms (2002: 53-54), "the *sine qua non* condition for membership in the EU" and hence, the candidate countries' complete acceptance of EU laws and regulations is the central focus of CEE countries' current environmental legal and policy reforms, including the eight candidates whose environmental chapters have been closed and who must comply with implementation targets and timetables. But it would be wide of the mark to suggest that the accession process was the earliest inspiration for CEE countries to internalize Western European environmental norms. International treaty obligations, albeit in more limited ways than the EU accession process, shaped institutions for environmental protection in CEE and the former Soviet Union as far back as the 1970s. For example, the 1974 Convention on the Protection of the Marine Environment of the Baltic Sea Area (Helsinki Convention) is credited with helping foster environmental institutions in the Baltic Sea shoreline states of CEE during the Communist period, and in particular, in building up the capacity of scientific institutions (Broadus et al., 1992).

In practice, the 1974 convention was limited to managing pollution risks in the open waters of the Baltic Sea. (The Soviet Union was loath to cede any of its authority over Soviet land-based activities affecting the sea.) However, legal aspects of the convention were less consequential than were procedures for developing so-called recommendations for environmental management—politically binding "soft laws" governing activities as diverse as wildlife protection to prohibitions on industrial pollution emissions. The development of recommendations provided Soviet and other Eastern bloc scientists and environmental authorities entrée to broader discussions on the health of the Baltic, access to national and Baltic-wide environmental data, and exposure to Western environmental management practices. Among the most active participants in these soft law deliberations were scientists and midlevel civil servants from the Baltic States, and especially Estonia. Russian, Polish, and Estonian officials were also prominent in higher-level discussions taking place annually in the Helsinki Commission (HELCOM). Among other functions, HELCOM cast final votes on proposed recommendations.

A renewed convention, signed by all Baltic Sea states in 1992 is shaping domestic environmental institutions in ways that the old convention could not. Perhaps most importantly, the new convention unambiguously extended the treaty area to include land-based pollution sources. That provision had a clear impact on rule making in Latvia, where regulations governing the emissions of pollutants into waterways closely mirror Article 6 of the 1992 convention as well as various HELCOM recommendations (National Audit Office of Denmark et al., 2001: 101). Also, Russia strived to meet HELCOM recommendations governing sewage treatment. The wastewater treatment rate in St. Petersburg—the largest urban discharger of pollution to the sea—increased from 60 percent in the early 1990s to 78 percent at decade's end, with large decreases in phosphorus and nitrogen loadings over that period (National Audit Office of Denmark et al., 2001: 160-162). However, only with the provision of external aid, including through a HELCOM-related investment program,[10] has Russia been able to realize a small set of commitments made in the HELCOM regime.

The Helsinki Convention and related instruments, then, have shaped environmental institutions in Central and Eastern Europe and in Russia, serving to dispel the notion that prospective EU membership is the only significant external driver of environmental reforms in CEE. Other legal and extralegal instruments are also part of the complex international context in which CEE and Russian environmental institutions have evolved. To illustrate, dozens of regional and international environmental conventions have been ratified by CEE countries over the past ten to fifteen years, followed by the promulgation of enabling domestic laws, regulations, and programs. Estonia, for example, has responded to conventions on global scale problems such as stratospheric ozone depletion and climate change with domestic programs of its own (table 1.1).

CEE countries' accession to international environmental treaties does not necessarily guarantee improved environmental conditions in these countries. But international arrangements can jump-start domestic institutions for environmental protection and sustain institutions that are already in place. Consider, for example, the "Environment for Europe" process that commenced in 1991. That year, Josef Vavrousek, head of the Federal Environment Commission of former Czechoslovakia, invited environment ministers and other officials to discuss how to improve environmental programs in CEE through better intergovernmental and donor-recipient coordination. The meeting produced the Environmental Action Programme for Central and Eastern Europe and put in place a schedule of future high-level meetings.

Environment for Europe's mark on domestic environmental policy institutions was measurable, spurring the development of national environmental action plans in sixteen countries in transition (Kratovits and Punning, 2001: 446).

TABLE 1.1
Estonian Ratification of International Conventions and Subsequent Domestic Programmatic Activity

Title of Convention (year of ratification and accession by Estonia)	Title of Domestic Programme (year of promulgation)
Convention on Wetlands of International Importance Especially as Waterfowl Habitat (1971); Convention on Conservation of European Wildlife and Natural Habitats (1979); Convention on Biodiversity (1992)	National Biodiversity Strategy and Action Plan (1999)
Convention on the Control of Transboundary Movements of Hazardous Wastes and Their Disposal (1989)	National Programme for the Implementation of the Basel Convention for 2000-2005 (1999)
Convention for the Protection of the Ozone Layer (1995); Protocol on Substances that Deplete the Ozone Layer and Amendments (1987; 1990; 1992)	National Programme on Phasing out the Substances that Deplete the Ozone Layer for 1999-2002 (1999)
United Nations Framework Convention on Climate Change (UNCCC) (1992); Kyoto Protocol to the UNCCC (1997)	Climate Change Mitigation Programme (2002)

Source: Adapted from Kratovits and Punning, 2001: 444; 446.

It also proved indispensable to donors who had had trouble coordinating programs with counterpart agencies and whose activities did not always meet re-
cipient countries' needs. I witnessed firsthand the disciplining effect that the
Environment for Europe process had on CEE environmental programs sponsored by the United States Agency for International Development (USAID). Up
until 1993, USAID officials and contractors to that agency were confounded by
coordination problems in the field, including sponsoring activities that dupli-
cated other donors' programs. The Lucerne meeting of the Environment for
Europe process (1993) marked a watershed in U.S. bilateral assistance to the
region, as USAID reengineered several of its programs to complement the work
of other bilateral donors, international financial institutions, and local implementers. Hence, Environment for Europe provided institutional order not only for
actors in CEE, but also for donors and their partners.

Former Czechoslovak environmental officials took risks in launching Environment for Europe. Commissioner Vavrousek risked offending powerful donors with his candid remarks about the shortcomings of current aid programs.
Instead, donors almost universally concurred with his views and the meeting
helped stimulate renewed interest in donor coordination and the development of
national action plans. Former Czechoslovakia led this effort—an assertion of
leadership not unlike Sweden's hosting of the first-ever, global-scale intergovernmental environmental conference in 1972 and Finland's groundbreaking
meetings between East and West over the fate of the Baltic Sea environment in
1974. Perhaps some day the 1991 Environment for Europe process (and former
Czechoslovakia's central role in its founding) will be held in as high regard as
the 1972 Stockholm Declaration and the 1974 Helsinki Convention.

Boundaries for a Book

This volume's subtitle correctly identifies the geographical context for our enquiry, though we are less concerned with making a geographically coherent argument than in examining the experiences of countries that have encountered
similar challenges since the end of Communism.

Other students of environmental affairs in CEE have delimited the scope of
their investigation by invoking an explicitly historical or political rationale.
Baker and Jehlička, for example, exclude the Baltic countries from their survey
"on the grounds that they were part of the USSR itself and had consequently
rather different post-war histories" (1998: 2-3). In contrast, Klarer and Moldan
cluster the Baltic republics with CEE because "these countries are clearly pursuing an integration into the European Union and other Western institutions or
alliances" (1997: 63 passim). Pavlínek's and Pickles's study of environmental
transition in CEE draws primarily on information from Poland, the Czech Republic, Slovakia, Hungary, Bulgaria, Romania, and Albania (2000: 9), but the

authors are also attentive to subnational and regional institutional changes, noting that most surveys of CEE environmental affairs "overlook not only variations at regional and local levels, but also the fact that the transition operates unevenly in space and time" (Pavlínek and Pickles, 2000: 30).

Disparate constructs for the study of environmental reform and environmental transition in CEE and FSU belie the tenuousness of physical and political geography as organizing principles for comparative research. The Czech Republic is frequently associated with "Eastern Europe" though Prague is west of Vienna and Stockholm. The same is true of Ljubljana, Slovenia, and Zagreb, Croatia—seemingly Western locales on a Mercator projection—but more often viewed as Eastern outposts of Europe proper. The continent of Asia and more separates Vladivostok from European capitals, yet Russia is a council member in the North Atlantic Treaty Organization.

Indeed, of all the countries examined in this volume, it is Russia that may seem least well-matched for a comparison of post-Communist environmental reform experiences. Straddling two continents and eleven time zones, Russia has defied conventional political and geographical classification for centuries. The Russian coat of arms' two-headed eagle, peering east and west, is a metaphor for Russian transitiveness. As Huntington suggests (1993: 41-42), it is a "torn country," enamored by Western material wealth and the forces of modernity but also pulled by old patriarchal traditions and distinctly Russian (not European) mindsets.

Whether or not Russia is sui generis in either a historical or cultural sense, it is a suitable subject for our enquiry because like its CEE neighbors, it is a country in the midst of profound political and economic transition away from Communism and central planning. Top-down political decision making, weak civil societies, and mismanaged environments were common to all CEE countries and to Russia during the Communist period. For our purposes, Russia's "otherness" and its legacy of regional hegemony are only salient to the extent these factors are institutional determinants of the country's post-Communist environmental reform process.

Indeed, excluding Russia from our analysis on the basis that Russia is "different" is unfulfilling because it is *difference* that so clearly characterizes the CEE region and its constituent parts. CEE countries have distinct histories, different levels of economic development, different cultural traditions, and the region is a meeting place for four major religions: Orthodox Christianity, Protestant Christianity, Roman Catholicism, and Islam. These differences are pertinent to our study if they influence environmental institutions, and influence these institutions they do. Historical and cultural determinants of institutional arrangements are addressed in several chapters, and they include, for example, an examination of mutual reciprocity in Romania (chapter 4); language ties between Finns and Estonians (chapter 5); and norms governing personal trust in Russia (chapter 6).

A Preview of the Country Case Studies

Czechs, for one, have never been comfortable with "Eastern" Europe as an appellation for a country that was the seat of great "Central" European empires and monarchies, including those of Moravia and Bohemia. And the Czech Republic has worked assiduously to win back a place in "the heart" of Europe by, among other strategies, putting EU environmental norms into domestic practice. The Czech Republic was among the first CEE accession countries to provisionally close its environmental chapter.

An appraisal of the accomplishments and shortcomings of the approximation process are subjects of interest in the next chapter on the Czech Republic and other chapters to follow. Auer and Legro (chapter 2) find inadequacies in the Czechs' transposition efforts, and in particular, in the government's contradictory environmental and economic development priorities. These contradictions are reinforced, paradoxically, by rules, incentives, and procedures specified in the EU's own accession policies and programs.

Like the Czech Republic, Hungary is a major beneficiary of EU accession grants and technical assistance. And Hungary's dedication to the accession process resembles that of the Czech Republic. Hungary is also an innovator in the use of market-oriented instruments for environmental protection. Its embrace of economic tools may stem from the government's experiments with quasi-market reforms in the 1970s and 1980s, including the liberalization of prices for certain resources such as nonresidential fuels (Richet, 1989: 5-7). But as Ruth Greenspan Bell explains (chapter 3), the performance of market-oriented measures was compromised by weak environmental institutions meant to support these reforms. As do the authors of chapter 2, Bell queries whether Hungary's relatively nimble transposition of EU environmental laws translates into markedly better environmental management by state authorities, not to mention the millions of ordinary citizens who must be enrolled in new environmental institutions.

On balance, EU environmental laws and Brussels' grant programs for environmental protection will do much more good than harm for both the Czech Republic and Hungary, and will boost these countries' bids for EU membership—outcomes that seem all but certain as this book goes to press. Romania's prospects appear somewhat less certain. Not only do Romanian efforts lag behind in the transposition of EU laws, but more broadly, Romania struggles to convince other EU members of its commitments to the rule of law, to civil society, and to macroeconomic reforms. Novac and Auer (chapter 4) reveal how the perpetuation of Communist-era edicts have fostered mismanagement of one of that country's most precious natural assets. Informal institutions that helped citizens get by during the years of totalitarianism have worked at cross-purposes with new, formal rules meant to protect the environment.

While environmental protection efforts have stumbled in Romania, they have mostly prospered in Estonia (chapter 5). Environmental policy and management institutions function as well or better in Estonia than anywhere else in CEE. In the early 1990s, pollution pressures on air and water resources declined with the economic recession in Estonia, as was true elsewhere in CEE and in Russia. But economic recovery did not bring back the high emission loads of the 1980s. Less polluting trade and service industries became leading economic sectors, and large investments in wastewater treatment and major factory upgrades helped revive the environment.

But Estonia's cultural and language connections to neighboring Finland also facilitated environmental institution-building. Finns and Estonians worked side by side on what was arguably the single most successful international environmental project in the Baltic Sea region in the 1990s—the upgrade of the sewage treatment plant in Estonia's capital, Tallinn. Finland transferred to Estonia not only engineering know-how, but also Western-style business strategies for operating a public water and sewer company. Estonia's remarkable success at integrating its economy with Finland's and Sweden's inspired its foreign minister to declare Estonia a Nordic country first and a Baltic State second (*City Paper*, 1998).

Estonia is due west of a nation that is nearly its antithesis in environmental performance. Only a crippling economic depression in the 1990s gave Russia's environment a respite from years of neglect. An economic recovery in the early years of the new century allowed it to bring on-line environmental projects it had postponed for nearly a decade, such as the modernization of St. Petersburg's wastewater treatment systems. But environmental inspectorates from the national, to the oblast (provincial), to the municipal level remained understaffed and poorly equipped, and Russia's ruling class continued to cast environmental concerns far down the list of policy priorities.

Abrams's and Auer's chapter (chapter 6) focuses on a paradox in Russian environmental affairs: there are more environmental nongovernmental organizations (NGOs) in Russia than in any CEE nation. But even as the number of environmental NGOs has grown, popular interest in the environment has plummeted since the glasnost era, and the vast majority of NGOs boast only a handful of followers. The environmental community's problem stems from institutional missteps by Western donors. External grants to NGOs have created fratricidal competition for these resources instead of fostering collaboration. Moreover, ordinary Russians mistrust civic organizations, believing them to be fronts for Western interests and too far removed from the concerns of average citizens. With a weak civil society, few pressures on elected leaders to pay attention to environmental quality, and politicians who are instinctive autocrats, prospects for meaningful environmental protection are perhaps more bleak in Russia than in any country in CEE.

Contributors to this volume do not deal with the troubled reform processes in Albania or the countries of former Yugoslavia. With the exception of Slovenia, where environmental protection efforts bore fruit in the 1990s, reforms in much of the Balkans were on hold for parts or all of that decade, swept aside by crippling civil wars and conflicts fought in the name of Serbian pan-nationalism (and non-Serbian ethnic survival). Fighting between Orthodox Christians and Muslims in Macedonia and grinding poverty and ineffective governments in Albania held in check most intentional efforts to protect the environment; any measurable environmental improvements were second order effects of economic decline.

By virtue of its size and economic might, Poland more so than any of the Balkan nations is much more consequential as a shaper of regional environmental conditions in CEE. Yet, beyond this scene-setting chapter, Poland's post-Communist environmental experiences are not addressed in this book. Poland's story has been expertly told by others, including Daniel Cole's (1998) carefully researched legal institutional analysis of environmental policy failure and success in Communist Poland and post-Communist Poland, respectively; the various contributors to Cole's and John Clark's (1998) edited volume on environmental institutional reform in Poland; Magnus Andersson's (1999) study of environmental policy change in Poland as an illustration of the advocacy coalition framework; Halina Szejnwald Brown et al.'s (2000) analysis of Polish environment, health, and safety regulatory systems; and Barbara Hicks's (1996) study of Polish environmental activism before and after the fall of Communism. Indeed, in part because the Polish environmental policy experience is so thoroughly documented by others, we replaced it with other significant though less familiar cases, such as the troubled reform of forest management and conservation in Romania and the rapid restoration of Estonia's environment.

Arguments could be made for adding chapters to this volume on Poland, other Baltic States besides Estonia, on the Balkans, Slovakia, Bulgaria, Moldova, or Ukraine, Belarus, or even former Soviet republics that are unambiguously not part of Europe. After all, there are many nations in Eurasia that possess important characteristics that motivate our enquiry, namely, the struggle to repair environments damaged under Communism. Ultimately, however, the variety of country experiences covered in this book is determined by the expertise and knowledge of the various contributors. And in the end, we are less concerned about assuring complete geographical coverage than in illuminating the diversity of paths taken by Russia and CEE countries to restore their cursed air and water, forests and fields.

Notes

1. The corruption perceptions index is derived from survey data of perceptions of corruption from businesspersons and country analysts. Transparency International uses data sources from the World Economic Forum, the Economist Intelligence Unit, PricewaterhouseCoopers, and Freedom House, among others (Lambsdorff, 2001).

2. Several former Soviet republics have high levels of perceived corruption. Georgia, Azerbaijan, and Tajikistan were deemed the most corrupt, tied for 124th place in the 2003 corruption perception index; Moldova, Kazakhstan, and Uzbekistan were tied for

100th, and Russia was 86th. The CEE country with the lowest level of perceived corruption was Slovenia which ranked 29th (Transparency International, 2003).

3. For a thorough analysis of the impetuses for and outcomes of externally financed wastewater treatment projects in CEE, see Gutner, 2002.

4. In Russia, the real cost of pollution charges was eroded by price inflation. Moreover, Russian authorities dispensed generous waivers to enterprises that were actively investing in pollution abatement equipment. Issuance of waivers was so common, the total value of these waivers exceeded the revenues actually collected from polluters. In other cases, if enterprises turned in poor business results, pollution charges were capped (OECD, 1999: 107, 109).

5. Abrams and Auer in this volume cite sources documenting some 300,000 registered charitable organizations (including environmental organizations) in the Former Soviet Union.

6. The United Nations Economic Commission for Europe notes that Romanian citizens' limited access to information is not confined to the environmental arena: "Besides, there is no general law on access to information in general, which would give a clear definition of public information and state the precise rights of access to it" (UNECE, 2001b: 52).

7. These certificates verify that companies are instituting environmental management systems that conform to standards set by the International Organization for Standardization (ISO). ISO's certification is perhaps the most widely recognized voluntary environmental management accreditation scheme. Many European companies are also certified under a comparable arrangement known as the Eco-Management and Audit Scheme (EMAS).

8. A majority of voters in the 1996 referendum rejected the Kostroma nuclear power facility and construction activities ceased soon thereafter. However, the federal government held out the possibility of completing the plant in the future. As of 2002, construction at the site remained frozen.

9. Upon the Council's approval of an accession treaty with a candidate country and following the assent of the European Parliament, an approved treaty is sent to the candidate country for ratification, and in some cases, a referendum (EEA, 2003).

10. All contracting parties to the Helsinki Convention are participants in the Joint Comprehensive Environmental Action Program, created under the auspices of the 1992 convention, and which calls for a multiyear, multibillion euro plan to "ensure the ecological restoration of the Baltic Sea and [preserve] its ecological balance" (Helsinki Commission, 1992: 1). Cleaning up the sea entails remediating 132 hot spots of pollution in the Baltic Sea drainage basin. Four of those hot spots are in the St. Petersburg region; all involve installing or improving sanitary infrastructure. From 1995 to 1999, St. Petersburg received €10.7 million in grants from international sources while borrowing more than US$1 billion in 2000, alone, for the sewerage upgrade projects (National Audit Office of Denmark et al., 2001: 101).

References

Andersen, Mikael Skou. 2002. "Ecological Modernization or Subversion?" *American Behavioral Scientist*, vol. 45, no. 9: 1394-1416.

Andersson, Magnus. 1999. *Change and Continuity in Poland's Environmental Policy.* Dordrecht, Netherlands: Kluwer Academic Publishers.

Auer, Matthew. 1998. "Environmentalism and Estonia's Independence Movement." *Nationalities Papers*, vol. 26, no. 4: 659-676.

Auer, Matthew, and Anto Raukas. 2002. "Determinants of Environmental Cleanup in Estonia." *Environment and Planning C: Government and Policy*, vol. 20, no. 5: 679-698.

Auer, Matthew, Rafael Reuveny, and Lisa Adler. 2001. "Environmental Liability and Foreign Direct Investment in Central and Eastern Europe." *Journal of Environment and Development*, vol. 10, no. 1: 5-34.

Baker, Susan, and Bernd Baumgartl. 1998. "Bulgaria: Managing the Environment in an Unstable Transition," in Susan Baker and Petr Jehlička (eds.), *Dilemmas of Transition: The Environment, Democracy and Economic Reform in East Central Europe*. London: Frank Cass, 1-26.

Baker, Susan, and Petr Jehlička. 1998. "Dilemmas of Transition: The Environment, Democracy and Economic Reform in East Central Europe: An Introduction," in Susan Baker and Petr Jehlička (eds.), *Dilemmas of Transition: The Environment, Democracy and Economic Reform in East Central Europe*. London: Frank Cass, 183-206.

Bell, Ruth Greenspan, and Thomas Kolaja. 1994. "Capital Privatization and the Management of Environmental Liability Issues in Poland," in Gretta Goldenman (ed.), *Environmental Liability and Privatization in Central and Eastern Europe*. London: Graham and Trotman/Martinus Nijhoff, 109-123.

Broadus J., S. Demisch, K. Gjerde, P. Haas, Y. Kaoru, G. Peet, S. Repetto, and A. Roginko. 1992. *Comparative Assessment of Regional International Programs to Control Land Based Marine Pollution: The Baltic, North Sea, and Mediterranean*. Marine Policy Center, Woods Hole Oceanographic Institution, Woods Hole, MA.

Brown, Halina Szejnwald, David Angel, and Patrick Derr. 2000. *Effective Environmental Regulation: Learning from Poland's Experience*. Westport, CT: Praeger.

City Paper. 1998. "Selling Estonia: Part II." www.balticsww.com/news/features/selling_estonia2.htm. Accessed 8 August 2002.

Clark, John, and Daniel H. Cole. 1998. "Poland's Environmental Transformation: An Introduction," in John Clark and Daniel H. Cole (eds.), *Environmental Protection in Transition: Economic, Legal and Socio-Political Perspectives on Poland*. Brookfield, VT: Ashgate, 1-18.

Cole, Daniel H. 1998. *Instituting Environmental Protection: From Red to Green in Poland*. London: Macmillan.

Darst, Robert G. 2001. *Smokestack Diplomacy: Cooperation and Conflict in East-West Environmental Politics*. Cambridge, MA: MIT Press.

Estonian Environment Information Centre. 2001. *State of the Environment in Estonia: On the Threshold of XXI Century*. Tallinn: Estonian Environment Information Centre.

European Bank for Reconstruction and Development. 1994. "EBRD's First Environmental Loan Will Reduce Baltic Sea Pollution." Press release of the European Bank for Reconstruction and Development. 21 July. London: EBRD.

European Environment Agency. 2002a. *ETC Air and Climate Change*. National data submissions to CLRTAP/EMEP from the European Topic Centre on Air and Climate Change (Database version 2.0). etc-acc.eionet.eu.int/. Accessed: 14 March 2003.

———. 2002b. *The Europe Agreements*. europa.eu.int/comm/enlargement/pas/europe_agr.htm. Accessed 9 June 2002.

————. 2002c. *Accession Negotiations: State of Play*. europa.eu.int/comm/enlargement/ negotiations/pdf/stateofplay_28june2002.pdf. Accessed 24 June 2002.

————. 2002d. *Enlargement of the European Union: Guide to the Negotiation Chapter by Chapter*. Brussels: European Commission, Directorate-General Enlargement, December.

————. 2002e. *Enlargement and Environment: Questions and Answers*. Brussels: European Commission, Directorate-General Environment, May.

————. 2003. *Enlargement*. www.europa.eu.int/comm/enlargement/negotiations/ index.htm. Accessed 20 April 2003.

Fagin, Adam, and Petr Jehlička. 1998. "Sustainable Development in the Czech Republic: A Doomed Process?" in Susan Baker and Petr Jehlička (eds.), *Dilemmas of Transition: The Environment, Democracy and Economic Reform in East Central Europe*. London: Frank Cass, 113-128.

Garvey, Tom. 2002. "EU Enlargement: Is It Sustainable?" in Sabina A.-M. Crisen and JoAnn Carmin (eds.), *EU Enlargement and Environmental Quality: Central and Eastern Europe and Beyond*. Proceedings of the Conference: EU Enlargement and Environmental Quality in Central and Eastern Europe and Beyond, Washington, D.C.: 14 March 2002, Washington, D.C.: Woodrow Wilson International Center for Scholars, 53-62.

Gliński, Piotr. 1998. "Polish Greens and Politics: A Social Movement in a Time of Transformation," in John Clark and Daniel H. Cole (eds.), *Environmental Protection in Transition: Economic, Legal and Socio-Political Perspectives on Poland*, 129-153.

Gutner, Tamar. 2002. *Banking on the Environment: Multilateral Development Banks and Their Environmental Performance in Central and Eastern Europe*. Cambridge, MA: MIT Press.

Helsinki Commission. 1992. *The Baltic Sea Joint Comprehensive Environmental Action Programme (Preliminary Version)*, conference document no. 5/3, agenda item 5 of the Diplomatic Conference on the Protection of the Marine Environment of the Baltic Sea Area, Helsinki: HELCOM.

Hicks, Barbara. 1996. *Environmental Politics in Poland: A Social Movement between Regime and Opposition*. New York: Columbia University Press.

Huba, Mikuláš. 1997. "Slovak Republic," in Jürg Klarer and Bedřich Moldan (eds.), *The Environmental Challenge for Central European Economies in Transition*. New York: John Wiley and Sons, 229-270.

Hudson, Chris. 2001. "The Role of International Environmental Law in the Protection of the Danube River Basin: The Baia Mare Cyanide Spill." *Colorado Journal of International Environmental Law and Policy*, vol. 12, Summer: 367-393.

Hughes, Gordon, and Magda Lovei. 1999. *Economic Reform and Environmental Performance in Transition Economies*, World Bank Technical Paper no. 446, Washington, D.C.: World Bank.

Huntington, Samuel. 1993. "The Clash of Civilizations." *Foreign Affairs*, Summer, 22-49.

International Organization for Standardization. 2001. *The ISO Survey of ISO 9000 and ISO 14000 Certificates: Tenth Cycle up to and including 31 December 2000*. www.iso.org/iso/en/iso9000-14000/pdf/survey10thcycle.pdf. Accessed 6 June 2002.

Klarer, Jürg, and Bedřich Moldan. 1997. "Regional Overview," in Jürg Klarer and Bedřich Moldan (eds.), *The Environmental Challenge for Central European Economies in Transition*. New York: John Wiley and Sons, 1-66.

Kraav, Eva. 2000. "Removing/Restructuring Distortional Energy Subsidies in Estonia," Paper presented at the UNECE/OECD Workshop on Enhancing the Environment by Reforming Energy Prices, *Pruhonice near Prague, Czech Republic, 14 to 16 June.*

Kraft, Michael E., and Scott R. Furlong. 2004. *Public Policy: Politics, Analysis, and Alternatives.* Washington, D.C.: Congressional Quarterly Press.

Kratovits, Adres, and Jaan-Mati Punning. 2001. "Driving Forces for the Formation of Environmental Policy in the Baltic Countries." *Ambio,* vol. 30, no. 7: 443-449.

Lalasz, Robert, and Naomi Greengrass. 2002. "EU Enlargement and Environmental Quality in Central and Eastern Europe and Beyond." *Environmental Change and Security Project.* Woodrow Wilson International Center for Scholars. ecsp.si.edu/eugreen.htm. Accessed 7 May 2002.

Lambsdorff, Johann Graf. 2001. *Background Paper to 2001 Corruption Perceptions Index: Framework Document.* Berlin: Transparency International and Göttingen University. www.transparency.org/cpi/2001/dnld/methodology.pdf. Accessed 28 May 2002.

Lasswell, H. D., and M. S. McDougal. 1992. *Jurisprudence for a Free Society: Studies in Law, Science, and Policy.* New Haven, CT: New Haven Press.

Millard, Frances. 1998. "Environmental Policy in Poland," in Susan Baker and Petr Jehlička (eds.), *Dilemmas of Transition: The Environment, Democracy and Economic Reform in East Central Europe.* London: Frank Cass, 145-161.

National Audit Office of Denmark, the State Audit Office of Estonia, the State Audit Office of Finland, the State Audit Office of the Republic of Latvia, State Control of the Republic of Lithuania, the Supreme Chamber of Control of the Republic of Poland, Accounts Chamber of the Russian Federation, the Swedish National Audit Office. 2001. *Joint Final Report: Of Findings over Parallel Audits of Implementation of the Provisions of the Convention on the Protection of the Marine Environment on the Protection of the Baltic Sea Area (Helsinki Convention).* Warsaw: Supreme Chamber of Control of the Republic of Poland.

Nikodemusa, Alda. 2002. "Expert Meeting on Protection of the Mammal Species from Perspective of EU Nature Conservation Requirements," Birstonas, Lithuania, 16 April 2002. www.bef.lv/nature/pdf/species/02_04_16.pdf. Accessed 7 June 2002.

North, Douglass. 1990. *Institutions, Institutional Change and Economic Performance.* Cambridge: Cambridge University Press, 1990.

Nowicki, Maciej. 1997. "Poland," in Jürg Klarer and Bedřich Moldan (eds.), *The Environmental Challenge for Central European Economies in Transition.* New York: John Wiley and Sons, 193-227.

Organization for Economic Cooperation and Development. 1999. *Environment in the Transition to the Market Economy: Progress in Central and Eastern Europe and the Newly Independent States.* Paris: OECD.

Pavlínek, Petr, and John Pickles. 2000. *Environmental Transitions: Transformation and Ecological Defence in Central and Eastern Europe.* London: Routledge.

Podoba, Juraj. 1998. "Rejecting Green Velvet: Transition, Environment and Nationalism in Slovakia," in Susan Baher and Petr Jehliča (eds.), *Dilemmas of Transition: The Environment, Democracy and Economic Reform in East Central Europe.* London: Frank Cass, 129-144.

Richet, Xavier. 1989. *The Hungarian Model: Markets and Planning in a Socialist Economy.* Cambridge: Cambridge University Press, 5-7.

Rosenbaum, Walter A. 1998. *Environmental Politics and Policy.* Washington, D.C.: Congressional Quarterly Press.

Statistikaamet. 2003. *Air Emissions Database: Summary CO₂ Emissions, Gg, 2003.* Statistical Office of Estonia, Tallinn. www.stat.ee/statistics. Accessed 12 April 2003.

Thompson, Jon. 1991. "East Europe's Dark Dawn." *National Geographic.* June: 36-69.

Thomson, Alice. 2000. "One Dead Salmon Speaks Volumes." *Daily Telegraph* (London). 16 February: 26.

Transparency International. 2003. "Transparency International Corruption Perceptions Index 2003: Nine out of Ten Developing Countries Urgently Need Practical Support to Combat Corruption, Highlights New Index," Press Release of Transparency International. www.transparency.org/pressreleases_archive/ Accessed 16 January 2004.

United Nations. 1997. *Poland: Country Profile. Implementation of the Agenda 21: Review of Progress Made since the United Nations Conference on Environment and Development, 1992.* Information provided by the Government of Poland to the UN Commission on Sustainable Development, Fifth Session, 7-25 April 1997, New York. www.un.org/esa/earthsummit/pold-cp.htm. Accessed 6 June 2002.

United Nations Economic Commission for Europe. 1995. *Trends in Europe and North America 1995.* Geneva: UNECE.

———. 1999a. *Environmental Performance Reviews: Lithuania.* Geneva: UNECE.

———. 1999b. *Environmental Performance Reviews: Latvia.* Geneva: UNECE.

———. 2001a. *Trends in Europe and North America 2001: Excerpt 2001.* Geneva: UNECE.

———. 2001b. *Environmental Performance Reviews: Romania.* Geneva: UNECE.

Chapter 2

Environmental Reforms in the Czech Republic: Uneven Progress after 1989

Susan Legro and Matthew R. Auer

Czech authorities combat a type of environmental problem that ordinary Czechs seldom contemplate: light pollution. The nation's night sky is badly contaminated by the glare from street lamps, strobe lights, billboards, and neon signs, so claims astronomer Jenik Hollan. "Astronomers are having to use stronger and stronger equipment to view the Milky Way, and some never get to see small meteors or wispy nebulas any more," he complains (Connolly, 2002: 19). Failing to take adequate measures to prevent the occurrence of light pollution in the republic, including, for example, shielding lamppost lights, could result in a fine of more than US$4,000.

Efforts to scrub the night sky at once signal how far Czech environmental reforms have come and the work that remains to be done. Elected leaders are tackling secondary environmental problems like light pollution having already instituted laws and regulations to redress first order public health and environmental threats, such as air and water pollution. But lawmaking only partly addresses environmental problems. Challenges remain in implementing rules that address environmental hazards large and small.

The light pollution case also underscores a larger problem that countries confront worldwide: environmental priorities are often played off against development interests in a kind of zero-sum game. Infrequently are environmental and public health precautions central facets of development planning. For example, waste light emanating from the country's many new expressways is a planning failure. Officials never considered the problem of waste light in the night sky, and hence never bothered to explore the benefits of installing low-glare, flat-bellied street lamps during roadway construction.

Powerful politicians tend to be ambivalent about environmental protection, especially if it risks stifling capitalism. As a result, Czech environmental authorities have fought and lost major battles pitting development and environmental interests. Ironically, and as we contend below, certain accession programs sponsored by the European Union have occasionally reinforced the development versus environment dichotomy rather than reconcile it.

Shortcomings in the EU's environmental laws and preaccession programs are of particular concern to Czech environmentalists because EU norms more so than homegrown environmental institutions are the main shapers of Czech environmental policy. Moreover, in practice, environmental policy in the republic is often controlled by individual decision makers who are prone to corruption and conflict of interest.

Pressure on the environment from industries, and especially heavy industries, has subsided since the late 1980s, and environmental policy reforms are part of this success story. However, declining industrial pollution is rapidly replaced by pollution from other sources, and in particular, from automobiles. Section one of this chapter discusses these contradictory trends in environmental performance.

The second section considers the central government's mixed results in assuring the environmental integrity of economic development and the role of the EU in shaping interactions between the environment and the economy. In the early twenty-first century, Czech environmental authorities hewed closely to EU norms, so as to comply with preaccession legal and policy obligations. One result was that contradictory norms and ambiguities in EU legislation translated into weaknesses in Czech environmental law.

Section three examines environmentally questionable dimensions of EU preaccession grant programs that are billed as environmentally friendly. Lack of clarity in EU legislation and policies governing nuclear safety and the future of a controversial nuclear power facility in the Czech Republic are the subjects of section four. Civic organizations' struggle to influence both preaccession policies and broader public opinion are core themes in section five. The problem of corruption in environmental policy institutions is examined in section six.

Throughout the chapter, case material is presented to underscore the fragility of environmental norms in a nation that nevertheless met many of the environmental legal requirements for entry to the EU by 2001.

Perceptions of Environmental Quality in the Czech Republic

In terms of changes to environmental conditions since the era of central planning, the Czech Republic has followed a similar trajectory with that of its neighbors. The early economic downturn and painful industrial restructuring experience had a silver lining in the form of relief from pollution. Indicators of declining pollution loads pleased environmental authorities who reasoned that their policies were working. For example, the Czech republic's SO_2 emissions, which at one time were the highest in Europe, declined to the OECD average of around 40 kilograms per person per year by 1999—an "exceptional" accomplishment, according to Bedřich Moldan, a former Minister of Environment (Moldan, 2000).

Others were less impressed. Fagin and Jehlička note (1997: 113) that improved ambient environmental conditions since the Velvet Revolution were due mainly to economic recession. Moreover, in the late 1990s, the Czech Republic continued to emit a great deal of pollution per unit economic output. Its emissions of SO_2 per unit GDP exceeded the OECD European average by nearly four times and its CO_2 emissions per unit of GDP were more than twice the OECD European average (OECD, 1999: 49-50).

Sulfur emissions fell precipitously during the 1990s—by some 68 percent between 1987 and 1997 (OECD, 1999: 49). But Pavlínek and Pickles note that the downward sloping trend for SO_2 emissions began in the mid-1980s before the collapse of socialism.

In this sense, the political changes of 1989 did not represent a major turning point in pollution levels for SO_2 and particulate emissions, but instead were a continuation of an earlier trend that was in turn strongly reinforced by a pronounced industrial decline and increased efforts to combat air pollution after 1989 (Pavlínek and Pickles, 1999: 363).

But as was true of other advanced transition countries in CEE, the resumption of economic growth after 1993 was not accompanied by a reversal of these positive environmental trends. Emissions of SO_2, dust, CO, NO_x, and other air contaminants continued to decline early into the twenty-first century, suggesting that both policy reforms and environmental investments were consequential, after all. While some heavy polluters shut down in the early 1990s, never to re-open, many others modernized their production processes or instituted end-of-pipe environmental solutions. Fuel switching from coal and lignite to natural gas and higher fuel prices also helped clean up the air (Pavlínek and Pickles, 1999: 364-366). In addition, the Clean Air Act, which came into force in 1991, required large stationary source emitters to come into compliance within seven years, leading to major investments in pollution abatement.[1] By 1999, Czech authorities could boast an 86 percent reduction in SO_2 emissions from 1990 levels. NO_x from stationary sources also declined significantly to levels below the EU average. Moreover, CO_2 emissions fell by 25 percent from 1990 to 1999, indicating that Czechs were putting less stress on the global climate (Moldan, 2000).

Nevertheless, by decade's end, Czechs continued to churn out large amounts of pollution on a per capita basis—facts not lost on Czech citizens. In a poll taken as part of a series of surveys to commemorate the ten year anniversary of the Velvet Revolution, only 49 percent of Czechs were satisfied with the quality of the environment in their neighborhood. Only 20 percent expressed satisfaction with the quality of environment in the country as a whole (Tax, 1999). Czechs are uneasy about the environment, but during the 1990s few were troubled enough to pressure the government to take environmental concerns more seriously. Authors of the republic's National Strategy for Sustainable Development, which was developed for the 2002 United Nations World Summit on Sustainable Development, noted that while the overall state of the environment had improved since 1989, Czechs had only a token appreciation of sustainable development. The public's quiescent attitude toward environmental issues may signal to politicians that development can occur without thorough environmental planning. Hence, environmental aspects of formal economic and social policies are frequently addressed only superficially or not at all (Center for Environmental Studies, 2001: chapter 2).

Even when formal environmental policies are implemented, they do not necessarily reflect a sustainable development ethos. One set of observers described the government's environmental objectives as "defined strictly in technical and market terminology" (Fagin and Jehlička, 1997: 113). It is suggested that efficiency and the profit motive become ends in themselves in the design and implementation of environmental policies, with public health and ecological objectives taking a back seat. Authors of the National Strategy for Sustainable Development were similarly struck by the government's tendency to approach environmental problems as mere engineering puzzles. They contend that the predominance of regulatory instruments and end-of-pipe technological solutions had actually obstructed public understanding of sustainable development principles (Center for Environmental Studies, 2001: chapter 1).

The Primacy of Economic Development

Progress and setbacks in environmental policymaking in the Czech Republic cannot be understood without careful attention to the most pressing concerns and interests of successive post-1989 Czech governments, namely, economic development and accession to the European Union. From first appearances, Czech environmental protection institutions resemble those of Western European counterparts. Environmental affairs are governed by laws, regulations, directives, and market-oriented instruments dealing with air, water, waste, and nature protection, among others. Environmental policies are administered by numerous ministries and agencies, but most prominently by the Ministry of Environment and the Environmental Inspectorate.

But in practice, environmental compliance, and not merely environmental rule making, has been most thoroughly developed and applied in those areas that interfere least with economic development and that are prescribed most clearly in EU legal directives (for example, rules governing sulfur dioxide emissions from state-owned utilities). Examining how economic development priorities and prospective EU membership alternately enable and hinder environmental compliance is instructive for understanding the start-and-stop quality of Czech environmental reforms since the end of Communism.

Less than three years into the post-Socialist transition, more than one-third of Czech voters opted for center-right candidates in the 1992 parliamentary elections. The new prime minister, Václav Klaus, promised to accelerate market-oriented reforms but called for a reappraisal of environmental protection efforts. Klaus employed colorful language to amend otherwise positive public perceptions of the environmental movement and of environmental issues, generally. The environment, he quipped, was merely "whipped cream on the [economic] cake," (Pavlínek and Pickles, 1999: 371) and he labeled sustainable development "a bizarre leftist invention" (Horak, 2001: 318). "Ecology," he declared, "is not a science. It has nothing in common with science. It is ideology" (Pavlínek and Pickles, 1999: 371).

Klaus's skepticism about environmental protection was matched by his faith in the socially redeeming qualities of capitalism, the government's obligation to foster economic liberalization,[2] and conservative lawmakers' insistence that governmental bodies like the Ministry of Environment not encumber economic reforms.

A 1993 law gave the Ministry of Environment broad authority over water, forest, and landscape management, among other areas, but Klaus shifted many of these functions to other ministries. Land use planning moved to the Ministry of Economy; the Ministry of Industry and Trade took over supervision of environmental aspects of mining; several water protection functions shifted to the Ministry of Agriculture (Pavlínek and Pickles, 1999: 371).

However, Klaus's seeming hostility to environmental concerns was not so indelible as to supercede his even stronger commitment to nurturing and maintaining national economic security. Consistent with the norms prescribed in the nation's Clean Air Act (which was passed before Klaus assumed the prime minister's post), Klaus-led governments required environmental improvements from the country's main electricity producer (as well as its largest air polluter), the energy firm Ceske Energeticke Zavody (CEZ). By 1998, CEZ had spent around $1.7 billion on air pollution control equipment and on the decommissioning of old power stations (Horak, 2001: 320). CEZ did not resist this regulatory burden because, as the country's monopoly power producer, it was highly profitable and could afford to comply with the rules. Moreover, compliance improved its chances of passing muster with European regulators once the Czech Republic joined the EU, and it enhanced CEZ's competitiveness at the expense of smaller firms that might not pass EU-sponsored environmental inspections (Horak, 2001: 320). In this case, both advocates of national economic security and environmental protection realized a mutually satisfactory institutional outcome. But the CEZ case was an exception to the dominant pattern of conflict between environmentalists and economic development interests.

CEZ is not the only Czech organization sensitive to the EU's demands and expectations. As Horak observes (2001: 317), "from the outset" the Ministry of Environment used European Community standards as benchmarks for environmental rule making in post-Communist Czechoslovakia, and later, in the Czech Republic (see also, Madar, 1997). During the 1990s, MOE in conjunction with the State Environmental Inspectorate pressed industry to comply with new domestic laws, regulations, and decrees that were modeled after EU legislation. On paper, these efforts were quite successful: by the end of 1998 (a deadline for compliance) only 120 out of 2,500 large polluters transgressed pollution control laws enacted earlier in the decade, and less than 2 percent of the country's 27,000 medium-sized polluters failed to respect the compliance deadline (Horak, 2001: 320).

But in many cases, the government set a relatively low bar for enterprises to cross in order to achieve compliance. Consider, for example, the monetary charges for air pollution emissions that are set in large and medium-sized plants' environmental permits. According to the OECD,

> some of these charges have been set at relatively low levels; thus, they have little or no incentive effect on company management and do not stimulate investments that would prevent or abate pollution. For example, it is estimated that the charge for emitting one tonne of SO_x (CZK 1,000 in 1997) would need to be about ten times higher in order to have a possible incentive effect. (1999: 151)

The Republic's 400 plus environmental inspectors were in charge of monitoring compliance during the 1990s and assessing fines against out-of-compliance firms. Czech news agencies occasionally reported on the enforcement activities of the Inspectorate (e.g., CTK Business News, 1994), and the Inspectorate made readily available its annual tally of inspections and punishment activities (e.g., CTK Czech News Agency, 2000). However, journalists seldom made finer distinctions in appraising enforcement activities, namely, the extent to which penalties against polluters were conclusively applied. The OECD found (1999: 128) that approximately only 60 percent of assessed fines were actually paid through the mid-1990s.

Economics and the Environment Square Off:
The Problem of Urban Sprawl

The Environmental Inspectorate's relatively small staff has struggled with a hefty inspection load, and also rules that have hemmed in their ability to abrogate environmentally destructive acts. Its formal authorities include inspecting facilities for violations of air, water, and waste management rules as well as enforcing nature conservation laws. However, in practice, it has been prohibited from enforcing penalties for illegal construction activities in protected areas or areas not zoned for development—activities that conservative Czech lawmakers were reluctant to regulate during the 1990s. One consequence is that authorities are confronting a growing problem of urban and even rural sprawl. The 2001 State Environmental Policy recognized sprawl as one of the nation's most pressing dilemmas. That policy states,

> At the edges and beyond the boundaries of built-up settlement areas and even in the open landscape, new industrial, storage and commercial areas, petrol stations, billboards, isolated groups of houses and other structures are emerging, in spite of the fact that within existing settlements a great many buildings with the same purpose are gradually falling into disrepair; and properties equipped with services and roadways are left unused. Thus agricultural land and natural areas are being used up, leading to new requirements for transportation and causing the economics of investment and operation in urban areas to deteriorate. (Czech Ministry of the Environment, 2001a: 15)

Ironically the laissez-faire approach favored by Prime Minister Klaus gave rise to public goods problems he hoped to avoid. Sprawling residential and commercial developments on the outskirts of cities lacked the tax base to permit construction and maintenance of needed infrastructure, such as roads. But were the roads extended and improved, they would tend to reinforce rather than relieve pressures from sprawl, even as public infrastructure in well-established urban areas decays.

Here is an example where learning from and avoiding the mistakes of other OECD countries, and in particular, the United States, did not occur. In the United States, in the 1980s and 1990s, a new generation of urban architects and planners condemned old planning rules that fostered urban and suburban sprawl, sparking a renaissance of "community-friendly" planning and a return of the ethic of the "traditional town" (Duany and Plater-Zyberk, 1992). But outskirts of larger Czech municipalities are beginning to resemble the sprawling urban hinterlands of many American cities—a result of institutional rules that provide easy title to unclaimed land and are permissive of all types of built property uses.

EU legislation offers no remedy for urban sprawl because EU directives do not contain clear standards for urban land use. Instead, during the late 1990s and in the first years of the twenty-first century, member states developed voluntary agreements through an initiative called the European Spatial Development Perspective. The Perspective contains sixty "policy options." On a parallel track, the Council of Europe—an intergovernmental body distinct from the European Union but that counts all EU states as members—adopted the "Guiding Principles for Sustainable Spatial Development of the European Continent" which outlines measures for sustainable development of cities and towns, but contains no legally binding provisions (Expert Group on the Urban Environment, 2001: 7-8).

Not surprisingly, rules governing management of urban growth are relatively weak in the Czech Republic, and extant EU policies have not provided especially clear reference points in domestic debates between the Ministry of Environment and prodevelopment interests, nor between municipal authorities and developers. In the late 1990s, for example, the government proposed reducing the area of land with "protected landscape" status by up to two-thirds—a proposal that curried favor with developers seeking to weaken already minimal spatial planning rules. In this case, the Ministry of Environment's insistence on preserving norms for protected areas prevailed; its strongest argument was that current domestic rules were consistent with relevant EU standards. But as Horak points out, the ministry unintentionally reinforced the notion that compliance with EU legislation is the main reason for protecting the environment. Environmental protection for the sake of human or ecological well-being was beside the point.

> By relying upon the integration argument, the defenders of environmental policy reform transformed the rationale for such reform into an instrumental one. Initiatives were no longer assessed on their own merits, but primarily as a means to an entirely separate end. As a result, developing environmental policy that went significantly beyond compliance with minimal European standards became a politically indefensible position. (Horak, 2001: 319)

The EU's Spatial Development Perspective provides advice and moral support to accession states to promote sustainable urban development. But the most powerful incentives from Brussels for strengthening urban environmental institutions, and environmental institutions generally, are standards-based directives whose transposition into domestic legislation is obligatory.

Soft pledges by Prague to promote sustainable development in and around cities have not reversed the urban sprawl trend, as admitted by the government in its State Environmental Policy. Among the undesirable consequences of this trend is the increased need for motor vehicles. Between 1990 and 1996, the total number of cars and trucks in operation in the republic grew by 40 percent (OECD, 1999: 60). But swelling traffic was especially obvious in major cities like Prague. The number of motor vehicles in the capital increased 72 percent between 1990 and 1998. No other large city in CEE has more vehicles per person; in the late 1990s, Prague had 513 cars per 1,000 inhabitants (Pavlínek and Pickles, 1999: 372). In the country as a whole, ridership on public transport declined by 19 percent between 1990 and 1997 as travelers switched to cars and as the government cut subsidies for the improvement of mass transit systems. Moreover, state-supported trains ran less regularly on many rural routes, forcing passengers to purchase cars—often older, used vehicles with poor gas mileage and primitive pollution controls (Pavlínek and Pickles, 1999: 372-373; Czech Ministry of the Environment, 2001a: 45).

The EU has voiced concern about the explosive growth of cars on European roads, but its preaccession funding has done little to reverse the problem. In the Czech Republic, the EU approved a plan to build 1,000 kilometers of new highways by the year 2000 (Horak, 2001: 322).

Moreover, EU directives only partly amend the problem of air pollution from automobiles. Community legislation requiring all new gasoline-propelled cars to be equipped with catalytic converters led to a steep rise of such cars on Czech roads (from 7.5 percent in 1994 to 18.3 percent in 1996). Also, ambient lead levels decreased 75 percent between 1989 and 1994 thanks to growing numbers of cars using unleaded gasoline (as well as lower lead levels in leaded gas) (OECD, 1999: 60). However, EU directives do not create economic disincentives for overuse of vehicular fuels, and there are no rules limiting the use of urban roadways.

Compared to EU directives governing mobile source emissions, prohibitions on stationary source emissions are stronger, though the focus tends to be end of pipe (Horak, 2001: 321). Common industrial air pollutants from stationary sources such as suspended particulates and sulfur dioxide—contaminants that are the subject of unambiguous, numerical standards in EU legislation—dropped precipitously in the Czech Republic during the 1990s (figure 2.1).

During that same period, mobile source emission trends were more complex (figure 2.2; see also, Horak, 2001: 322-323). Oxides of nitrogen from cars and trucks decreased in absolute terms between 1990 and 2001 (from 210,356 m.t. to 168,283 m.t.). But emissions of NO_x from vehicles as a percentage of total NO_x (i.e., from stationary and mobile sources combined) climbed steeply during the period, from 28.4 percent in 1990 to 50.7 percent in 2001. Carbon monoxide emissions from mobile sources rose in absolute terms until the mid-1990s before declining; CO pollution from cars and trucks remained higher in 2001 than in 1990 (333,119 m.t. versus 210,269 m.t., respectively). Mobile source emissions of CO as a percentage of total CO emissions rose steadily over the course of the 1990s, from 23.6 percent in 1990 to 51.4 percent in 2001 (Czech Ministry of Environment, 2002).

Environmental Implications of EU Accession Programs

Complying with EU environmental norms is an expensive undertaking for the Czech Republic. The government estimates that by the time all EU

FIGURE 2.1

Stationary Source Pollution Emissions in the Czech Republic, 1990-2001

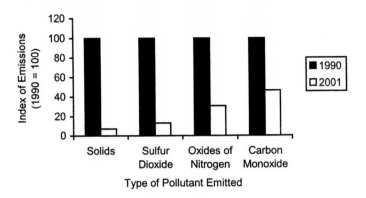

Source: Czech Ministry of Environment, 2002.

FIGURE 2.2

Mobile Source Pollution Emissions in the Czech Republic, 1990-2001

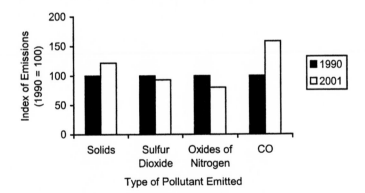

Source: Czech Ministry of Environment, 2002.

environmental directives are fully implemented, 400 billion Czech crowns will have been spent on new or improved environmental infrastructure and other investments (approximately US$11.6 billion) (OECD, 1999: 163). For the sake of comparison, the European Commission estimated that the Czech Republic needed to spend approximately 315.3 billion Czech crowns or around US$9.14 billion to modernize the nation's public and private transport infrastructure (CTK Czech News Agency, 1998). Among other major costs, and a burden that other CEE countries confront, is providing wastewater treatment services to sparsely populated towns and rural villages. These projects may cost more than 110 billion crowns (US$3.19 billion) alone (OECD, 1999: 163).[3]

Easing this great financial burden are loans and grants from various bilateral and multilateral sources, but by far the most important are from EU accession programs. Funds from these programs are key not only for environmental protection efforts, but also for economic development. The missions of major EU aid programs such as PHARE, SAPARD, and ISPA[4] all embrace the principle of development that minimizes environmental impacts or even en-hances environmental values. But this goal has not always been easy to realize.

Reconciling conflicts between prodevelopment and environmental interests has been particularly challenging for projects sponsored under the EU's Instrument for Structural Policies for Accession (ISPA) which was launched in April 2000 and focuses on transport and environmental initiatives (DG Regio-ISPA, 2000). The republic was scheduled to receive more than €1 billion per year from 2000 to 2006 from this fund. Among the key environment-oriented ISPA projects are wastewater treatment upgrades for three large cities and one region. Transport grants include three for road construction and two for railway line upgrades.

A key objective of most ISPA transport projects in the Czech Republic is to improve interconnections with larger TransEuropean Transport Network (TEN) and Transport Infrastructure Needs Assessment Scheme (TINA) projects that link up or otherwise enhance interusability of highways, railways, airports, and waterways throughout the EU and accession countries (ISPA, 2001). Hence, ISPA transport-related grants intentionally benefit not only direct country recipients, but also citizens throughout the EU.[5]

This broad targeting of aid benefits is defensible to the extent that the EU promotes economic development in states that will become members of the EU itself. From this perspective, economic and environmental problems in CEE and in the EU are one and the same. If the EU is persuaded that candidate members are incapable on their own of modernizing their economies or protecting their environments, but that EU aid will ultimately enable greater economic and environmental self-reliance, it is in the EU's interest to help, today. Moreover, it is equitable to make investments that promise benefits to broad sets of actors in the EU and not just in targeted Central and Eastern European countries.

However, the question remains whether EU-sponsored projects that are in the interest of the EU at large are also in the interest of Czechs. Czech environmentalists and some environmental authorities, for example, are not enthusiastic about road transport projects made possible by EU grants. Former Minister of Environment Bedřich Moldan asserted,

> the consequences of extending the current EU perverse incentives in transport and agriculture to the candidate countries would be disastrous for environment, biological diversity, social structure and economies of Europe as a whole. (Moldan, 2000)

Controversy over the proposed ISPA-sponsored Prague and Dresden roadway—
the so-called D8/A17 motorway—illustrates how Czech authorities have struggled to translate conflicting EU policy objectives into environmentally sensitive
policies and programs in the Czech Republic. One segment of the D8/A17 motorway would pass through a protected landscape in the Czech *stredohori* (Middle Mountains) and through a nature park. Planned construction also conflicts
with waterway conservation activities on the Elbe River. The project would also
traverse densely settled urban areas (CEE Bankwatch Network, 2001: 16;
Robes, 1996). Environmentally problematic aspects of the project inspired a
coalition of NGOs and citizens to bestow the "Polluter of the Year" (*Ropak
roku*) award on the Czech Minister of Environment in 2001. Ironically, one of
the main objectives of the 1998 Transport Policy of the Czech Republic (413/98)
was to support public transport projects over private transport projects. The policy also stated that future transport infrastructure must abide by strict environmental protection principles (Czech Ministry of Environment, 2001b: 28-29).
However, even in the face of intense public criticism, the government was reluctant to perform a transboundary environmental impact assessment for the project
(CEE Bankwatch Network, 2001: 7).

Relevant European Union laws and policies sent mixed signals to Czech authorities. The EU's Regulation 2236/95 of 1995, which authorized a process for
applying for TransEuropean Transport Network funds, stated that projects must
be consistent with applicable EU norms, including environmental laws. However, the regulation established no standards nor incentives to favor public
transport projects. The Ministers' failure to prioritize the availability of project
funds based on energy or environmental criteria all but contradicted a key objective of the EU Sustainable Development Strategy, namely, to "[markedly re-
duce] the share of finance given to road transport" (CEE Bankwatch Network,
2001: 7).

Only in 1999, with Regulation 1655/99, did the Council of Ministers formally incentivize the process of applying for environmentally friendly public
transport projects. The new regulation specified that between 2000 and 2006,
only 25 percent of TEN funds would be set aside for roadway projects compared
to at least 55 percent for railways (European Union, 2002).

Most Czech applications for EU-sponsored transport funds were developed
before the 1999 regulation, and not coincidentally, the Czech government spent
considerable time, energy, and money developing requests for motorway improvements such as the D8/A17 and R48 expressway projects. Critics complained that environmental considerations in these applications were mostly per-
functory and that environmental interests had been shut out of key policy
deliberations. The validity of these allegations can be discerned by examining
Czech institutional arrangements for preparing ISPA applications.

The government assigned different application-writing duties to different
Czech ministries, with the Ministry of Transport overseeing a working group for

transportation projects and the Ministry of Environment leading a group on environmental projects—this notwithstanding the environmental implications of transport projects and vice versa. In the D8/A17 case, NGOs were instructed that the Ministry of Transport's working group served only in an advisory capacity to the vice minister of Transport. Hence, the working group would be composed solely of representatives from the ministry itself (CEE Bankwatch Network, 2001: 16). As a result, NGOs and other civic organizations were excluded from relevant policy discussions.

This approach to constituting ISPA working groups contrasts with the provisions for multistakeholder participation developed in the EU's Chapter 22 (environmental law) accession negotiations with the Czech government. Moreover, the D8/A17 proposal process did not adhere closely to European Union norms on public access to environmental information. However, as one review of ISPA project development procedures notes,

> The guidelines for accession funds do not provide an obligatory demand for public participation in the process of setting up and implementing accession mechanisms. Where opportunities are given by law, the wording "where appropriate" is often used, making enforcement difficult. (CEE Bankwatch Network, 2001: 5)

The Ministry of Transport had an interest in backing the D8/A17 application, among other reasons, because it promised to increase the policy-making leverage of that ministry vis-à-vis the powerful Ministries of Economy and Foreign Affairs. An approved grant would bring in millions of euros for the ministry and its contractors to oversee, and for the construction of a key transport corridor through Central Europe. In 2000, the EU authorized an ISPA grant to assist in the preparation of technical designs, financial analyses, and environmental impact statements; these documents will be used by the Czech government to apply for a larger, capital-assistance ISPA grant for the motorway.

Nuclear Power and Accession Politics

The EU has played a role in another controversial Czech project: the completion and operation of the Temelin nuclear power station—a plant vigorously opposed by neighboring Austria. Indeed, Austria vowed to block the Czech Republic's path to accession were the plant to come on-line. The EU struck a more conciliatory tone, but its actions raised concerns about Brussels's purview over matters that are poorly defined in community law, namely, those governing nuclear safety and the future of nuclear energy in Europe.

Inspired as much by the need for reliable sources of electricity as the desire to showcase Soviet advanced technology, the Temelin project was initiated in the late 1970s, as part of a scheme to build one nuclear power plant in each of the six regions of Czechoslovakia. Southern Bohemia, near the Austrian border, was selected as the site for Temelin in 1980. Construction commenced in 1983 but more than fifteen years elapsed before nuclear fuel was loaded into the plant. During the first years after the Velvet Revolution there was lively discussion about the merits and drawbacks of moving ahead with Temelin. But the government ultimately braved projected cost overruns and other concerns and renewed its commitment to bring the plant on-line. In 1992, the government of Václav Klaus finalized a provisional decision made by Petr Pithart, Czechoslovakia's first post-Communist prime minister, to pare down the number of planned reactors from four to two. In part, this decision reflected Czechoslovakia's desire to mollify neighbors (and especially Austria) who worried about the plant's Russian-designed instrument, control, and safety systems.

The plan called for completing construction by 1995 at a cost of 68.8 billion crowns (US$2 billion in 1998 dollars) (World Information Service, 2000). Revised estimates put total construction costs at around 98.5 billion crowns (US$2.86 billion) which, environmentalists pointed out, exceeded the break-even costs for the plant that the government calculated in 1993 (Pachner and Horner, 1998: 1). The U.S. government pledged US$317 million in loan guarantees to enable Westinghouse Electric Corporation to graft Western-style containment facilities and other safety features onto both reactors (Jehl, 1994: A1).

Austrian officials began campaigning to halt completion of the reactors shortly after the awarding of the Westinghouse contract, and won support from anti-Temelin allies in the German government and European NGOs. In 2000, the Austrian Parliament passed a resolution linking safety features of Temelin with the Czech drive for EU membership. Unless modern safety measures were guaranteed at Temelin, lawmakers insisted, the Austrian government should block its neighbor's entry to the EU. The Austrian chancellor made similar demands. But as Axelrod (2002: 44) points out, there are no EU directives covering nuclear safety except those governing ionizing radiation, transportation of nuclear fuel, and rules on nuclear preparedness derived from other European agreements.

Divergent energy strategies in the EU partly explain the lack of well-defined EU legislation on nuclear issues. Seven of the fifteen member states possess nuclear power plants (Axelrod, 2002: 42), though a subset intend to phase out nuclear power. Other members, like Austria, have renounced nuclear energy for decades. However, the *acquis*'s lack of clarity on nuclear safety, and member states' disparate views on the future of nuclear power, did not dissuade the European Parliament from recommending a draft, nonbinding resolution to close Temelin and to dismantle the facility via an EU-financed bailout. This resolution recommended that the EU's main advisory body, the European Commission, consider Temelin's status in evaluating the Czech Republic's readiness for accession. But the EU Commission rejected this advice, refusing to make Czech accession negotiations contingent on heretofore legally-unspecified safety standards.

Shortly thereafter, Austrian pressure on both the EU and its Czech neighbor subsided. Austria realized it lacked support in both the EU Commission and the EU's executive decision-making body, the European Council of Ministers (Axelrod, 2002: 47). Moreover, it knew it risked being labeled a bully. A leading Czech daily warned, "The instrument of self-defence has turned into a weapon against ourselves" (*Die Presse* quoted in CTK National News Wire, 2003). Perhaps indicative of a more accommodating mood in Vienna, there were no recriminations when, in May of 2003, the two reactors at Temelin were powered to full strength.

Environmentalism: The Struggle to Excite Public Interest

The dying down of controversy over Temelin also reflects environmental NGOs' uphill struggle to appeal to lawmakers and the public at large. In 2000, several NGOs collected signatures for a referendum on Temelin. Activists hosted national news conferences, issued press releases, gave speeches throughout the country, and even retained popular musical artists to rally against the plant at concerts designed to appeal to young people. However, the referendum movement all but collapsed when the Czech Parliament failed to pass a law on referenda (legislation that remained bogged down in the Senate in 2001). As far as enshrining a place for grassroots petition by popular initiative, little had changed since the early 1990s, when environmentalists called for an open vote on the D8/A17 motorway. More than ten years after the Velvet Revolution, a reliable process for drafting and authorizing popular referenda remained elusive.

Making matters worse for environmentalists, public interest in Temelin and other environmental controversies had long since ebbed. The underlying explanations are familiar to students of post-Communist environmentalism in CEE and the FSU and include: the emergence of acute economic problems, such as soaring unemployment rates; environmentalism's irrelevance as a safe harbor for opponents of Communism; and the formation of divisions between environmental activists, Green Party advocates, and nationalists, in what previously had been a unified movement.

Early stumbles in the campaign against D8/A17 foreshadowed waning public interest in environmental affairs. Though environmentalists called for a referendum, regional and national authorities did not yield, and NGOs did not push more aggressively, realizing they might lose the vote anyway. Existing roads connecting Prague and Dresden were in poor condition and there was considerable public support for a new modern highway. Moreover, while national authorities felt compelled to respond to the environmentalists' challenges, most local governments were mute. The Ministry of Transport felt confident in pressing ahead once it realized that officials in towns along the route would not voice strong opposition.

Efforts to reenergize public interest in the environment have met with mixed results, and the reasons can be traced to lapses and setbacks in institution-building by the state and by environmentalists themselves.

The center-right government that took office in 1993 aimed to assert discipline over official policy-making institutions that had been, according to the conservatives, open to so many interests and points of view as to be ineffectual. Former Environment Minister Bedřich Moldan's "Green Parliament"—a forum for state and civil society actors to exchange views on environmental policies—was jettisoned, with the Ministry of Environment inviting public opinion and sharing information with NGOs only as mandated by law. Vaclav Klaus's administration renounced the broad-based approach to policy-making that had been employed by the country's first post-Communist leaders; democratic participation was redefined in narrower, functional terms. The main opportunity for public participation in governmental affairs was voting at parliamentary elections (Fagin, 1999: 99). As Fagin contends,

> in such a climate it is hardly surprising that environmental associations were denied any constructive role in the political process and were viewed as an opposition force rather than as potential partners in the policy process. (1999: 102)

Nineteen ninety-five was a low point for environmentalists when four environmental organizations were added to an internal security "watch list" of alleged subversive groups—a list shared with police and other public organizations (Fagin, 1999: 102).

More constructive ties between state and civil society actors reemerged with the passing of the Klaus administration. Environmental ministers in the late 1990s and their subordinates have invited environmentalists to weigh in on and even draft new regulations and policies—for example, Greenpeace wrote part of a new code governing disposal of wastes (Fagin, 1999: 103).

Still, in the early years of the twenty-first century, the environmental movement struggled to regain a central stage in public affairs—an endeavor complicated by the declining influence of environmental leaders. In the early 1990s, new political parties and interest groups siphoned off many of the most politically active and well-connected members of the Green movement, sapping strength from environmental organizations. The ultimate cause of these defections was the unfettering of democratic participation and the opening up of a previously closed political system—outcomes that environmentalists had sought all along.

NGOs themselves are also partly responsible for their own diminishing influence. Many environmental civic organizations had trouble adjusting to the new political landscape of post-totalitarianism. There were growing pains for groups that had favored organizational plans with flat management structures and fluid memberships, and that relied primarily on confrontational strategies to promote organizational interests. The impromptu public demonstrations and spontaneous protest activities that had proven so effective in the late 1980s became anachronistic in an increasingly politically open Czechoslovakia, and later, the Czech Republic. Institutional problems occurred at the microlevel as mass-based coalitions of environmentalists failed to adopt rules to regularize ordinary but nevertheless critical organizational functions such as personnel, financial accounting, and program auditing.

Environmental NGOs were handicapped by funding problems throughout the transition period and beyond—a dilemma faced by environmentalists in all CEE countries. Those fortunate enough to obtain funds often relied on foreign sources, including from bilateral aid agencies, private foundations, and large, international environmental organizations. Reliance on external sources of financing created public relations problems for local NGOs in the Czech Republic, much as they did in Russia (see chapter 6). Corporate polluters and slow-moving environmental agencies parried attacks by environmentalists, accusing the latter of doing the bidding of foreign backers and promoting Western interests over that of ordinary Czechs. The notion that environmental organizations lacked patriotism was an especially well-worn theme during the Klaus administration.

The government has adopted both formal and informal conventions to determine which NGOs receive state grants and under what circumstances. Generally, government funds do not constitute the main revenue sources for civic organizations. Nevertheless, it has been suggested that competition for such funding shapes NGO missions and political orientations. Fagin notes (1999: 104):

> Competition for securing limited state funding is fierce and it is widely perceived that the more apolitical conservation-oriented organizations are favoured over the more ostensibly political groups. As a result, certain environmental associations who initially campaigned on radical agendas have subsequently modified their political stance in a quest to attract (often unsuccessfully) state funding.

Moreover, the most important statute creating legal status for civic organizations, the 1995 Law on Public Benefit Societies, does not enshrine the rights of many politically oriented civic associations. The law and its amendments primarily protect organizations with specific, charitable functions.

> The more overtly political organizations and interest associations that do not exist to provide a specific public benefit, do not own property, or distribute grants, remain in a legal abyss. Their right to exist as non-profit organisations and their capacity to receive and solicit donations is uncertain. (Fagin, 1999: 98)

Here is an instance where institutional rules create incentives that allow particular organizations to prosper at the expense of other organizations. Politically cautious NGOs have succeeded while activist organizations have declined in importance—a response to laws that recognize and subsidize service-oriented NGOs but that marginalize political NGOs. Meanwhile, the policies and programs of the successful organizations tend to reinforce the existing set of institutional rules. As per North, (1990: 5):

> Both what organizations come into existence and how they evolve are fundamentally influenced by the institutional framework. In turn, they influence how the institutional framework evolves.

Critics imply that governmental grant-making procedures homogenize the political personalities of the country's environmental NGOs and that a kind of regression toward the mean occurs whereby the most financially stable civic organizations are ones that maintain relatively uncontroversial political agendas and are less prone to forcefully challenge government policies.

However, external actors' political agendas and grant-making policies may be no less important in shaping local NGOs' values and program missions. The United States Embassy in Prague and the Open Society Fund, for example, have sponsored NGO efforts to expose corrupt practices in the public arena. These programs do not win universal praise from Czech authorities; in fact, anti-corruption programs threaten certain entrenched political and bureaucratic interests. If, in fact, local NGOs that depend on Czech governmental funds are reluctant to challenge the government's policies, externally sponsored NGOs seem less timid in this regard.

Corruption

There are reasons to doubt that the government is conspiring to co-opt NGOs through its institutions for grant making. Each ministry administers its own grant competitions—arrangements used by governments in other European countries and in North America. Different Czech government agencies have different interests and policy agendas, and especially since the Klaus years, do not share a universal antipathy for environmental activism and grassroots involvement in public policy making. There is no compelling evidence of an intergovernmental scheme to defang radical, politically oriented civic associations, not to mention mainstream politically oriented civic associations.

However, there are darker passages in the corridors of official policy making that do raise concerns for environmentalists and for the public at large. Environmental policies or policies that affect the environment are not impervious to dishonest deal making, conflicts of interest, and other "extralegal" practices. Graft in government is sufficiently worrisome that one expert likened Czech public policy making to a marriage of convenience between bureaucracy and institutionalized corruption (Kabele, 1999: 212).

As argued by other contributors to this volume (see, in particular, chapters by Bell and Novac and Auer), corruption in the form of illegal rent seeking is relatively common in the environmental policy-making realm in CEE.

Before relating how corruption affects Czech environmental decisionmaking, it is incumbent to define it and to establish its institutional character. We adopt Nye's (1967: 444) definition of corruption as

> behavior which deviates from the formal duties of a public role because of private regarding (personal, close family, private clique) pecuniary or status gains; or violates rules against the exercise of certain types of private regarding influence. (Nye, 1967: 419)

Nye proposes that corrupt acts violate rules that prohibit private abuse of public roles. We offer an amendment: corrupt acts, themselves, tend to conform to particular institutional rules or practices. But the rules obeyed by corrupt actors are nonauthoritative. Indeed, the rules that bring order and predictability to corrupt acts are also intentionally corrosive to official rules. They are designed to elude, undermine, or nullify the norms that define acceptable behavior for public officials.

According to North (1990: 3-4, 7), institutions define and limit the choices available to institutional actors, constrain possible modes of interaction between these actors, and determine economic opportunities. Corruption resembles an institution because it functions by way of constraints, and these constraints shape social interaction. People who engage in corrupt acts, for example bribery, tend to follow certain self-confining protocols and procedures. A bribe is generally not performed in an open, public setting; bribes are extracted quietly, clandestinely, behind closed doors. A premium on secrecy and the need to limit information about the bribe to small numbers of actors are ordinary conventions followed by extractors and takers of bribes. Another institutional feature of corrupt acts is that they tend to reduce uncertainty: an actor who provides an under-the-table payment or an illicit favor might expect a future gratuity or privilege in return. If formal institutions fail to deliver desired economic benefits, the gaps may be filled by informal institutions of graft.

After the Second World War and over the next several decades, corruption thrived in Communist Czechoslovakia. Kabele (1999: 214) links that era's pervasive graft to popular allegiance to the Communist Party itself. Corruption, he writes, "commonly meant 'trade': tolerance for petty corruption and shadow business was paid for with loyalty to the Communist party" (Kabele, 1999: 215). Under Communism, writes Kummerman,

> anyone who entered politics did so with the aim of serving personal interests. There existed a wide consensus that the last idealists within the highest circles of the regime—if there ever were such people—must have quietly withered away in the early 1950s. The concept of conflict of interest was replaced by the

subconscious concept that serving the state meant the pursuit of power and the pursuit of filling one's own pockets. (1994: 1)

The political and economic reforms that ensued after 1989, however, did not fundamentally redress corrupt institutional rules and conventions. Indeed, the chaos of economic transition created new, lucrative prospects for graft (Kabele, 1999: 220). The restructuring and privatization of industry, the restitution of state-owned property, the decentralization of governmental functions, and state financing to facilitate these reforms presented ample opportunities for people and organizations to bend and break new, unfamiliar, official rules. Transactions in both the public and private sectors affecting environmental quality became susceptible to corruption, too.

Consider, for example, the pervasive problem of conflict of interest and its relevance to natural resource management. Czechs are familiar with high profile cases of alleged conflict of interest in the energy sector, in particular. In 1994, the wife of then–Prime Minister Václav Klaus was appointed to the board of directors of the country's largest energy company, Ceske Energeticke Zavody (CEZ) which operates Temelin as well as power plants in environmentally degraded Northern Bohemia. Klaus was roundly attacked by the media for condoning his spouse's appointment to the CEZ board. Many worried that the government would be tempted to relax regulatory oversight of coal-fired power plants and take a hands-off approach to Temelin (Crockford, 1994: 1). A similar case involved a former Czech minister who oversaw the distribution of heating oil nationally, and whose wife was the director of an Austrian heating oil company that cheated the government out of billions of crowns of tax revenues (Kummerman, 1995: 1).[6]

Czech laws dealing with conflict of interest apply solely to government ministers and members of Parliament, and even for these officials prohibitions are poorly articulated and punishments are weak. Observing high officials' compliance with a statute requiring government executives to publish their annual wages, one journalist quipped,

> Keeping in mind that the conflict of interest policy provides zero punishment for lawbreakers, government officials met the requirements of declaration, and that's that. (Kummerman, 1996: 1)

The Czech Republic's albeit weak conflict of interest rules do not apply to lower-level public officials, such as town council members, midlevel civil servants, or others with managerial duties in the public sector. Hence, various day-to-day tasks of government, including environment-related tasks, are susceptible to mismanagement by officials who have conflicting roles. These activities, include, for example: the selection of sites for construction activities that may have adverse environmental impacts or may be performed in environmentally sensitive areas; procurements of services that may have environmental impacts or the hiring of environmental services; invocation and collection of environment-related fees and fines; and other important functions.

The Czech state began devolving these types of responsibilities to administrative regions in the early twenty-first century, with the intention of giving provincial authorities more flexibility to shape local economic development. But the decentralization process is also an inadvertent experiment to test the honesty of regional and local governmental units. Hundreds and perhaps thousands of elected officials and civil servants are acquiring decision-making powers that are especially vulnerable to corruption and conflict of interest.

Strikingly, rules that are ostensibly intended to protect the environment are sometimes invoked by corrupt individuals and organizations. New construction projects often trigger environmental assessment proceedings, and the rules are liberal regarding who may complain about the proposed construction work. According to the head of the Czech government agency overseeing foreign direct investment, many of these complaints lack merit, but nevertheless they must be investigated and addressed by the applicant for the construction permit. In many cases, complaints about noise or pollution are not legitimate, but instead reflect a "corrupt motivation." Petitioners often attempt to siphon bribes from the investor or seek to delay the project indefinitely or to destroy economic rivals (Orol, 1998).

Ferreting out corruption in state agencies and enterprises whose operations affect the environment is stymied by rules and procedures that preclude public scrutiny. To illustrate, in recent years, the Czech government has instituted procedures to make procurement of major construction projects even less transparent than in the past. A government-wide directive issued in 2000 gave ministries the option to forgo public bidding procedures for major projects. State agencies may select contractors directly for large public works projects, such as highway construction. As one pair of critics observed, "The more the contract is worth, the more negligible the cost of the bribe becomes" (Bouk and Gonderinger, 2001). Moreover, since bids are not examined by actors other than the procuring agency, environment-related aspects of the bids remain secret.

Conclusion

A student asked to check facts and figures on post-1989 Czech environmental quality might conclude that the environment is on the mend. Levels of emissions of conventional air pollutants like particulates and sulfur dioxide have plunged by as much as 75 percent or more, and in a most encouraging sign, these pollutants have not resumed an upward climb with the revival of the economy. In the realm of water protection, the Czech Republic earned high marks from an OECD audit that lauded the state's efforts to integrate environmental concerns in agricultural policy reforms; to protect rivers; and to approach clean drinking water as a cross-sectoral policy problem. It also praised the government's multilateral cooperation with neighboring states to protect the Elbe, Morava, and Odra river basins (OECD, 1999: 76). Moreover, the Ministry of Environment could take great pride when in 2001 the environmental chapter of the *acquis* was provisionally closed by Brussels.

Yet behind the headlines and the apparent good news, the sturdiness of environmental reforms remained subject to question and it was unclear how deeply environmental norms had penetrated state and societal institutions.

Even as stationary source air pollutants diminish, these benefits are partly nullified by growing emissions from mobile sources. The latter are diffuse and emanate from millions of cars and trucks whose owners strive for high-consumption lifestyles that were denied under socialism.

The OECD's positive review of integrated management efforts in the water sector is contradicted by the Czech Ministry of Environment's grim assessment of intergovernmental dysfunction in the environmental sector, generally. The government's self-criticism mentioned several major shortcomings in policy-making institutions, including:

- ineffective operation of the state administration and unsatisfactory enforcement of legislative requirements in practice;
- inadequate implementation of economic instruments in the framework of environmental protection;
- unsystematic financing of environmental protection from public budgets;
- inconsistent implementation of environmental considerations in sectoral policies;
- inadequate environmental education; poorly informed public bodies (Czech Ministry of Environment, 2001a: 20).

The government also recognized the monumental tasks of devolving environmental functions to regional and local levels, part of a larger administrative devolution process that began in the early twenty-first century. According to the Ministry of Environment,

> In connection with the new regional structure and the need to harmonize Czech environmental legislation, it will be necessary to restructure the existing system of state administration, and to greatly improve its performance in implementation of legislation, inspection and enforcement of compliance. (Czech Ministry of Environment, 2001a: 68)

Indeed, implementation, inspection, and enforcement of environmental laws are key facets of environmental protection that are not clearly addressed and incentivized in EU accession rules. Hence, it was refreshing to find the Ministry of Environment abjuring self-congratulation over the provisional closing of the environmental chapter in the *acquis*, and instead, calling for more vigorous efforts to implement rules and regulations that, in some cases, remain paper prescriptions.

The government also made a candid appraisal of the poor state of public awareness of and participation in environmental institutions (Czech Ministry of Environment, 2001a: 20). These problems are partly a function of institutional practices that the state perpetuates at the expense of environmental activists and organizations. The Czech Republic is a bona fide, functioning democracy; especially since the Klaus years of the mid-1990s, authorities have demonstrated an appreciation of both the abstract political and substantive service-oriented roles performed by civic organizations, both in formal policy-making arenas and in society at large. Nevertheless, the state faces critics who believe that government grant-making procedures favor NGOs that refrain from criticizing governmental policies and actions. Ministries and other official grantors can dispel these complaints by opening up and making more transparent the selection of grant awardees.

Motivating public interest in environmental policy is actually part of a larger undertaking to raise public confidence in government, generally. Widespread conflict of interest among government officials and weak laws to discourage such behavior reinforce citizens' misgivings about public servants and public service, generally. Public disdain for politicians and lawmakers provokes general apathy toward official norms, such as environmental laws.

The Ministry of Environment, for one, appears to understand that having a winning environmental record is not the same as winning approval from either European environmental auditors or Czech citizens. Restoring the nation's environmental quality requires a deeper inculcation of caring in Czech society than has been achieved so far. But convincing people to care requires clearer signals from the state that environmental protection is a worthy end in itself and not merely a litmus test for EU admission, and moreover, that environmental authorities in the Czech Republic are honorable and are up to the task of leading sustainable development efforts.

Notes

1. In its environmental performance review of the Czech Republic, the OECD notes,

From a cost-effectiveness point of view, the decision to require large plants to meet emission limits within a relatively short period of seven years, however desirable in itself, was certain to lead to non-optimal measures being taken, e.g. retrofitting old production facilities and resorting more often to end-of-pipe than to clean production technologies. (1999: 62)

2. Even as Klaus touted the need to liberate market forces in the Czech Republic, patent governmental and political interventions in certain economic sectors were common during the mid-1990s. For example, Klaus had considerable influence over individual privatization decisions made in the banking sector (Čulík, 2000).

3. The 2001 Czech State Environmental Policy contains somewhat different, and generally lower, cost estimates for compliance with EU norms than those cited by OECD,

1999. According to the former, during 2000-2003, the Czech government estimated that it would spend 32 billion crowns (US$928 million in 1998 dollars) for wastewater treatment (EC Directive 91/271/EEC), 13 billion crowns (US$377 million) to treat waterborne hazardous substances (76/464/EEC), and 11 billion crowns (US $319 million) to comply with the EU drinking water quality directive (98/83/EEC) (Czech Ministry of Environment, 2001b: 48).

4. SAPARD (Special Accession Programme for Agriculture and Rural Development) addresses a wide range of rural development issues, such as modernization of arable crops and livestock sectors, soil conservation, and forestry. Until the late 1990s, PHARE (Poland and Hungary Assistance for the Restructuring of the Economy) covered the broadest array of economic development, institution-building, and environmental themes of the major accession programs; its focus has narrowed with the coming on-line of SAPARD and ISPA (Instrument for Structural Policies for Preaccession)—the latter which provides financing for major transport and environmental infrastructure projects. Since 2000, new investments from PHARE in transport, agriculture, and some environmental areas have declined. Yet another EU-sponsored accession grant program, TACIS (Technical Assistance to the Commonwealth of Independent States) supports environment-related projects, but the Czech Republic is not eligible for these funds.

5. Similarly, foreign investments have helped reduce sulfur dioxide emissions from Czech industries. But since most Czech sulfur emissions end up traversing national borders, emissions reduction generates larger environmental benefits for neighboring countries than for Czechs (Pavlínek and Pickles, 1999: 368).

6. Accusations of conflict of interest in the energy sector are not the Czech government's bane, alone. In the United States, for example, Wendy Gramm, the wife of former Senate Banking Committee Chairman Phil Gramm, was a member of the board of directors of the energy company Enron. During his wife's tenure at the company, Senator Gramm sought to reduce regulatory oversight of energy trading. Ms. Gramm earned her seat on Enron's board just five weeks after resigning as chairwoman of the Commodity Futures Trading Commission where she enacted an important regulatory exemption that benefited Enron (Benac, 2002).

References

Axelrod, Regina S. 2002. "Nuclear Power and European Union Enlargement: The Case of Temelin," in Sabina A.-M. Crisen and JoAnn Carmin (eds.), *EU Enlargement and Environmental Quality: Central and Eastern Europe and Beyond*. Washington, D.C.: Woodrow Wilson International Center for Scholars, 41-50.

Benac, Nancy. 2002. "Gramms Entangled in Enron's Collapse." *Chattanooga Times/Chattanooga Free Press*, 24 January: C2.

Bouk, Frantisek, and Lisa Gonderinger. 2001. "Prague Changes Bid Rules." *Prague Post*, 11 April. Lexis/Nexis News/World News/Europe Library. Accessed 9 July 2002.

CEE Bankwatch and Friends of the Earth. 2001. *Billions for Sustainability? II: The Use of EU Accession Funds and Their Environmental and Social Implications—Second Briefing*. Brussels: CEE Bankwatch Network.

Center for Environmental Studies. 2001. *Report for World Summit on Sustainable Development (Rio+10). Chapter II*. Prague: CES.

Connolly, Kate. 2002. "Unbearable Lightness of Being." *Manchester Guardian Weekly*, 17 April: 19.

Crockford, Ross. 1994. "Klaus Family Dismisses Conflict of Interest." *Prague Post*, 29 June: 1.

CTK Business News. 1994. "Skoda Engergetika Fined for Atmospheric Pollution." *CTK Business News*, 29 December. Lexis-Nexis World News/European News Library. Accessed 24 June 2002.

CTK Czech News Agency. 1998. "EC Estimates Czech Transport Infrastructure Costs at KC315BN." 24 June. Lexis-Nexis World News/European News Library. Accessed 24 June 2002.

———. 2000. "Polluters Fined 60 Million Crowns Last Year—Inspection." 6 November. Lexis-Nexis World News/European News Library. Accessed 24 June 2002.

CTK National News Wire. 2003. "Vienna Inconspicuously Back-Pedals on Veto Threat." 9 April. Lexis-Nexis World News/European News Library. Accessed 21 July 2003.

Čulík, Jan. 2000. "Czech-style Mafioso Capitalism." *Central Europe Review*, vol. 2, no. 26. www.ce-review.org/00/26/culik26.html. Accessed 13 July 2002.

Czech Ministry of the Environment. 2001a. *State Environmental Policy*. Prague: Czech Ministry of Environment.

———. 2001b. *Statni politika zivotniho prostredi: Leden 2001*. [State Environmental Policy: January 2001]. Prague: Czech Ministry of Environment.

———. 2002. *The Statistical Environmental Yearbook 2002 of the Czech Republic*. Prague: Czech Ministry of Environment.

DG Regio-ISPA. 2000. *ISPA Mandate, Programming and Implementation: State of Play*. 15 September. Brussels: DG Regio.

Duany, Andres, and Elizabeth Plater-Zyberk. 1992. "The Second Coming of the American Small Town." *Wilson Quarterly*, Winter: 19-48.

European Union. 2002. "Rules on Financial Aid to the TEN-T." europa.eu.int/comm/ transport/themes/network/english/tn_3_en.html. Accessed 7 July 2002.

Expert Group on the Urban Environment. 2001. *Toward More Sustainable Urban Land Use: Advice to the European Commission for Policy and Action*. Brussels: European Union, 2001.

Fagin, Adam. 1999. "The Development of Civil Society in the Czech Republic: The Environmental Sector as a Measure of Associational Activity." *Journal of European Area Studies*, vol. 7, no. 1: 91-108.

Fagin, Adam, and Petr Jehlička. 1997. "Sustainable Development in the Czech Republic: A Doomed Process?" in Susan Baker and Petr Jehlička (eds.), *Dilemmas of Transition: The Environment, Democracy and Economic Reform in East Central Europe*. London: Frank Cass, 113-128.

Horak, Martin. 2001. "Environmental Policy Reform in the Post-Communist Czech Republic: The Case of Air Pollution." *Europe-Asia Studies*, vol. 35, no. 2: 313-327.

ISPA. 2001. *ISPA Information Sheet: Measure No. 2001 CZ 16 P PT 012*. Brussels: DG Regio.

Jehl, Douglas. 1994. "Ukraine Hints It Won't Close Nuclear Plants at Chernobyl." *New York Times*, 13 June: A1.

Kabele, Jiri. 1999. "VII. Ceska byrokracie and korupce" [Czech Bureaucracy and Corruption] in Pavol Fric, Michal Burian, Jirí Kabele, Quentin Reed, Ales Rozehnal, and Václav Zak et al. (eds.). *Korupce na cesky zpusob* [Corruption—Czech Style]. Prague: Nakladatelstvi G plus G, 211-252.

Kummerman, Daniel. 1994. "Still Few Checks on Corruption in Government." *Prague Post*, 25 May: 1.

————. 1995. "New Law: What's Crucial? The Conflict or the Interest?" *Prague Post*, 15 November: 1.

————. 1996. "Official's [*sic*] Extra Pay Is Merely a Sign of Their Tireless Work Ethic." *Prague Post*, 10 January: 1.

Madar, Zdenek. 1997. "Harmonization of National Environmental Law with EU Legislation: Case of Czech Republic." *Environmental Policy and Law*, vol. 27, no. 4: 336-341.

Moldan, Bedřich 2000. "Environment after Ten Years of Transition." Presentation at Tenth Anniversary of the Regional Environment Centre, Szentendre, Hungary, 18 June 2000. Available at www.rec.org/REC/Programs/10th_anniversary/Speech.html. Accessed 30 July 2002.

North, Douglass. 1990. *Institutions, Institutional Change and Economic Performance*. Cambridge: Cambridge University Press.

Nye, Joseph S. 1967. "Corruption and Political Development: A Cost-Benefit Analysis." *American Political Science Review*, vol. 61, no. 2: 412-427.

Organization for Economic Cooperation and Development. 1999. *Environmental Performance Reviews: Czech Republic*. Paris: OECD.

Orol, Ron. 1998. "Under the Table and out of Mind." *Prague Post*, 25 November. Lexis-Nexis News/World News/Europe Library. Accessed 9 July 2002.

Pachner, Klara, and David Horner. 1998. "Latest Cost Hikes Intensify Temelin Debate." *Prague Post*, 13 May: 1.

Pavlínek, Petr, and John Pickles. 1999. "Environmental Change and Post-Communist Transformations in the Czech Republic and Slovakia." *Post-Soviet Geography and Economics*, vol. 40, no. 5: 354-382.

Robes, Martin. 1996. *Part II: Case Examples from Central and Eastern Europe: Motorway Brno-Dresden, Czech Republic, Regional Environment Center*. www.rec.org/REC/Publications/BndBound/Czech.html. Accessed 7 July 2002.

Schilling, Theodor. 1995. "Subsidiarity as a Rule and a Principle or: Taking Subsidiarity Seriously." *The Jean Monnet Working Papers*, no. 10/95, New York: NYU School of Law.

Tax, Vladimir. 1999. Transcript of "The Environment." RFE-RL Weekly Edition of *Ten Years After: 1989-1999*. Prague: Radio Free Europe-Radio Liberty.

World Information Service on Energy News Communique. 2000. "Temelin: Criticality after Seventeen Years of Construction?" 15 September. Amsterdam: WISE-Amsterdam.

Chapter 3

Hungary: Developing Institutions to Support Environmental Protection

Ruth Greenspan Bell

When Hungary emerged from the Soviet bloc, it did so with environmental laws and institutions already in place. Hungary had a Ministry of the Environment, a framework environmental act dating from 1976, and a set of ambitious environmental standards. It is generally agreed that these were mostly paper institutions, created partly in response to pressure from environmental groups whose members advocated not merely for environmental reforms, but for revolutionary political changes. The Hungarian state's main objectives, like most governments in the Soviet bloc, were growth, production, and national security. Robust environmental implementation took a backseat to these priorities. Nevertheless, in part to mollify domestic agitators, Hungarian authorities were compelled to appear to be addressing the nation's environmental woes.

More than ten years later, Hungary put into place an even bolder set of environmental requirements, this time in response to its application for entry into the European Union. The process, variously known as approximation and harmonization, required Hungary to demonstrate that its laws were consistent with European Union (EU) directives, including those for the environment. Some commentators likened Hungary's new legal and regulatory edifice to a Potemkin village, analogous to the pre-1989 legal strictures, and worried that the new institutions, like the old, would be paper only (Jacoby, 1999). Others fretted that Hungary's response was top-down and did not reflect domestic will nor meaningful public commitment. But even critics, paradoxically, note that EU membership and its related requirements seem to be the strongest impetus for environmental protection in Hungary.

This chapter examines whether or not the pressure to adapt domestic laws in Hungary to EU requirements will ultimately provide a foundation for real environmental protection. Environmental efforts before and after 1989 took place within broader Hungarian political and economic contexts. Thus, this chapter begins with a brief discussion of Hungarian politics after 1945 and the Communist-era environmental protection regime. The next section reviews the period since 1989, including the environmental dimension of the EU accession process. It goes on to assess Hungary's prospects for establishing robust environmental regulatory regimes and requirements.

The chapter concludes that while improving the environment does not have the same priority in Hungary as maintaining the social safety net or nurturing economic growth, there is reason to hope for improved environmental conditions and more potent and effective environmental protection efforts. Among the most positive developments are the increasing savvy and effectiveness of non-governmental actors (broadly defined), who are gradually becoming participants rather than merely protestors in the evolving civil society. As Jancar-Webster notes,

> if cynicism is the proper attitude for the person living under Communism, positive activism is more appropriate for the person living under democratic institutions. The shift from protest to positive participation cannot be made overnight, because it demands a fundamental shift in attitude towards the nature of government. (Jancar-Webster, 1998)

These attitudinal shifts are under way in Hungary, but the rate of change is variable and where those changes will lead remains unclear.

Political Background to Hungary's Environmental Transition

From the end of World War II until 1956, Hungary's political and economic life closely resembled that of many other CEE nations. Soon after the war, the Communist Party (MSZMP) forced its rivals out of the political scene, and established itself as the sole political and civil actor. Civic groups could only function under the auspices of the Party. Hungary was so successful at adopting the Soviet model of rapid industrialization, collectivized agriculture, and authoritarian politics that Matyas Rakosi, the leader of MSZMP, earned the nickname "Best Pupil of Stalin."

Following Stalin's death in 1953, Nikita Khrushchev permitted greater decision-making autonomy in various arenas of political and economic affairs in the Soviet Union and tolerated like-minded reforms in the satellite states. Power struggles ensued in Hungary. Hungarian citizens, weary of political terror and economic hardships, demanded more comprehensive political reforms and greater rights. Public discontent reached a climax with the October 1956 uprising, which was repressed by the Soviet army.

Janos Kadar, who sided with the Soviets and assumed leadership after the uprising, nevertheless embarked Hungary on a path of "socialism with a human face." Although power remained centralized through the late 1980s, Hungary's economy was among the most market oriented of the Soviet bloc regimes. It eventually developed reforms such as a two-tier banking system and adopted Western-style company, bankruptcy, competition, and tax laws (Elster et al., 1998). These reforms were part of the so-called New Economic Mechanism (NEM)—a scheme that also allowed limited development of a private economic sphere. Kadar tolerated "under the table" economic activities. Perhaps one-third of the Hungarian GDP was generated by this "second economy" (Rotschild and Wingfield, 2000).

The Kadar regime also softened prohibitions on political dissent, reasoning that those who did not actively oppose the Party could be considered allies. This gave new hope to non-Party member intellectuals, in particular. The regime amnestied some political prisoners, allowed greater freedoms in the cultural arena, and invited non-Party experts to help with the relatively uncontroversial task of economic development (Rotschild and Wingfield, 2000). As a result, Hungarians were somewhat freer than were most other CEE citizenries to travel to the West.[1] Those who visited Western Europe and North America developed private and professional connections with Westerners and were exposed to liberal cultural and political ideas. While the role of the Party remained dominant and unchallenged, intellectuals were able to express their opinions on a wide variety of "politically neutral" issues, such as environmental policy.

Thus, in contrast to CEE countries such as Romania and Bulgaria, where radical political transformations occurred almost overnight in late autumn 1989, the process of regime change in Hungary was gradual. It would be a mistake, however, to overstate the degree of change that occurred before 1989. Rigid, centralized policy-making institutions offered only limited opportunity for dissent or independent political discussion, not to mention genuine bottom-up political participation.[2] But precedence for challenging the state had been established, and gradually there was more open questioning of policies in certain sectors, particularly in the environmental sector. Finally, in the summer of 1989, opposition groups sponsored a series of roundtable discussions, leading to the first free elections in 1991, as well as the symbolic action of renaming the country.

The transition to capitalist democracy, though gradual, was not always smooth. Hungary endured a period of withering price inflation, a substantial drop in GDP, and the debilitating effects of unemployment in a formerly "full employment" society.[3] In the post-1989 period, not only did Hungary need to reform its economy, but also to develop governmental and administrative institutional capacities and public trust in these institutions.

The drive for EU membership created another set of high hurdles.[4] The process of "approximation" is complicated and challenging, requiring the adoption of about 1,700 EU directives (core laws of the *acquis communitaire*) (Jacoby, 1999). All this has happened in the midst of political uncertainty, if not political instability. Between 1991 and 2001, three parties and their coalition partners, all with different administrative philosophies and ideological leanings, governed.[5] There were three environment ministers in the period 1997 to 2001 alone, and substantial turnover in the professional staffs of environment-related agencies.

Environmental Protection before 1989

The official attitude toward environmental protection in Hungary before 1989 resembled that of other Soviet bloc regimes, and indeed, recalls the U.S. government's mind-set in the first half of the twentieth century. Great factories spewing orange smoke evidenced a vibrant economy and a society "on the move." Air and water were thought to be essentially free goods—resources to be exploited for the greater good of society. These attitudes were apparently consistent with earlier Hungarian traditions (Enyedi and Szirmai, 1998).

Plant managers and workers were ordered to meet or exceed quotas; less emphasis was placed on quality, efficiency, or preventing pollution. The centralized command economy operated without any market or price mechanisms, drew freely on natural resources, and paid almost no attention to the resulting social costs. Weak productivity and economic inefficiency could be easily concealed in Hungary's secretive political system.

The 1960s saw early efforts at environmental protection in the form of subsidiary environmental regulations that were inserted into rules governing economic activities (Erdey and Karcza, 1996). The first stand-alone environmental legal rules—standards and fines for discharges of wastewater—were promulgated in 1964 (Berg, 1999). Other norms followed. These standards were frequently more symbolic than real. Often unreasonably strict, they lacked effective implementation mechanisms (Bándi and Wajda, 1996) and were repeatedly disregarded in favor of maximizing output.

This record of neglectful environmental management and enforcement raises an interesting question: Why did Hungary bother to have environmental laws, standards, and penalties at all, much less such tough requirements? Alternative answers have been proffered.

Some call these norms "aspirational." They are part and parcel of an idealized society and proclaim goals that seem unimpeachable. But as laws and regulations, they were never meant to be operational or consistently enforced.[6]

Others say that the legal situation can only be understood in the context of the important fiction of Party infallibility and the Party's unwavering commitment to self-preservation. Having declared every citizen's right to a healthy environment, as it did in the 1972 Constitution, it was impossible for the Party to admit that it had failed to deliver. Therefore, on paper, environmental protection was presented as a success story. In fact, the laws were sublimated to Party control, as were all other parts of society. The Communists established a hierarchy of values, with emphasis on full employment and maximum economic production—all in an effort to consolidate and maintain power (Cole, 1998; Kosztolanyi, 1999). A third explanation posits that environmental regulations were established not to improve the performance of economic entities, but rather for political purposes, to placate intellectuals and complainers (Bándi and Wajda, 1996).

What role, if any, did the public play in helping establish environmental policy during this period in Hungary? There was scarcely any public input in environmental law- or policy-making. It was not important to the process of law creation whether public support, understanding, or willingness to comply with environmental rules existed (Bándi and Wajda, 1996).

The government's secretive ways and disregard for public opinion was reciprocated by public deviance and contravening of laws and formal requirements, generally. So just as factory managers flouted laws governing pollution control, ordinary citizens routinely undermined official rules through hidden acts of sabotage such as tax evasion, theft, or sloppy work discipline. These acts resembled a kind of three-way battle between the people, the government, and the law. Selective rule breaking was often abetted by networks of intimates or trusted associates. Outcomes from the battle were eroded trust and respect for law, and deep skepticism about authorities' will and capacity to manage complex challenges such as environmental protection.

In the absence of reliable legal frameworks, people decided on a private basis, and sometimes at great personal risk, what norms would or would not be adhered to. At various times, complex personal connections were used for basic economic activities such as obtaining food.[7] These informal institutions strongly resemble those in Communist Romania, as described in chapter 4 of this volume. Pervasive graft could be justified by the uneven and unreliable provision of goods and services under totalitarianism. But, shadow economies and networks of corrupt actors did not vanish with the fall of the Berlin Wall. Old habits of skirting the law and cynical attitudes toward government, nurtured under Communism, posed lasting obstacles to the implementation of new laws, post-1989.

With Kadar's gradual relaxation of the Party's monopoly on the "truth" in the 1960s and 1970s, scientists and experts were invited to advise the government on "politically benign" issues, such as the environment. In return, they received privileged information and data and financial and technical support not available to the general public—indulgences that the state dispensed with the apparent hope of appeasing and perhaps even co-opting intellectual critics.

Hungary was also influenced by international environmental movements in the 1970s. Following the 1972 Stockholm Conference on the Human Environment, the Hungarian Academy of Sciences sponsored the country's first major environmental conference (Berg, 1999) and the government revised the Constitution to include a right to a healthy environment (Enyedi and Szirmai, 1998).

In the mid-1970s, Kadar's National Patriotic Front (NPF), an offshoot of the Communist Party that recruited non-Communist intellectuals for the task of governing, used environmental issues as part of its public appeal. NPF's Green agenda resulted in the 1976 Environmental Framework Act—the first comprehensive Hungarian environmental protection law. The act institutionalized environmental management—at least on paper—for such functions as monitoring and enforcement.

At that time, Hungary also instituted resource-use fees and fines for violation of environmental norms. The fines were added to a set of unrealistically strict requirements governing pollution discharges, which were routinely violated (O'Toole and Hanf, 1998).

Before 1989, pollution fees were generally treated as soft budgetary items and were prepaid by state-owned companies. Rather than genuinely motivating change by eroding company profits, they more closely resembled a transfer from one government pocket to another. Since they were predetermined entries in an enterprise's expense ledger, they were mostly ignored by plant managers. As such, they enabled pollution-intensive behavior.

In sum, during the 1980s, Hungarian environmental requirements were strongest on paper, not in practice. They were undercut by policies favoring unfettered economic production, and by avoidance of cumbersome legal requirements where possible. Moreover, during the 1980s, the government's attention to the environment waned in the face of mounting financial and economic crises (Enyedi and Szirmai, 1998). Environmentalists and intellectuals realized their advice was going unheeded as the environment deteriorated. In addition to openly discussing technical aspects of environmental protection, they began to question the undemocratic character of environmental decision making, and policy making generally.

In the 1980s, environmental grievances grew louder, bolder, and focused in on a controversial project: the Gabčíkovo-Nagymaros Dam. That case illustrates how environmental concerns became intertwined with political dissent and ended up nurturing institutions of civil society.

The dam was a joint project between Czechoslovakia and Hungary; it promised to bring electric power to underdeveloped districts of Slovakia, and also to help Hungary wean itself off foreign oil. Before the engineers got to work, scientists and experts began questioning the purported benefits of the dam. When the government did not respond, critics leaked information to opposition groups.

The latter circulated petitions, issued newsletters, and complained not only about technical facets of the dam, but also about anticipated social impacts. Other groups joined the fray, including most prominently the Danube Circle, which cooperated with Austrian Greens in efforts to stop Austrian financing for the project.[8]

Through much of the 1980s, the Hungarian government rejected environmentalists' demands. It also tried to weaken the movement by forming its own "environmental" organizations.[9]

Despite setbacks, the dam protest gave voice to nonstate actors heard from the bottom-up, and for the first time a modicum of direct public involvement in state affairs. Increasingly, environmental groups were allowed to form and operate. Although their most outspoken leaders were periodically harassed, they were not arrested. Environmentalism opened the way for scientists and dissidents to challenge—albeit indirectly—political and economic rules and practices affecting the environment.

By the end of 1985, a number of independent environmental groups were operating in Hungary, each with its own goals and strategies. Some, like the Danube Circle, the Blues, or the Foundation for the Danube, concentrated on the construction of the Nagymaros Dam (the Hungarian portion of the joint project) and directly confronted the system of one-party decision making. Others from universities and regional bases collected and disseminated information to solve local environmental problems (REC, 1997). By 1988, the Communist Party was dominated by a reformist faction which voted to stop preliminary work on the dam. Not only was this a significant victory for the environmental movement, but it also signaled the beginning of a different, more democratic era.

Environmental Protection since 1989

In view of Hungary's history of environmental activism, many observers in the West thought that strengthening environmental protection would be among the highest priorities of the post-1989 governments. The environmental effects of central planning and heavy industrialization provided obvious and dramatic demonstrations of the failures of socialism and an early rallying point for democratic opposition. It seemed logical that these realizations would inspire new laws, policies, and programs to clean up the mess. President George H. W. Bush famously (at least, in the environmental community) gave a speech in 1989 in Budapest pledging U.S. help for environmental revitalization efforts. That promise led to the creation of the Regional Environmental Center for Central and Eastern Europe (REC), originally located in Budapest (now in Szentendre).

International resources for environmental protection were made available from disparate sources including the European Union through its PHARE program and from individual Western European and North American countries. The

European Bank for Reconstruction and Development (EBRD), a bank created to assist the regional transformation, wrote a commitment to environmental protection in its charter. The U.S. Agency for International Development and U.S. Environmental Protection Agency, founders and early supporters of the REC, provided support for Hungarian projects as varied as the reconstruction of wetlands, clean production in industry, and environmental education and environment-related training programs. The REC itself supported the development of new environmental laws and institutions and market-based instruments for environmental protection. Reflecting on the roles played by external actors on environmental institution-building in Hungary, Bedřich Moldan, chair of the board of the REC observed,

> Within a few years, a series of new environmental programs, environmental laws and institutional reform followed the democratic changes. . . . [t]he CEE countries tried to use the best practices and ideas from the West, helped by the various assistance programmes of donor countries and projects of the International Financial Institutions. (Moldan, 2000)

But despite donor enthusiasm, Hungary was not really ready for environmental reform. Like its neighbors, Hungary had no choice but to shift its attention to the depressed economy, badly frayed social safety nets, and widespread concerns about social unrest. Exhilaration about the collapse of Communism was swiftly eclipsed by the enormity of the challenges on every possible front. The difficulty of doing everything at once (including instituting environmental reforms) in a time of sweeping social and economic change has been well documented.

> The situation of panic, surprise, extravagant aspirations as well as paralyzing uncertainties, triggered by the sudden breakdown, is not the most conducive one to furthering the huge constructive and cooperative effort of institution building that society [was] now challenged to perform. (Elster et al., 1998)

Moreover, some of the air went out of the environmental movement's sails. The combination of pressing economic problems and diverted public attention pushed environmental concerns to the periphery. With the demise of Communism, opposition leaders no longer had to hide behind environmental camouflage and could participate directly in political arenas. Environmental issues became the domain of a smaller group of activists—many of whom were genuinely interested in the issues, but were generally less powerful and "well connected." Some of the attitudes and habits of old guard environmentalists also needed adjustment. Environmental NGOs tended to be top-heavy with technical experts and scientists, and relatively dismissive of the broader public's role in environmental decision making. While they were effective in using science to support their arguments, these groups often had difficulty communicating with and connecting to broader movements for policy reform.[10]

Challenges to Institutional Reform

While environmentalists searched for ways to regain their role as effective policy advocates, environmental authorities in Hungary and elsewhere in CEE contended with a new set of problems. In the early years of transition, environmental officials were urged by Western advisers that they could leapfrog over the mistakes committed in the name of environmental protection in the West. The Organization for Economic Cooperation and Development (OECD) and others pushed them to develop economic instruments for environmental protection so as to avoid the excesses of so-called "command and control" environmental regulations (Lehoczki and Balogh, 1997).[11]

The effort to move directly to market-based instruments offers an illustration of the disconnect between hopes, expectations, and on-the-ground institutional realities—a classic case of optimism and good intentions trumping good sense. Briefly, the optimists never really considered institutional constraints.

Consider, for example, shortcomings of a system for trading rights to emit pollution, a concept pressed on Hungary in the early 1990s. Tradable permit schemes are promoted to industrial polluters as cheaper and more efficient ways to achieve compliance versus the command and control approach. But without consistent monitoring and enforcement, the incentives to reduce compliance costs through permit trading are substantially diminished. There is little incentive for the polluter to strive to save money on regulatory compliance if it is not spending any to begin with and does not expect to in the future.

Trading also requires verifiable knowledge—not guesswork—of specific contaminants that each facility discharges and in what quantities. Believable, reliable, end-of-the-pipe monitoring assures that real, not imaginary, pollution credits are traded. But Hungary used ambient measures of pollution, and its monitoring efforts were not performed in a systematic manner. In truth, no one could be sure what types of pollution firms were emitting, nor how much, nor whether enterprises were complying with permitted emissions ceilings. All of these problems undermined the prospects of a full-fledged pollution trading scheme (or even an experimental program).

A range of institutional assurances is necessary to assure the integrity of trading and to discourage cheating. An especially important one in the United States is transparency. This is achieved by making emissions data, and the specifics about what emissions are traded, by whom, and when, available for inspection by the public, including by the regulated firm's competitors. Efforts to develop public trust are requisite if regulators, economic competitors, and environmentalists are to accede to unconventional programs like markets for tradable emissions. Transparency is not a Hungarian (nor even necessarily a European) tradition. Hungarian NGOs still struggle to obtain emissions and other environmental data—information that, by law, is accessible to the public, but in practice is often difficult to acquire.[12]

Hungary, particularly in the early 1990s, lacked sufficient market experience to adopt highly sophisticated economic instruments like pollution permit trading regimes. Pollution permits are complex intangible property rights embodying a right to pollute in the future. Buying and selling them is not the same as buying and selling ordinary commodities. More than theoretical knowledge was necessary to successfully deploy such complex arrangements.

Before 1989, Hungarian scholars studied non-Marxist economics, but the actual, functioning economy, even with the relatively liberal market reforms instituted in the 1980s, remained highly centralized and unresponsive to real market forces. Economic decision makers were not sensitive to profit and loss, not held to Western business accounting standards (which suffered their own legitimacy crisis in the United States in 2001-2002), and not responsive to shareholders or the stock market. In general, economic managers lacked the experience and on-the-job skills necessary to participate effectively in an emissions trading system.

Over the last ten years, many Hungarian entrepreneurs have received MBA-style training and have gained practical market experience. But business practices have not changed without a great deal of pain, including the "unlearning" of Communist-era enterprise management. Industrial managers have endured a steep learning curve. It is unlikely that most enterprises were ready, especially in the early part of the transition, to take on market-based environmental responsibilities, generally.[13]

In sum, in order to adopt market-based environmental reforms, both regulators and economic actors in Hungary had to disown Communist-era ways of managing (or mismanaging) the environment, while rapidly adjusting to new rules and incentives that were novel even in the West. It is certainly debatable whether the single-minded push of some donors and Hungarians to institute sophisticated, market-based environmental tools (such as tradable emissions programs) was a disservice to the nation, diverting resources from more productive policy reforms and sending confusing signals to regulated actors.

Mixed Outcomes from Law Drafting

Despite some ill-advised initiatives, such as the tradable emissions idea, some reforms performed reasonably well—for example, the implementation of charges on certain types of wastes—a topic addressed in later paragraphs. First, however, it is instructive to appraise the accomplishments and shortcomings of law drafting efforts that enabled environmental programs like the system of waste charges.

Early in the transition, the Ministry of Environment was reorganized into the Ministry of Environment and Regional Development (it was reorganized again in 2002 when it was combined with the Ministry of Transport and Water Management). In 1992, the ministry set out to write a new framework environment law. Hungary's decision to revisit this law was encouraged by donors and influenced by the Pan-European Environmental Ministerial Meetings held in the early and mid-1990s. I was one of a number of foreign and Hungarian experts who not only provided support to the framework law drafting exercise, but also testified in one of the first Hungarian Parliament Ecology Committee meetings that was open to the public. The meeting was called to solicit public views on the draft document, and was covered by the media. Although the entire drafting process was not marked by such dramatic transparency, the work concluded, after many twists and turns, with a relatively progressive 1995 Law on the General Rules of Environmental Protection (AGREP).

While AGREP replaces an outdated 1976 Environmental Framework Act and provides a useful basis for future legislation, it *is* fundamentally a framework act. Among other provisions, the 1995 Act contains general norms promoting sectoral and intragovernmental cooperation; the public's right to access environmental information; the government's responsibility to collect data on the state of the environment; citizens' rights to environmental education; and the requirement that significant environmental impact assessments (EIAs) be subject to public hearing (Lehoczki and Balogh, 1997). AGREP also recognizes the "polluter pays principle"—a foundation for the institution of economic incentives for environmental protection.

Extended discussion of AGREP's effectiveness in advancing environmental protection is difficult because significant pieces of implementing legislation are still missing. With a few important exceptions noted below, Hungary has been slow to write the necessary additional laws, and it also has not yet reconciled much of its pre-1989 environmental legislation with the more progressive provisions in AGREP (Erdey and Karcza, 1996). The European Commission pointed out in 1997 that much of the existing subsidiary legislation, especially concerning water and waste, is consistent with the old system rather than the framework legislation (European Commission, 1997).

AGREP did not change Hungary's fundamental reliance on noncompliance fees and fines (and on shutting down polluting enterprises) for environmental enforcement purposes. As discussed previously, fees and fines were essentially programmed into the budgets of state enterprises in the socialist economy. Penalties were nominal, and have essentially remained so.

Since 1989, many companies have preferred to pay fines rather than make expensive changes to environmental management systems (OECD, 1999: 109). There have been credible rumors for years about enterprises that were acquired by neighboring countries so as to shift production into Hungary and away from states with more aggressive environmental enforcement regimes. A June 2001 interview with an official of a major multinational corporation with plants in Hungary indicated that the Hungarian facilities would pay fines rather than make comprehensive, plantwide changes to environmental infrastructure—at least until it became clear how the strict and oddly calculated standards dating from the 1980s would be reconciled with EU environmental requirements (Interview, Bori Sari, General Electric, Budapest, 16 June 2001).

Although the system of fines and fees has done little to promote meaningful pollution reduction, it does generate government revenue, which is reinvested in the environment. But these recycled monies only go so far; environmental authorities, who have been ordered to generate their own revenues without relying wholly on intergovernmental transfers, find it difficult to execute their responsibilities. Environmental inspectorates, the enforcement arm of Hungarian environmental protection, are only partially funded by the state budget. The balance must be made up through other means; consulting is the most important secondary income source. It is easy to imagine the pernicious effects of this policy—for example, situations where the inspection process is compromised because inspectors are at once enforcement officers and paid authors of companies' compliance documents. Is it possible that this inherent conflict of interest might lead to situations in which an inspector offers an environmentally unfriendly enterprise a clean bill of health in hopes of winning future consulting work with the firm?

Other significant post-1989 laws include 1995 and 1996 acts on the restoration of protected natural areas and nature conservation; a 1997 decree on confiscated protected natural assets; a 1996 decree that provides for voluntary and mandatory environmental audits; and a 1995 act and a decree establishing procedures for environmental impact assessment (EIA).

Hungary has also participated in a number of continental and international environmental efforts that have led to domestic environmental commitments. These include the Environmental Action Programme for Central and Eastern Europe and the various regional agreements to clean up the Danube River. Hungary also ratified the Aarhus Convention on May 29, 2001, reinforcing its promise to provide open access to environmental information collected by the government (UNECE, 1998).

As discussed above, domestic environmental law has also provided for the institution of various market-oriented environmental instruments, some of which have performed relatively poorly. But one instrument winning plaudits is charges for goods that generate pollution as a by-product of their use.

Levies were put on gasoline, packaging, tires, and refrigerators in the early 1990s. The proceeds were paid to the Hungarian Environmental Fund (CEPF). As a result of the charge on gasoline, petrol prices rose higher than in any other nation in the region. Nevertheless, these charges have had only a modest effect on demand for fuel, and vehicular traffic has increased. The tire product charge and a fee for used batteries raised revenues for the environmentally friendly disposal of these products. Charges on refrigerators and refrigerants helped finance the phaseout of ozone-depleting substances. The government also provided corporate tax concessions to companies that invested in abatement technologies (Lehoczki and Balogh, 1997). Although not always leading to dramatic improvements in environmental quality, these instruments were serious-minded attempts to encourage consumers and others to internalize the costs of pollution generation.

In contrast, the pollution fee/fine system continued to suffer from some of the problems that undermined it in the Communist era. In particular, the imposed fees tended to be too small to encourage pollution prevention or pollution control. The fees' impacts were further blunted by delays in collections, allowing firms to take advantage of inflation. As noted earlier, in some instances, it was less expensive for companies to pay the fees and fines than to install pollution abatement devices.

Revenues from these tools go to important functions, including providing operating funds for government environmental authorities and investment resources for pollution prevention projects. But at best, the fee/fine systems send only weak signals to polluters to change their behavior. Through the early years of the new century, there was little political will to strengthen these signals.

Policy Reforms and Effects on the Environment

During the 1990s, polluters in Hungary often shrugged at the trade-offs created by official fees and fines. Most chose to pollute and to pay the resulting charge or penalty. Nevertheless, in terms of actual pollution reduction, Hungary could report measurable progress by decade's end.

Improved air quality has been a major, if largely incidental, success story in Hungary and other CEE countries. Between 1989 and 1995, many former eastern bloc nations had drastically reduced their emissions of SO_2, CO_2, and NO_x. During the early to mid-1990s, SO_2 declined in CEE countries by 58 percent compared to only 33 percent in the EU (Moldan, 2000).

These achievements were due largely to the collapse of old, often outmoded state-owned enterprises; decreased reliance on heavy industry; the emergence of a dynamic service sector; and gains in energy efficiency as end users began purchasing energy at market rates (OECD, 2000). The latter is an example of an "active" pollution reduction strategy, as elaborated in chapter 1. Pollution reduction due to the demise of pollution-prone factories and shifts in leading economic sectors, however, is pollution reduction by default.

As was true in many parts of CEE, environmentally beneficial trends in Hungary were sustained in the late 1990s, even as the economy picked up steam.

OECD has noted that major reforms in the energy sector contributed to decoupling of SO_2 and NO_x emissions from economic growth (OECD, 2000). Despite this hopeful development, at the end of the decade, about half of Hungary's population continued to be exposed to serious or moderate levels of air pollution (Commission on Hungary's Process Toward Accession, 2002; OECD, 2000).

The complete phaseout of lead in gasoline, achieved in April 1999, was an unqualified policy-driven success, leading to sharp declines in ambient lead levels in Budapest's and other cities' busy corridors. On the other hand, mobile source air pollution increased substantially during the 1990s as car ownership reached more deeply into Hungarian society. Growing automobile use will also drive up CO_2 emissions. The 2000 EU Commission Agenda cites urban traffic as the fastest growing source of air pollution in Europe, and the OECD has condemned this trend. Hungary is not the only CEE country struggling with the pollution downsides of increased car ownership. In the Czech Republic and Estonia, for example, auto emissions are major concerns, as described in chapters 2 and 5.

Compared to the mostly downward trends in air pollution levels, Hungary had less success in reducing water pollution loads. At the end of the twentieth century, only 22 percent of the population was connected to sewage treatment networks (OECD, 2000). In Budapest, most sewage was deposited directly into the Danube River and one of its tributaries, the Tisza. The problem was complicated by diffuse pollution loadings from large-scale livestock and other agricultural operations.

Hungary has committed to clean up the Danube. It is an active participant in the Environmental Programme for the Danube River Basin (EPDRB) launched in 1992 (Botterweg and Natchkov, 2000). Among other accomplishments, Hungary and other EPDRB parties harmonized an emergency warning system. This played a positive role in managing cyanide spills from Romania into the Tisza River in January and March 2000.[14]

Environmental Professional Organizations and NGOs in Hungary

An important development in the arena of environmental management in Hungary is the emergence of influential nongovernmental actors of all stripes and persuasions. One set of actors is familiar to students of CEE environmental affairs: research, policy, and advocacy-oriented environmental NGOs. A less well recognized group is private sector professionals who provide environmental management services. Both sets of actors play key intermediary roles between environmental authorities and individuals and organizations whose behavior affects the environment. We consider the institution-building functions of the less well known group of intermediaries first.

An environmental service sector developed in Hungary after 1989. Before long, several of these firms earned a reputation for understanding the environment-related needs of foreign investors in Hungary, possessing the skills to serve these customers, and providing services at a discount to those offered by Western European and North American companies.[15]

Some purveyors of environmental services have formed associations to market their trade. A prominent example is the Hungarian Association for Environmentally Aware Management which serves companies seeking ISO 14000 certification. (ISO 14000 is a voluntary environmental management scheme.) Other organizations, like the Association of Environmental Producers and Service Providers in Budapest, provide information and other support to environmental service companies and/or lobby for association members' shared interests and concerns.

The development of private sector environmental associations is illustrative of the expansion of civil society in Hungary. It also demonstrates that the environmental movement is much more eclectic than during the period of the struggle over the Gabčíkovo-Nagymaros Dam. Environmental advocates represent many predispositions, preferences, and social and economic interests.

An example of this more diverse and inclusive environmentalism is in the area of citizen access to environmental information. Originally, the major advocates were Green NGOs who kept tabs on state environmental activities. However, for-profit interests also came to realize the value of obtaining regulatory and compliance data from the government. Hence, the Hungarian Association of Environmental Producers and Service Providers became an important advocate for open access to official, environment-related data.

Another key trend is the increasing sophistication of environmental nongovernmental organizations and the way they go about meeting their objectives. While environmental NGOs have lost the high profile they had in the late Communist period, in recent years, they have become more politically adept, and have increased their effectiveness as promoters of policy change.

Since 1989, the environmental movement has had to regroup, rethink its purpose, and reengineer its modes of operating. Environmentalists gradually realized that demonstrations and street protests produced diminishing returns. By the mid-1990s, many NGOs were interacting constructively instead of combatively with government. New strategies included providing information to lawmakers; commenting on legislative proposals; lobbying; participating in governmental advisory committees; and partnering with the state on discrete, environment-oriented projects.

Interacting with government in expert and other professional capacities, promoting politically informed perspectives, and taking activities from the streets to the corridors of power were major changes of approach and attitude for Hungarian environmentalists. These were big steps for Hungarian organizations that were formed as opposition groups, and whose members believed, instinctively, that government was the enemy.

The shift began when Green political parties, including the Hungarian Green Party, the Green Alternative, and the Blues, sought representation in Parliament. After unsuccessful campaigns in 1991 and 1994, the environmental political movement reinvented itself as a Western-style association of lobbyists. It exercised rights that were codified in heretofore untested framework laws on public participation dating from the late 1980s[16] and early 1990s.[17] The activities of the Levego Munkacsoport (Clean Air Working Group) illustrates this more Westernized approach to advocacy. The group produced a newsletter, position papers, and other informational materials that were sent to politicians and other influential actors in policy making. In the late 1990s, it was not uncommon for NGOs like Levego Munkacsoport to be invited to meetings of high environmental officials, and occasionally they were allowed to contribute to the formal debate.

However, the ability of NGOs to participate is very much dependent on the disposition of the Ministry of Environment and Regional Development. The ministry's willingness to work with NGOs changes from administration to administration. For example, civic organizations were asked to comment in 1992 on the developing Environmental Framework Act. But they were excluded from environmental policy-making deliberations during the administration of Pepo Pal between 1998 and June 2000 (Szabo, 2000). The situation appeared to be improving in the early years of the new century, and many of the major environmental organizations including Levego Munkacsoport, Humusz, and Gaia were increasingly optimistic about their ability to contribute in meaningful ways to environmental policy making. Levego Munkacsoport, for example, claims that it has influenced legislation dealing with the Environmental Fund (CEPF), product charges, and transportation issues (Levego, 2000).

Various Green associations have formed umbrella organizations to increase their lobbying effectiveness. Prominent NGO leaders believe that cooperation between environmental groups is vital for influencing the legislative process (Szabo, 2001b). Green networking exists in different forms, including the "Green Spider" Internet network and the Annual Meeting of Environmental and Nature Conservation Groups. Top decision makers from the environmental ministry have participated in these networks (REC, 1997).

Meanwhile, NGOs and their associations have remained steadfast about improving citizens' access to environmental information. The activities of the Tisza Klub, an NGO formed to protect the Tisza River, are a case in point. The much-publicized cyanide spill upstream in Romania (and before that, the impacts of NATO bombing on environmentally protected areas of Yugoslavia) discouraged tourism and in turn threatened the economic well-being of the region. A Tisza Klub member played a key role in preparing a Hungarian language "Citizen's Handbook" designed to help individuals and groups write information requests in ways that are difficult for the government to reject. The guide offers an extremely practical approach for would-be advocates. It includes model request letters as well as information about what to do if the government responds negatively.

Despite the increasing sophistication and capabilities of NGOs, much of the Hungarian public deems them ineffective and their activities inconsequential. Public opinion polls from 1998 indicated that around 68 percent of respondents considered NGOs to be useless to society, and only about 12 percent believed that NGOs played an important role in democratization (Anderson, 2000). On the other hand, 5 percent of Hungarians were members of an environmental organization, and younger respondents with postsecondary school training were relatively more sanguine about NGOs as effective promoters of a cleaner, better environment.

Perhaps Hungarian citizens are holding NGOs to an unfair standard. Often, environmental progress is achieved only at a glacial pace. In Western democracies, even small changes and improvements to environmental policies can require complex political maneuvers and trade-offs. Proponents must build coalitions and work out compromises. In the United States, for example, reauthorization of the Clean Air Act required drafts and debates in four separate congresses, spanning more than eight years, before the law itself was passed in 1990. Subsequently, USEPA had to write and issue relevant regulations, set standards in individual permits, and defend legal challenges to many rules. It was only after the USEPA had issued final regulations that actual plant-level implementation began taking place. If this start-and-stop process is typical of a prosperous country like the United States, with its centuries-old legacy of democratic governance and wealth of environmental protection experience, it may be unfair to criticize Hungarian environmental actors, including both state agencies and NGOs, for failing to achieve more impressive environmental results.

The Effort to Join the EU and Its Role in Stimulating Environmental Reform

Gyula Bándi, a leading Hungarian environmental lawyer, opines that between 1998 and the middle of 2000 "nothing important happened" in the realms of environmental legislation or regulatory implementation in Hungary (Bándi, 2002). This spell of inactivity ended mostly because of Hungary's desire to enter the European Union. In order to gain admittance, Hungary had to adopt all European Community legislation including all environmental rules and regulations. Arguably, prospective EU membership became the main driver of reforms in Hungarian environmental law and policy institutions.

During the late 1990s, official reports from the EU repeatedly pinpointed environmental management as one of the most problematic areas in Hungary's adoption of the *acquis*. Some 200 major environmental directives had to be adapted, and Hungary was afforded little room to negotiate the terms of the transposition nor to discuss the applicability of the directives themselves (European Commission, 1997). The environment ministry had to compare existing domestic legislation with the EU *acquis* ("the screening process" step in the transposition process) and then bring domestic laws in line with those of the EU. In order to ensure that the *acquis* was not only adopted but also implemented, the screening process included assessments of the organizational, monitoring, reporting, and communication needs of relevant government agencies (Jacoby, 1999; Lynch, 2000). As in most of the countries seeking EU membership, the approximation process became something of a cottage industry. Hungarian experts who poured over domestic and EU laws were tutored extensively by Brussels, and became skilled at drafting conforming requirements.

The European Commission's "Agenda 2000" report indicated that Hungary moved forward on such disparate matters as: laws for nature protection; industrial pollution; petrol and diesel fuel (including banning the sale of leaded petrol); waste management; environmental product charges for oil products; collection and processing systems for waste oils and used batteries; lawnmower and household appliance noise standards; large combustion plants; and control of major environmental accidents. On the other hand, the EU's November 2000 report indicated the need for additional work to adopt and adjust legislation on environmental impact assessment; access to environmental information; drinking and bathing water quality; wastewater treatment; prevention and reduction of industrial pollution; protection and reduction of environmental pollution by asbestos; control of certain noise emissions; and completion of legislation on waste management (Commission on Hungary's Process Toward Accession, 1999; 2000).

Following publication of the November 2000 report, Hungary instituted twenty-six new regulations, mostly in the area of air pollution prevention and water management, in a process so swift that the country provisionally closed its environmental chapter in June 2001. The European Union granted extensions for the implementation of a number of specific environmental directives and regulations. In striking this bargain, Hungary provided a detailed proposal complete with timetables and targets and financial particulars for four different areas where concessions were granted.

The details of these extensions provide some idea of the complexity and expense involved in Hungary's EU accession, and how these commitments will drive Hungary's environmental agenda. One concession involved the incineration of hazardous waste. None of Hungary's biomedical waste processors and only two of twenty-two other hazardous waste incarcerators comply with EU standards. The EU, which had only just implemented the relevant law, allowed Hungary until 2005 to come into compliance, recognizing that it will take time to upgrade these plants or to build new ones. A second concession gives a seven- to fourteen-year extension on biological treatment of wastewater for large settlements. Other allowances include upgrading of certain types of air pollution filters and instituting a recycling system for packaging materials by 2005.

It is estimated that these improvements will demand investments of nearly US$8 billion or about 1.5 percent of the country's GDP each year until 2015 (Szabo, 2001a) of which 93 percent must be committed by domestic sources. (PHARE aid and other EU aid programs may cover the balance.) The EU will closely scrutinize Hungary's efforts in these areas and may block accession if it deems the nation's progress unsatisfactory (Szabo, 2001a). Clearly, the drive toward EU membership and Brussels's environmental demands place a sizable claim on Hungary's discretionary environmental expenditures and are highly influential in shaping Hungary's domestic environmental policy agenda.

Does Prospective EU Membership Abet Domestic Environmental Performance?

Hungary, like its Soviet bloc neighbors, proved very adept before 1989 at placing environmental laws on the books only to subvert those laws by pursuing other imperatives. Today, the subtext of environmental law adoption in Hungary is EU accession. An existing and well-defined legal system is essentially being imposed from outside. The process, and the speed with which Hungary is incorporating EU standards into domestic policy institutions, raises fundamental concerns. What reason is there to believe that the accession process will produce laws that are more effectual than the "Potemkin village" of the pre-1989 period?

There is reason to be pessimistic about prospects for serious environmental reforms. One Hungarian expert argued by analogy to Hungarian treatment of the Roma community (the Gypsy minority). She pointed out that Hungary boasts excellent laws concerning the fair and equitable treatment of Roma. In fact, however, Roma are systematically deprived of a variety of rights and benefits, including education, health care, and housing (interview, Eva Bakonyi, former director, Soros Hungary, Budapest, Hungary, 26 August 2002). That such huge disparities still exist between formal rules and policies on the ground make it important to examine whether EU environmental requirements—not to mention European legislation, generally—will prove illusory and empty or real and consequential.

One mostly unexplored issue both within and outside Hungary is whether there is bottom-up support for EU-dictated environmental reforms. To function properly, environmental regulation typically requires large numbers of actors to change their behavior in significant ways. Beyond the duties required of companies and municipalities, environment-oriented responsibilities flow widely and deeply into society. Ordinary citizens must take actions that may cause them inconvenience or expense, at least in the short term. Reducing the flow of toxins to the Danube, for example, requires environmentally proactive participation by industry, agriculturalists, and homeowners tending their private gardens, among many others. Is there general public willingness to undertake these efforts, and in some cases, to make sacrifices? Do citizens, who are foot soldiers in the war on pollution, have sufficient trust and confidence in the new rules and requirements that they will accept the burdens these requirements impose?

Ordinarily, in a modern democracy, these questions are answered through the legislative process. If there is sufficient popular support, the legislature will act. Enforcement is the process of assuring that those who are least willing to comply—including lawbreakers—will be compelled to answer to the law-abiding majority. Approximation, in contrast to a democratic process of law-making, puts into place requirements that have been defined and adopted by an external actor—in this case, European Union lawmakers. Most current EU members have participated in the process of formulating EU laws. But Hungary, like other accession states, has not, and is in effect buying a bundle of prepackaged norms. Hungary is missing out on an important confidence-building process that may be necessary for developing public trust in rule making. Ordinary Hungarians' exclusion from this decision-making process may have implications for environmental compliance (Tyler, 1990). Ironically, the importation of EU requirements resembles the old socialist practice of law creation, in that both processes lack meaningful public participation and are essentially dictated from above.

On the other hand, through the early twenty-first century, Hungarian attitudes toward EU accession, generally, were positive. Public concern that aspects of the approximation process were antidemocratic were neutralized by most citizens' aspirations for membership. A larger lesson may be derived from Hungary's and other CEE countries' accession experiences. If a majority of citizens desire integration with a union of otherwise democratic states, those citizens may deem membership sufficiently valuable that they will tolerate undemocratic rule-making processes.

Notwithstanding concerns about constitutive aspects of the harmonization process, there are reasons to be hopeful for the success of the new laws. Joining the EU introduces four levels of scrutiny on the specifics of Hungary's compliance with EU directives. Before 1989, there was no remedy when the Hungarian government failed to honor its own laws and no oversight mechanism for frustrated citizens to invoke. This will change with EU membership.

Each of the European Community policing mechanisms has its own unique features.[18] Some must be initiated by the European Commission, while individuals can call upon others. Together, they could help assure environmental compliance.

The first is the European Commission's power to bring "infringement proceedings" in the European Court of Justice against Member States. If a Member State found to have violated Community law has not remedied this situation over a specified period, the Commission can impose a daily penalty and commence proceedings concerning national situations not in substantive conformity with EC legislation.[19] Individuals do not play a role in these proceedings, but individuals can bring complaints directly to the attention of the Commission by letter, or indirectly by complaining to Parliament.[20] The European Commission has also made it clear that it will monitor Member States on their implementation of the directives, and it has already issued some warnings.[21]

Another level of review is found in the European Court of Justice's doctrine of "direct effect." Individuals can invoke provisions of Community law against public authorities (but not against individuals) before national courts. The provisions invoked must be sufficiently clear and precise.[22] Directives, which are the main legal instruments for EC environmental law and are orders to Member States to act, can create rights for individuals.[23]

Because directives cannot be invoked against individuals, the Court has created the doctrine of "sympathetic interpretation" to close that "legal protection gap." In cases involving individuals, national courts and authorities must interpret national legislation as much as possible in conformity with the EC legislation.

Finally, an individual can seek damages before a national court against an EU Member State for violations of Community law caused by that state. This doctrine emerges from a groundbreaking 1991 case: *Frankovich and Bonifaci v. Italy* (European Court of Justice Reporter, 1991). The European Court ruled that it is a principle of Community law "that the Member States are obliged to make good loss and damage caused to individuals by breaches of Community law for which they can be held responsible."[24]

The Frankovich decision is a promising precedent for domestic Hungarian constituencies unsatisfied with the pace of national implementation of the directives. To understand why, it is useful to examine parallel experiences in the United States. When U.S. federal agencies were slow to implement environmental laws, particularly those for which the Congress set specific deadlines, public interest environmental groups brought "mandatory duty lawsuits" that compelled action.[25] These cases were instrumental in moving the environmental agenda forward and forcing EPA to act in a timely manner.

The Frankovich line of cases in Europe presents an analogous opportunity for Hungary's environmental NGOs.[26] Without waiting for the European Commission to take action, and so long as they meet the conditions set out in the Frankovich case, environmental interest groups can file lawsuits to hold Hungary responsible for its failure to implement the environmental directives. The result of a successful case will be damages, not an injunction. Nevertheless, those dissatisfied with the Hungarian government's environmental performance can use this tool in the same way environmental advocates did in the United States, to compel real and earnest implementation of the law. At a minimum, the very fact of a lawsuit or even a threatened lawsuit can create unfavorable publicity, forcing a state to meet its commitments.

The availability of these new legal tools hinges on Hungary's accession to the EU—an outcome that is highly probable as this volume goes to press. But whether these instruments will be used to fulfill the promises contained in the environmental directives will depend on Hungary's legal culture. It remains uncertain what path Hungary will follow as it moves from transposing environmental laws to implementing those laws. Perhaps, for example, it will adopt the model of the Netherlands, where many legal environmental cases have been adjudicated, in part or in whole, using Community law as a basis. Or perhaps Hungary's approach will resemble that of Spain's, where citizens and the legal profession seem less familiar with EC law or less eager to invoke it.

Reinvigorated Hungarian civic associations, with their diverse concerns and interests, could play instrumental roles in monitoring Hungary's environmental performance, advancing the objectives specified in national environmental action plans, and ensuring the state's and industry's obeisance to EU law. In the past, the realization of environmental policy objectives was contingent on centralized decision-making processes and Communist Party fiat. State-owned industries and the Ministry of Environment had little opportunity to act independently, and the ability of the nongovernmental community to challenge official actions or inactions was severely limited. The provisions of EU law discussed above could enable NGOs to press their case more effectively against polluters, but the decisive tests remain in the rigor with which Hungary implements newly transposed EU laws and whether the EU uses its authorities to insist on Hungary's compliance.

As regulators and NGOs pressure industry to be better environmental stewards, enterprise managers are gradually recognizing the economic advantages of good environmental behavior. Clean production and pollution prevention measures are increasingly popular, in no small part because they can positively affect the bottom line. ISO 14000 certification is picking up in Hungary because it is often demanded by customers or by others in the supply chain. It is also a useful public relations tool.

Hungarian enterprises *can* grow and prosper amidst a strict regulatory regime. An entire industry segment flourished in the United States when laws were passed that regulated the disposal of waste; a similar scenario could come to pass in Hungary as it implements certain EU directives on waste. When, in the early 1980s, a new administrator of USEPA threatened to slow down implementation of relevant environmental requirements, prominent economic interests felt threatened and made their views known to Congress.[27] It is difficult for members of Congress to ignore corporate constituents who complain that regulatory "relief" actually causes economic harm, but we can only speculate about how Hungarian parliamentarians might react in a similar situation.

Conclusion

Environmental reform is just one piece of the important process of economic and political transition, but it is also a bellwether. To put into place a working system of environmental regulations, Hungary must build—or rebuild—institutions and ultimately redefine the concept of law and how it works in everyday practice.

As this chapter and others in this volume attest, institutions are constituted by both formal and informal rules and procedures. Some of the informal institutions developed in Hungary during the socialist era must be renounced in order for real environmental progress to be achieved. One is the practice of winking at official laws and regulations; before 1989, adherence to strict environmental norms was the exception rather than the rule. Informally, plant managers expected lax enforcement. Formally, fines were precalculated in enterprise budgets. In the post-totalitarian era, Hungary must dispense with environmental requirements that only look good on paper. It can no longer afford to relegate laws to the category of "aspirational"—including the ambitious norms it has transposed from the EU.

Eliminating these institutional perversions and replacing them with smoothly operating systems of enforcement and compliance will occur only gradually—and perhaps too slowly for environmental advocacy groups and critics of the EU enlargement process. Expectations that post-Communist Hungary would leapfrog over the mistakes and inefficiencies of Western-style command and control regulatory institutions were never realistic. Leapfrogging in the realms of environmental law, policy, and management presume rapid learning across many parts of society, since successful environmental protection requires widespread societal efforts, not just changes in one government body or set of rules or practices. But discovering what makes institutions work well involves trial and error. Government, regulated actors, NGOs, and ordinary citizens must be enrolled in the trial-and-error process of making and administering policies that will eventually produce desired outcomes. Hungary like its neighbors must conduct its own experiments with environmental reform and learn from its own mistakes in order to develop policies and programs that flourish.

There is reason to hope that the EU accession process will accelerate the implementation of environmental laws and nurture other environmental institutions in Hungary, such as civic participation in different arenas of environmental policy making. The EU provides tools to adroit NGOs and citizens for the latter purpose.

But the EU also maintains unrealistically high expectations about Hungary's and other CEE countries' capacities to comply with EU environmental norms. To illustrate, Hungary is hard-pressed to implement the Integrated Pollution Prevention and Control (IPPC) Directive, 96/61/EC. IPPC sensibly recognizes that poorly integrated environmental management systems may encourage pollution to be shifted from one to another environmental media (e.g., from air to water), rather than protecting the environment as a whole. But integration that takes into account the *whole* environmental performance of an enterprise (i.e., emissions to air, water, and land; generation of waste; use of raw materials; energy efficiency; noise pollution; prevention of accidents; risk management; and so on) is exceedingly difficult to achieve. Wealthy nations with sophisticated regulatory institutions are only beginning to tackle the many political, bureaucratic, and economic obstacles that impede successful implementation of integrated environmental management norms. These requirements will be especially difficult to satisfy by underfunded, poorly staffed regulatory bodies like the Hungarian Ministry of Environment and Regional Development, particularly in light of its limited experience issuing and enforcing environmental permits.

Even if Hungary's progress toward achieving EU standards proves slow, the accession process has elevated environmental protection priorities higher than they otherwise might have risen, as the environment competes with other interests and demands in the transition process. Environmental protection's political profile can be raised higher still if the government takes its EU-mandated environmental duties seriously. The latter is unlikely to occur unless Hungarian NGOs and citizens are vigilant and make use of the very tools that EU directives provide for civic involvement in environmental affairs.

Notes

1. Generally speaking, Yugoslavians were freer than were Hungarians to travel to the West.

2. Even after reform-oriented members of the Communist Party replaced Kadar in 1988, they hoped that his successor Karoly Grosz would overhaul the economy while maintaining the predominant role of the Party.

3. GDP fell 20 percent between 1989 and 1993. Only in 2000 did Hungary's economic output recover to its 1989 level. The country experienced 15 to 30 percent yearly inflation in the early years of transition with a consequent decrease in real wages and a steep rise in poverty. Around 1.5 million people in a nation of 10 million left the workforce during this period. In addition, Hungary began repaying its foreign debt (which was among the highest in the region) (Andor, 2000). In contrast, Poland negotiated away much of its debt, and created a fund for environmental improvements as a quid pro quo for debt relief.

4. The Hungarian desire to join the EU was comparatively strong in the early years of the new century. According to polls, 54 percent of Hungarians would vote for accession while only 15 percent opposed it, and there was general consensus about the desirability of EU membership among different political factions. These figures surpass similar polled responses from other CEE citizenries (Radio Free Europe/RL Newsline, 2001).

5. The first governing party, Hungarian Democratic Forum (MDF), adopted a gradualist approach to economic reform and was widely criticized for achieving little in the area of privatization or of environmental policy. In 1995 the neoliberal Hungarian Socialist Party (MSZP) took over, which in spite of its name used unpopular austerity

measures to revive the economy. Economic shock therapy was unpopular, but the MSZP-led government advanced the country toward EU accession more so than any other administration. In the early years of the twenty-first century, the country was governed by the moderate right FIDESZ-MMP. In spite of its latent nationalistic and populist agendas, it managed to keep the country on track toward joining the European Union.

6. Clearly, all laws are aspirational to the extent they reflect societal goals, but the issue is whether there are dependable provisions and mechanisms that permit relatively consistent adherence with the laws' requirements.

7. See Janine Wedel's (1998) discussion on the development of "alternate" institutions for day-to-day economic livelihood. She writes of the

> labyrinth of channels through which deals and exchanges were made, both between people as 'themselves'—private individuals—and as representatives of economic, political and social institutions . . . informal relationships [that] pervaded the official economy and bureaucracy. . . . People became adept at operating in a twilight world of nods and winks, in which what counted was not formalized agreement but dependable complicity . . . enduring relationships, frequent contact, and the ability to verify reputation made trust a critical component. (Wedel, 1998: 104)

8. For its efforts, the Danube Circle received the Right Livelihood Award in 1985. The prize, established by Jakob von Uexkull, recognizes high environmental achievement. The award is often called the "alternative Nobel Prize."

9. For example, in 1988, the Society for Environmental Protection was founded to "provide support for state policy and to channel popular concern into acceptable activities" (Berg, 1999: 30; Waller, 1998).

10. This phenomenon has been commented on by others. See, for example, Jancar-Webster, 1998. For a discussion of parallel attitudes in Poland, see H. Brown et al. (2000: 56) which asserts:

> In practice, however, there are still serious obstacles to broad participation in policy making and implementation, especially by the general public. . . . [One is] the Bureaucracy's deeply entrenched administrative resistance to external scrutiny and its disdain for the value of lay persons' contribution to data analysis and policy making. . . . [Also] all parties are strongly influenced by the prevailing cultural mores, which, in Poland, favor delegating problems to experts who solve them in closed meetings.

Brown and her colleagues also note that "the independent ecological organizations have no traditions of participative legal process and are too fragmented to mobilize their limited resources necessary for such participation" and that enterprises continue to be recipients of regulations rather than participants in their formulation. Brown noted, however, that the situation was slowly changing.

11. The OECD, World Bank, USAID, and others pushed very hard for the creation and implementation of market-based instruments in CEE, including, for example, a program administered by the Harvard Institute for International Development that placed environmental economists in policy-advising roles in CEE governments. My own home institution, Resources for the Future, adopted a similar strategy (Toman, 1994).

12. I was coleader of a GEF-UNDP funded project in 2000-2001 that assisted the Hungarian Ministry of Environment and NGOs' efforts to develop procedures to respond to public requests for environmental information, such as emissions data. Hungary has also promised to institute rules that will allow any person or organization to ask for and

receive environmental information collected by the government. These commitments come under the UNECE Aarhus Convention (UNECE, 1998) which was ratified in May 2001. An EU directive incorporates the Aarhus obligations and makes them obligatory for member and accession states.

13. Similarly, the results of Hungarian national elections in 1990, 1994, and 1998, in which most voters supported candidates "that appeared less enthusiastic about dismantling the socialist institutions," demonstrated the public's ambivalence about market reforms (Andor, 2000).

14. The Tisza is Hungary's second largest river. In 2000, an Australian-Romanian mining company's waste pond burst near Baia Mare, Romania. This led to the release of approximately 100,000 m^3 of wastewater containing as much as 120 metric tons of cyanide and heavy metals into the Tisza. The spill had a very severe effect on plants and wildlife along the river. Some 1,240 metric tons of fish were killed. Thanks to the emergency warning system and the work of local authorities, the accidents did not cause any human deaths or acute illnesses (International Task Force for Assessing the Baia Mare Accident, 2000). For additional commentary on the Tisza River accidents, see chapter 4.

15. Interview, Bori Sari, June 16, 2001, Budapest, Hungary.

16. The 1987 Act on Lawmaking states that "bodies of public administration, social organizations and labor unions should be included in the process for preparing the drafts of those laws which concern interests represented and protected by them or which concern social conditions" (Stec et al., 1994).

17. A 1990 government decree directs the minister of environment to "keep in touch with citizen's organizations and movements"; a 1992 act enshrines the protection of personal data and free access to information (Stec et al., 1994).

18. EC legislation comprises the first and most central "pillar" of the three pillars of EU law, and includes environmental directives. The first pillar covers arrangements set out in the European Community Treaty (1957), the European Coal and Steel Community Treaty (1951), and the Euratom Treaty (1957). The second pillar deals with foreign policy and security policy, and the third with policy and judicial cooperation in criminal matters (European Union, 2002).

19. The authority for this is contained in Article 226 of the EC Treaty. Many of these proceedings concern whether Member States have put national legislation in place to transpose EC directives.

20. Procedures for complaining to Parliament are elaborated on the basis of Article 194 of the EC Treaty. The Commission retains full discretion to decide whether and when to start a case against a Member State.

21. For example, the European Commission recently decided to send Reasoned Opinions to France, Belgium, Germany, Italy, United Kingdom, Greece, Spain, and Portugal for failing to adopt and communicate the texts that are necessary to implement the 1999 directive on consumer access to fuel economy and CO_2 emissions data.

22. If there are questions of interpretation of EC law, the national court can (or in certain circumstances must) direct questions to the European Court of Justice (ECJ) in the form of a preliminary ruling. The ECJ responds to these questions and the national court then has to apply the answers in its ruling.

23. The rule is that where there is a discrepancy or contradiction between national law (including constitutional law) and EC law, EC law takes precedence and must be applied by national courts and authorities. However, directives cannot be invoked be-

tween individuals, only regulations and decisions, both of which are legal instruments which are directly applicable in the national legal order.

24. Frankovich involved Italy's failure to implement certain labor directives. The case established conditions which had to be met in order to obtain relief, namely: (1) the result prescribed by the directive should entail the granting of rights to individuals; (2) the contents of those rights must be identified on the basis of the provisions of that directive; and (3) "the existence must be established of a causal link between the breach of the State's obligation and the loss and damage suffered by the injured parties."

25. For example, the U.S. NGO, Natural Resources Defense Fund, brought a seminal law suit against U.S. EPA in the mid-1970s which resulted in a U.S. Federal District Court ordering EPA to promulgate effluent guidelines under the Clean Water Act, and to follow a strict schedule. (See Environmental Law Reporter, 1976.) The case was modified numerous times as the EPA struggled to issue effluent guideline rules on the court-ordered schedule. An extremely high percentage of the rules promulgated by EPA are issued pursuant to Court orders resulting from such suits.

26. For other cases related to Frankovich, see European Court of Justice Reporter (1993).

27. Private provision of solid waste management services became a major industry in the United States with the enactment of the Resource Conservation and Recovery Act of 1976. The act established legal requirements for the disposal of solid waste. The solid waste management industry protested vigorously when EPA began dismantling the act in the early 1980s. During the Reagan administration, EPA also rankled many enterprises when the agency proposed relaxing various environmental regulatory standards. Industries that had complied with heretofore strict regulations worried about free riding by competitors who had been slow to adopt these stringent rules.

References

Anderson, Brian (ed.). 2000. *Nations in Transition 1999-2000: From Post-Revolutionary Status to Incremental Progress. Country Report: Hungary.* New York: Freedom House.

Andor, Laszlo. 2000. *Hungary on the Road to the European Union: Transition in Blue.* Westport, CT: Praeger.

Bándi, Gyula. 2002. Recent Development of Environmental Law in Hungary. Avosetta Group. www-user.uni-bremen.de/~avosetta/bandidevenvlaw.html. Accessed 7 May 2002.

Bándi, Gyula, and S. Wajda. 1996. "Approximation of European Union Environmental Legislation. Regional Overview." Budapest: Regional Environmental Center.

Berg, M. 1999. "Environmental Protection and the Hungarian Transition." *Social Science Journal,* vol. 36, no. 2: 227-250.

Botterweg, Teun, and Ilya Natchkov. 2000. *Summary of Progress. Environmental Programme for the Danube River Basin (EPDRB), 2000.* www.rec.org/DanubePCU/Improvements.html. Accessed 28 August 2002.

Brown, Halina Szwjnwald, David Angle, and Patrick G. Derr. 2000. *Effective Environmental Regulation: Learning from Poland's Experience.* Westport, CT: Praeger.

Cole, Daniel H. 1998. *Instituting Environmental Protection: From Red to Green in Po-land.* New York: St. Martin's.

Commission on Hungary's Process Toward Accession. 1999. *1999 Regular Report.* Brussels: European Council. www.europa.eu.int/comm/enlargement/report_10 _99/pdf/en/hungary_en.pdf. Accessed 28 August 2002.

———. 2000. *2000 Regular Report.* Brussels: European Council. www.europa.eu.int/ comm/enlargement/report_11_00/pdf/en/hu_en.pdf. Accessed 28 August 2002.

———. 2002. *Environment: European Communitie, 2002.* europa.eu.int/scadplus/leg/en/ lvb/e15103.htm. Accessed 28 August 2002.

Elster, Jon, Claus Offe, and Ulrich K. Press. 1998. *Institutional Design in Post-Communist Societies.* Cambridge: Cambridge University Press.

Environmental Law Reporter. 1976. *Natural Resources Defense Council v. Train* (1976). 6 ELR 20588 (D.D.C. June 9, 1976).

Enyedi, Gyorgy, and Viktoria Szirmai. 1998. "Environment Movements and Civil Soci-ety in Hungary," in Andrew Tickle and Ian Welsh (eds.), *Environment and Society in Eastern Europe.* New York: Longman, 146-155.

Erdey, Gyorgy, and Mariann Karcza. 1996. "Approximation of European Union Envi-ronmental Legislation: Hungary Country Report." Budapest: Regional Environ-mental Center.

European Commission. 1997. *Commission Opinion on Hungary's Application for Mem-bership to the European Union.* Brussels: EU.

European Court of Justice Reporter. 1991. *Frankovich and Bonifaci v Italy (1991)* ECR I-5357 (1993) 2 C.M.L.R. 66.

———. 1993. *Cases C-46/93 and C-48/93 Brasserie du Pêcheur and Factortame III (1996)* ECR I-1029. 1 C.M.L.R. 889.

European Union. 2002. *Pillars of the European Union.* europa.eu.int/scadplus/leg/en/cig/ g4000i.htm#i5. Accessed 17 June 2002.

International Task Force for Assessing the Baia Mare Accident. 2000. "Report of the International Task Force for Assessing the Baia Mare Accident." Brussels: European Commission.

Jacoby, Wade. 1999. "The Reality behind the Potemkin Harmonization: Priest and Peni-tent: The European Union As a Force in the Domestic Politics of Eastern Europe." *East European Constitutional Review,* vol. 8, no. 1-2: 62.

Jancar-Webster, Barbara. 1998. "Environmental Movement and Social Change in the Transition Economies," in Susan Baker and Petr Jehlička (eds.), *Dilemmas of Tran-sition: The Environment, Democracy and Economic Reform in East Central Europe.* London: Frank Cass, 69-90.

Karatnycky, Adrian. 2000. *Nations in Transit 1999-2000: From Post-Revolutionary Stasis to Incremental Progress.* New York: Freedom House.

Klarer, Jurg, Patrick Francis, and Jim McNicholas. 1999. *Improving Environment and Economy: The Potential of Economic Incentives for Environmental Improvements and Sustainable Development in Countries with Economies in Transition.* Szenten-dre, Hungary: Regional Environmental Center.

Kosztolanyi, Gusztav. 1999. "Hungary: Where There's Muck There's Brass." *Central Europe Review,* vol. 1, no. 12. www.ce-review.org/99/12/csardas12.html. Accessed 6 January 2004.

Lehoczki, Zsuzsa, and Zsuzsanna Balogh. 1997. "Hungary," in Jurk Klarer and Bedřich Moldan (eds.), *The Environmental Challenge for Central European Economies in Transition.* New York: John Wiley, 131-168.

Levego. 2000. Reszletes Beszamolo a Levego Munkacsoport Orszagos Kornyezetvedo Szovetseg, 1999, evi kozhasznu tevekenysegerol (Detailed Report about the Activities of the Clean Air National Environmental Association Workgroup in the Year 2000). www.levego.hu/EVJEL99A.htm. Accessed 21 August 2002.

Lynch, Diahanna. 2000. "Closing the Deception Gap: Accession to the European Union and Environmental Standards in East Central Europe," in *Proceedings: Europe in the Global Economy: The Impact of Globalization on Policy-Making.* Berkeley, CA: California International and Area Studies Digital Repository, 426-437.

Moldan, Bedřich. 2000. *Environment after Ten Years of Transition.* Szentendre, Hungary: 2000. www.rec.org/REC/Programs/10th_anniversary/Speech.html. Accessed 21 August 2002.

OECD. 1999. *Environment in the Transition to a Market Economy: Progress in Central and Eastern Europe and the New Independent States.* Paris: OECD.

———. 2000. *OECD Environmental Performance Reviews: Hungary.* Paris: OECD.

O'Toole, Laurence J., and Kenneth Hanf. 1998. "Hungary: Political Transformation and Environmental Challenge," in Susan Baker and Petr Jehlička (eds.), *Dilemmas of Transition: The Environment, Democracy and Economic Reform in East Central Europe.* London: Frank Cass, 93-112.

Pawlik, Wojciech. 1992. "Intimate Commerce," in Janine Wedel (ed.), *The Unplanned Society Poland during and after Communism.* New York: Columbia University Press, 78-94.

Radio Free Europe/RL Newsline. 2001. *Radio Liberty Newsline,* vol. 5, no. 140, part 2.

Regional Environment Center. 1997. *Problems, Progress and Possibilities: Needs Assessment of Environmental NGOs in Central and Eastern Europe.* Szentendre, Hungary: Regional Environmental Center.

Rotschild, J., and N. Wingfield. 2000. *Return to Diversity.* New York: Oxford University Press.

Stec, Stephen, Magdolna Tóth Nagy, Margaret Bowman, Jiri Dusik, Jerzy Jendroska, Karel van der Zwiep, and János Zlinszky (eds.). 1994. *Manual on Public Participation in Environmental Decision Making: Current Practice and Future Possibilities in Central and Eastern Europe.* Budapest: Regional Environmental Center.

Szabo, G. 2000. "Pepo Egyszeruen Felszamolta a tarsadalmi kapcsolatokat" (Pepo Simply Cut All Ties to the Public). *HVG,* 10 June.

———. 2001a. "Tisztulo Levego" (Clearing Air). *HVG,* 9 June.

———. 2001b. "Otleteinket Viszontlatjuk az Allami Koltsegvetesben" (We See Our Ideas Appear in the National Budget). *HVG,* 20 January.

Toman, Michael A. (ed.). 1994. *Pollution Abatement Strategies in Central and Eastern Europe.* Washington, D.C.: Resources for the Future.

Tyler, Tom R. 1990. *Why People Obey the Law.* New Haven, CT: Yale University Press.

United Nations Economic Commission for Europe. 1998. *Convention on Access to Information, Public Participation in Decision-making and Access to Justice in Environmental Matters.* Aarhus, Denmark: UNECE.

Waller, Michael. 1998. "Geopolitics and the Environment in Eastern Europe," in Susan Baker and Petr Jehlička (eds.), *Dilemmas of Transition: The Environment, Democracy and Economic Reform in East Central Europe.* London: Frank Cass, 29-52.

Wedel, Janine. 1998. *Collision and Collusion: The Strange Case of Western Aid to Eastern Europe 1989-1998*. New York: St. Martin's.

Chapter 4

Forestry Resources in Transition: The Romanian Experience

M. Cristina Novac and Matthew R. Auer

One winter day in 2002, while walking through the Transylvanian countryside, a shepherd happened upon a cardboard box sheltering a most unexpected occupant. Inside was a naked, shivering boy who had lived alone in the woods for so long that he had forgotten how to speak and who appeared to have survived for months—perhaps longer—on meat scavenged from wild dogs (Leidig, 2002: 26). Romanians dubbed the child "Mowgli Boy" after the beloved hero of Rudyard Kipling's *Jungle Book*, and they marveled at his survival skills even as they condemned the abusive father from whom the Mowgli Boy sought refuge in the woods.

But if the boy's story struck some as fantastic and bizarre, to others it seemed quintessentially Romanian. Few forests in Europe are as vast and wild as those of Romania. They are certainly large enough to swallow a little boy, especially this one who was of Romany descent and poor social circumstances and who disappeared without anyone really noticing. To survive, he had to run with the carnivores, for Romania's forests are home to more large meat eaters, like lynx and bear, than any other in Europe.

Both the boy and the forest have suffered at the hands of bad parenting. Evidently, the child took refuge in the woods, fleeing an abusive father. In the case of the Romanian forest, the parental figure is the state, and in the 1990s, the government's forest service came to symbolize all that was dark and sinister about the Romanian public sector. According to one critic, the post-Communist

Romanian forest service was "one of the most corrupted authorities in Romania" (Bănăduc et al., 2002: 4).

For all their alleged corruption, it is unfair and inaccurate to suggest that Romanian government agencies have destroyed that nation's forests. Indeed, the woods are vast, lush, and boast great biological diversity. But over the years, the reform of the Romanian forestry administration has stumbled with harmful consequences for forests, the forest-based economy, and the integrity of Romanian public administration. In this chapter, we examine more than ten years of reform of Romanian forest management. We find that new, formal institutions for forestry have allowed older, informal institutions to flourish, and at the expense of sound natural resource management.

In determining who benefits from and who pays for the development and harvesting of Romania's forests, informal institutions—many of them rooted in the coping mechanisms that citizens used for "getting by" during the Communist era—are no less important than are formal institutions. In many cases, informal rules and procedures have led to forest mismanagement such as shady dealings between forestry officials and forest harvesters and widespread transgression of forest conservation rules by public and private actors alike. Before turning to an analysis of post-Communist Romania's record of forest management, that experience is placed in the broader context of Romania's contemporary natural resource and environmental policy reforms.

Environment in Transition: An Overview

Beginning in 1990, Romania overhauled its environmental statutes and policies as part of the grand overall tasks of creating Western European-style laws and governmental institutions. Early on, the industrial and urban environments received more attention than did the natural environment. Several severe pollution problems were addressed, though on an ad hoc basis. Moreover, the general approach to environmental reform was disorderly and incoherent, and rule making and new policies were made in piecemeal fashion. Communist-era policies and procedures for environmental protection, which tended to be stronger on paper than in practice, nevertheless cast a shadow on the first years of the post-Communist reform process. Since many of the pathologies of recent forest management institutions are rooted in Communist-era rules and procedures, it is instructive to highlight distinguishing features of the latter.

Environmental Policies under Communism

In the early 1970s, concurrent with the founding of environmental regulatory institutions in many industrialized countries, Romania's Communist leaders adopted a variety of environmental laws and policies that resembled those of the West. Among other accomplishments, water and air quality monitoring systems were instituted and were functioning by the late 1970s (Turnock, 1996); caps were set for pollution discharges from industry and fines were levied for non-compliance; and a handful of national parks and nature reserves were created.

However, environmental management in Romania was greatly undermined by misguided public investments that saddled Romania's economy with foreign debt. Resources for environmental protection became even more scarce as Communist officials determined to pay down the debt in the shortest time possible and at all costs and as the global economy slowed in the late 1970s and early 1980s. Environmental policies, which were never applied rigorously, were further handicapped by obtuse and contradictory implementation procedures. For example, to decrease consumption of energy in industrial plants, pollution control equipment was switched off at night. Bad policies produced disappointing results. In the field of energy efficiency, energy intensity in Romania was as many as five times the level of other OECD countries in the 1980s (ÖKO Inc./REC, 2001).

Policies promoting economic self-sufficiency meant that Romanian industry became increasingly reliant on antiquated technologies, including many pollution-prone manufacturing methods that were abandoned years earlier in the West. Chemical plants, steel and iron works, and nonferrous metal processing industries were major sources of air and water pollution. Concentrations of heavy metals in the soils in and near industrial towns such as Copşa Mică, Baia Mare, Zlatna, Bucharest, and Slatina greatly exceeded the maximum permissible levels, often by orders of magnitude (Ognean and Vădineanu, 1992: 245-258; Pavlínek and Pickles, 2000: 40-41; 71-72). Incidence of cancer and other illnesses were far higher among peoples living in severely polluted areas than in the country as a whole. Elevated levels of respiratory ailments, skin cancers, and a variety of diseases and illnesses in children such as lead poisoning, neurological impairment, and growth retardation were pervasive in Romanian hot spots during the 1980s (Pavlínek and Pickles, 2000: 153). With an autocratic regime in Bucharest and a well-financed internal security apparatus, there was little public outrage about the environmental situation until the mid-to-late 1980s. Concerned citizens had little or no reliable environmental or public health information and they were poorly served by the country's sole environmental agency, the National Committee for Environmental Protection.

Myopic economic policies and half-hearted environmental management procedures had devastating effects on natural resources. Overuse and inappropriate application of fertilizers, wastes generated by huge livestock farms, and urban and industrial pollution spoiled both waterways and aquifers (Tomescu, 1996). Wetlands along the Danube River and the Danube delta were drained and transformed into farmland, destroying wildlife habitats, reducing the filtration of polluted runoff from farms, and impairing groundwater recharge.

Environmental Policies in Transition

With the fall of Communism in Romania and the emergence of democratically elected governments at national, regional, and local levels, officials promised to confront the nation's environmental problems in an integrated fashion. Very early during the transition, social pressure and political will to issue new environmental regulations and procedures were strong—trends common in many CEE countries (OECD, 1999). Complementing and sometimes competing with the pro-environmental efforts of Romania's many NGOs were two Green political parties, the Romanian Ecological Movement and the Romanian Ecological Party. With support from urbanites in industrialized areas, both of these parties gained a handful of parliamentary seats in the elections of 1990 (Turnock, 1996).

However, relatively high public awareness and concern about the environment did not translate into effective and coherent governmental action. Among the key problems were the national and municipal governments' chronic financial problems and their triage approach to public investments which relegated environmental concerns near the bottom of the list. Romania was a prime destination for bilateral environmental aid; together with the Czech Republic, Hungary, and Poland, Romania received about 50 percent of all technical assistance to the CEE region through 1994 (OECD, 1999). However, external aid did not make up for the relatively small sums from Romania's treasury. Lack of political will and authorities'—especially local authorities'—limited experience and ill preparation for environmental management duties often further compromised the performance of the meager investments that *were* dedicated to environmental concerns.

Facilitating official efforts to tamp down urban and industrial pollution was the otherwise unwanted phenomenon of economic recession. As was true in countries throughout CEE, in the 1990s, and especially in the early 1990s, great reductions of air and water pollution and hazardous wastes came in the wake of decreased domestic and regional demand for heavy-industrial goods and the collapse of trade between CEE countries and between CEE and NIS countries. Even as pollution-prone factories and power plants began operating at half capacity or simply shut down, the Romanian government took active measures to abrogate pollution from the worst industrial offenders. Some notoriously heavily polluting manufacturing plants were shuttered, such as the artificial fiber plant of Suceava. Enterprises in Romania's vast industrial park of Copşa Mică were overhauled, and less polluting fuels were substituted in a power station in Braşov (Turnock, 1996; Government of Romania, 1992b).

As the government partially retrofit or shut down some of the major pollution emitters, Parliament drafted new environmental legislation, including a comprehensive environmental law in 1995 (Parliament of Romania, 2000b). Additional laws were passed in 1997 and 1998, but in some cases regulatory details, including specific prohibitions on pollution, rules governing pollution discharge permits, and acceptable levels of contamination in the environment were reserved for various governmental agencies to develop. Even when these detailed rules were specified, implementation stumbled as agencies made do with thin operating budgets and small, inexperienced staffs.

Perhaps the most poignant examples of spotty environmental monitoring and enforcement were well-publicized environmental accidents that occurred in the 1990s, and in particular, a spill of cyanide from an overflowing lagoon filled with toxic mining wastes. The spill killed aquatic plants and animals along several miles of the Tisa River[1] and farther west in the Danube River, and the accident temporarily strained relations between Romania and Hungary. Wrangling over legal liability for the accident continued into the twenty-first century as the spill occurred from the operations of a newly privatized enterprise that was partly foreign owned and managed.

As Romanian environmental authorities struggled with monitoring and enforcement duties, they experimented with new pollution fees and charges. Such levies existed during Communist times, but as a rule, were too small to inspire pollution-conscious behavior by industrial managers. Even in the 1990s, most fees remained nominal and much lower than the cost of pollution abatement equipment, hence polluters willingly paid the former to avoid investing in the latter. For example, in 1997, a US$11 charge was assessed on each ton of BOD (biochemical oxygen demand) discharged to waterways—a level much lower than in other former Communist countries (e.g., Lithuania, US$220/ton; Poland, US$1,000—US$4,000/ton) not to mention in advanced industrialized OECD countries (e.g., France, US$54,000) (OECD, 1999: 110). These charges served mostly to raise revenue rather than influence polluters' behavior. Moreover, proceeds from the charges were not channeled to national or regional environmental funds, as was the case in other CEE countries such as Poland and Hungary (Klarer et al., 1999).

Much as pollution fees and fines were too low to inspire major changes in polluters' behavior, post-Communist era water pricing procedures gave end users little incentive to conserve water. Along with paying for water officials' salaries, the state covered all costs for pumping and distributing water (ÖKO Inc./REC, 2001). Final users paid only for water consumed, and even then, the state charged less from residential customers than from industrial users. However, homes are seldom equipped with water meters, or for that matter, gas meters. State-owned water and energy companies take advantage of this situation by charging residential owners for water and gas distribution losses—charges that can add large increments to monthly bills. Hence, by decade's end, the state's efforts to rationalize retail prices for water and other natural resources, and more broadly, to improve delivery of essential services like water and gas, remained a work in progress.

However, in no natural resource sector were rent-seeking opportunities for the state, among other institutional shortcomings, more obvious than in forestry. Early during the transition, the Romanian legislature decided to preserve state ownership over the vast majority of forest resources (roughly 95 percent of for-estland) and gave management and control over the resource to a public-run corporation (Government of Romania, 1991c). Laws and regulations on forest conservation and management developed during the 1990s effectively strength-ened state control over forest resources. The middling quality of Romania's natural resource management efforts is poignantly illustrated in the forestry sec-tor as the physical effects of post-Communist era policies became apparent to ordinary Romanians and as foresters and other actors directly affected by these policies spoke out about problems with the reforms. Understanding the mixed results of forestry reforms in Romania requires analysis of both formal and in-formal policy institutions in that country. First, however, essential physical and productive characteristics of Romania's forests are examined and are character-ized vis-à-vis forest resources in the CEE region and Europe, generally.

Romania's Forest Resources

Around 29 percent of Romania's territory is covered by forests and other wooded vegetation. This places Romania below the European national average of about 33 percent forest cover, although differences among countries are con-siderable (table 4.1).

Only a small proportion of Romania's forests consist of ancient trees—around 5 percent—but this is a higher percentage of primeval forest land than in many other European countries (UNECE/FAO, 2000). Moreover, on a tract-by-

TABLE 4.1
Forest and Other Wooded Lands in Selected European Countries

Country	Forest and Other Wooded Land (% of land area)	Forestland/Capita (hectares/capita)
Austria	47.6	0.47
Britain	10.3	0.04
Bulgaria	35.8	0.43
Czech Republic	34.0	0.26
France	31.4	0.26
Germany	31.0	0.13
Hungary	19.9	0.18
Italy	36.9	0.17
Poland	29.4	0.23
Romania	29.1	0.28
Spain	51.9	0.34

Source: UNECE/FAO, 2000: 47, 63.

tract basis, Romania's ancient forests are among the largest in Europe (World Bank, 2002: 3). Forests and other natural resources provide habitat for several thousand different species of plants and animals in Romania. Among CEE nations, only Bulgaria boasts greater total biodiversity than Romania (table 4.2).

The Carpathian Mountains, most of which reside in Romania, are surrounded by the largest contiguous forest ecosystem in Central and Eastern Europe. Though it covers less than 1.5 percent of Europe's surface area west of Russia, nearly one-third of Europe's large carnivores, including wolf, lynx, and bear, reside there (Carpathian Wildlife Foundation, 2002). Those forests provide habitat for other depleted fauna in Europe, including wildcats, stag, and wild boar.

As was true in other CEE countries, after the Second World War, most forest land in Romania was expropriated by the state. Romania was largely self-sufficient in forest resources and at no time was it a major importer of wood products during the Communist period. For many years, this trend had as much to do with policies to maintain timber harvests at or below the forests' natural regenerative capacity as it did to constraints on the supply of wood products and relatively low levels of consumption (UNECE/FAO, 1996a).

The ratio between growing stock and harvest volume remained relatively stable in Romania until the 1980s, when harvesting pressures picked up. At the same time, species diversity in the forests declined (Turnock, 1996). These were setbacks for foresters who had busily reforested much of the countryside in the 1960s and 1970s, all in an effort to correct the effects of extensive clear-cutting that occurred decades earlier (Parliament of Romania, 1999f).

In the early 1990s, wood production and consumption slumped in most of CEE, mirroring the contraction of the region's economies and downward-sloping real income levels (UNECE/FAO, 1996b). Romania did not diverge

TABLE 4.2
Biodiversity in Selected CEE Countries, Late 1990s

Country	Mammals	Birds	Fish	Plants	Total Number of Species
Bulgaria	94	383	207	3,700	4,384
Czech Republic	90	186	65	2,520	2,861
Estonia	64	331	76	1,560	2,031
Hungary	83	373	81	2,500	3,037
Latvia	69	320	95	1,678	2,162
Poland	84	418	48	2,300	2,850
Romania	102	364	191	3,700	4,357
Slovakia	85	352	78	3,352	3,867

Source: UNECE, 2001: 191.

from these trends. Between 1993 and 1995, net annual increments to forest stock exceeded wood removed from harvesting by roughly 160 percent (UN-ECE/FAO, 1997). The advice of Communist-era forest managers proved instrumental in the early transition period as these actors warned against the hasty privatization of forests and cast doubt on the state's ability to control overharvesting on private land. Romanian officials were also learning about environmental problems ensuing from forest privatization policies in Hungary, Latvia, and as discussed by Auer in this volume (chapter 5), in Estonia.

Virtually all foresters from the previous regime were retained in Romania's post-Communist forestry agency. Not coincidentally, many of the basic organizational forms and functions of the agency remained intact from the Communist era. Most salient, the state determined to retain its near monopoly over management and conservation of forest resources in Romania (see Government of Romania, 1991c; see also State Council of Romania, 1982). During the 1990s, virtually all decisions concerning which forests were harvested and by whom remained in state hands. However, in practice, the authority of the forest service was gravely undermined by the self-interested behavior of state managers and workers who profited by relying on old, informal, and in many instances, illegal ways of transacting official business.

Informal Institutions for Forest Management

As was true of other Communist regimes in CEE, in Romania, the hierarchical structure of the Communist Party was replicated in administrative bodies at central as well as local levels of government. Moreover, party "cells" were organized and propagated in almost every aspect of political, economic, and social life. Hence, in each economic unit (e.g., extractive industries, finished good processing, goods and services provision, etc.) and public body (e.g., schools, hospitals, public libraries, and so on) a microscale party hierarchy functioned, authorized to ensure that policy directives and plans were obeyed. Moreover, political and production-oriented functions were responsibilities of the same individual, with the expectation that party doctrine would permeate all political, economic, and administrative activities (Berend, 1996; Kaminski, 1992; Kornai, 1992). Managers of industrial plants, commercial enterprises, and public service units also held positions in the party structure. Thus, they could be held accountable for both political and economic functions as per the direction of the party. Moreover, important party officials were rewarded for their loyalty by being entrusted with economic managerial roles. Through this party-state structure, centrally planned policies and procedures were administered. At the same time, a conflict of interest was institutionalized by the establishment of dual identities (political actor/economic manager) in the same individual.

Since the same person often performed policy-oriented *and* economic functions, there was a strong temptation for managers and workers alike to exploit their position for personal gain. Graft in Communist-era Romania was pervasive at both the administrative level and among line staff and in virtually every arena of production. So universal was this corruption, it effectively transformed a de jure nationalized economy into a "privatized" economy (Kaminski, 1992) and well before the fall of Communism. Privatization meant the fabrication and operation of shadow markets by private individuals, with persons occupying particular roles and operating by rules, albeit informal rules, understood and obeyed by other actors in the market. There was always the risk of getting caught, but law enforcement officers were also public servants, and prone to be corrupted. Top-to-bottom graft in public institutions was common throughout CEE countries during Communist times (Kaminski, 1992; Los, 1990) and Romania was no exception to this trend, particularly with its relatively lower living standards and chronic shortage of consumer goods.

In those millions of jobs in Communist Romania tied to the production and distribution of goods, bribery was so pervasive as to be deemed a normal part of doing business and was for all intents and purposes destigmatized.[2] The removal of odium to corrupt acts was abetted by the fact that the most basic units of the shadow economy were networks of family and friends (Sampson, 1984; Verdery, 1983). But even outside of these close, friendly exchange networks, corrupt acts such as bribery were so commonplace that bribes were seldom conceived as such; instead, to offer or take a bribe was to give or receive a "gift." Trafficking of gifts was especially critical when coveted goods were in short supply—a not infrequent occurrence in Romania, especially in the 1980s. A worker in a retail sales enterprise—for example, a store selling furniture—might be compelled to offer gifts to a furniture wholesaler. Generally, those gifts were in the form of goods that were in short supply at the wholesaler's end. For the retailer, obtaining that scarce furniture was critical because there were one-year or five-year revenue targets to meet, and workers might not be paid until planned targets were satisfied.

Customers, themselves, might be enrolled in this system of graft. Extralegal devices were important for moving products and satisfying demand. For example, bribes and "speed money" could help place a customer's name on a waiting list for coveted wood products or move that name up the list. Graft also greased transactions in the rural, local, and neighborhood economies where wood was essential for heating, cooking, and construction. As was true of other consumer goods, wood products of all varieties, including even fuelwood, were frequently in short supply since they were rationed by the state. These circumstances "encouraged corruption among foresters who might accept bribes to overlook unauthorized cutting or grazing" (Turnock, 1996: 155).

Formal Institutions for Forest Management

In the early 1990s, in newly democratized Romania, there was a consensus among forestry officials that the country's forests had been overexploited in the 1980s, and more broadly, were not well cared for (FAO, 1997; FAO, 1995). In response, the government strengthened state control over forest resources during the 1990s, and in the process, perpetuated many of the institutional and bureaucratic forms and functions that prevailed during the Communist era. This section describes the formal institutional reform experience of the 1990s followed by an analysis of the effects of these reforms on Romania's forests, on the welfare of its forest-based economic actors, and on the integrity of its state forest management agency.

The struggle between the state's demand for stronger official oversight and bottom-up pressure for private control of forests played out early in the decade. Forestry regulations adopted after 1990 emphasized forest resource conservation and protection (Government of Romania, 1998b; 1991b; Parliament of Romania, 1992). Reduction of state forest land was prohibited with few exceptions (such as the formation of right-of-way for utilities and other public infrastructure). Clear-cutting of trees was restricted (Parliament of Romania, 1996).

At the same time, rules governing restitution of property were enacted. Regulations adopted in 1991 included provisions for returning agricultural and forested plots of up to 1 hectare (approximately 2.5 acres) to pre-1945 owners or to their heirs. The implementation of these rules was fractious and many restitution claims required juridical action. Locations of old property lines were disputed between claimants or between the state and claimants, and in many cases, restitution was precluded by major changes to the land that occurred in Communist times. Restitution led to diversification of ownership over forest resources, but the percentage of forest land in private hands remained low. At the beginning of 2000, of Romania's 24,580 square miles of forest land, only about 5.4 percent was privately held. Compared to other European countries, in the 1990s, the area of forest and wooded land in private hands in Romania was small (table 4.3). The vast majority of forests and wooded lands were owned by the state and were managed by a state-owned corporation known as the Regia National a Padurilor (RNP) which is Romania's National Forestry Corporation (Parliament of Romania, 1999b; 1999c).

RNP,[3] which was established in the early 1990s, took over the assets and functions of the Communist-era Ministry of Silviculture. However, officially, RNP was not a wholly autonomous national agency, but under the auspices of a ministry that, after several bureaucratic reorganizations and name changes, became the Ministry of Agriculture, Food and Forests (Government of Romania, 2001; 1994; 1991c).[4]

RNP's mission was "to preserve, conserve and develop forestry resources, manage game and fresh water fishing resources, and ensure efficient economic

TABLE 4.3
Forest Land Area and Property Designation of Forests and Other Wooded Areas in Selected European Countries, 1990s

Country	Reference Period	Area of Forest and Other Wooded Land (1,000 ha)		Area of Forest (1,000 ha)		Number of Holdings	
		In public owner-ship	In private owner-ship	In public owner-ship	In private owner-ship	In public owner-ship	In private owner-ship
Austria	1995	1,502	1,790	1,502	1,790	7,286	227,307
Bulgaria	1995	3,903		3,590	0	177	0
Czech Republic	1996	2,212	418	2,212	418	4,566	137,260
France	1995-96	4,228	12,761	3,965	11,191	15,926	
Germany	1996	6,107	3,334			13,040	349,361
Hungary	1996	1,169	642	1,169	667	962	74,047
Italy	1995	3,686	7,156	3,352	6,505	2,241	815,586
Poland	1992-96	7,448	1,493	7,448	1,493	461	843,802
Romania	1997	6,320	360	5,961	340		
Spain	1990	5,608	20,376	4,235	9,274	8,718	661,992

Source: UNECE/FAO, 2000: 116.

use of the forests' other resources" (Government of Romania, 1991c). The agency was charged with developing, implementing and monitoring its own programs and operations. Its program costs would be subsidized from fees collected from harvested wood and revenue from consulting and other specialized services (Parliament of Romania, 1996; 1999a; Romanian Ministry of Water Resources, Forest Resources, and Environmental Protection, 1999a).

With the founding and enabling of RNP, the status quo condition of strong state control over forests was preserved. But in what seemed like a deliberate effort to counterbalance a trend toward statism, in 1991, Romania's legislature called for the liberalization of prices for uncut, standing wood (Government of Romania, 1991a). A year later, wood-processing equipment was exempted from import taxes and fees (Government of Romania, 1992c). These measures were intended to stimulate an indigenous, private wood-processing sector whose commerce would help determine prices for timber.

On the other hand, RNP continued to wrest control over timber harvesting decisions, and hence, over timber supply (Government of Romania, 2000c; 1995b; 1991b; Parliament of Romania, 1992). Moreover, RNP set starting bid prices for wood at timber auctions. Some harvesters claimed that these opening prices were set artificially high (Parliament of Romania, 1999d).

Meanwhile, the liberation of wholesale and retail prices for harvested wood, coupled with quotas on supply assured that prices for wood products, from saw-logs to finished products, rose steeply during the 1990s, though no less steeply than other nonfood commodities such as electricity and natural gas. Indeed, rising prices for wood occurred against a background of sharply rising prices for goods, generally. As late as 1999 through 2001, inflation in Romania hovered between 30 and 46 percent—highest in the CEE region with the exception of the former Federal Republic of Yugoslavia (UN, 2001: Annex 15). In the forest sector, revenues declined by as much as 40 percent between 1990 and 1998 (Institutul Naţional de Statistică, 2001).[5] Falling revenues were driven partly by a reduction in the volume of *legally* harvested wood: in the 1980s, fellings reached 23 to 26 million m³/year, declining to around 15 million m³/year in the 1990s (UNECE/FAO, 1996b: 6.7.1; FAO, 1997: 1). But in addition, the ratio of value-added revenue to total forest sector revenue declined in the 1990s as Romania's furniture and other high-end forest industries faltered and as unprocessed roundwood exports accelerated. In the 1990s, Romania became a net importer of furniture—a humiliating turnaround for what had been a major export sector and crucial hard currency earner in the 1970s and 1980s (Bănăduc et al., 2002: 5). Nevertheless, a decade after Communism, wood exports from Romania remained a vital economic engine, accounting for over US$1 billion or 10 percent of total exports in 2000 alone (World Bank, 2002: 3; Moroianu, 2001b; 2001c).

In the 1990s, the process of determining the total allowable annual timber yield was, in practice, highly devolved since RNP field level managers were the first actors in the decision-making chain to recommend caps on harvests. Unit level recommendations were funneled to the RNP's national office which made a final recommendation to RNP's home ministry. The latter promulgated an official yield, but seldom did this directive deviate greatly from the one recommended by RNP. After the allowable yield was established, timber harvest operations were scheduled two or three times per year by the RNP which awarded harvesting rights by auction. Also, RNP was authorized to organize additional auctions for "unanticipated situations" such as salvage operations after damaging windstorms, fires, or comparable natural events (Parliament of Romania, 1996; Government of Romania, 1995a).

RNP also had a large degree of de facto control over *who* was authorized to harvest in state forests. This is the case despite the state's establishment of a national committee whose sole purpose was to review the credentials of and award or deny applications to prospective timber harvesters (Romanian Ministry of Water Resources, Forest Resources, and Environmental Protection, 1999c). Even if a firm was awarded a tree-cutting permit, it had to obtain an additional certification from RNP. The latter preceded any given timber harvest auction, and it was a means for establishing (and reestablishing) a prospective harvester's fitness to operate in Romania's forests. To avoid potential conflicts of interest, persons employed as state foresters were prohibited from representing forestry companies in auctions.

In addition to organizing auctions to dispense harvesting rights, RNP was authorized to harvest trees in state forests at its own discretion; identify and mark trees to be harvested on both public and private lands (Romanian Ministry of Water Resources, Forest Resources, and Environmental Protection, 1999b); patrol state forests and police illegal harvesting activities (the latter in conjunction with local government officials and law enforcement personnel); manage forest health (i.e., protect trees against disease and infestation) in both public and private forests; purchase land under the preemptive right of the state to buy any forest area offered for sale; issue permits for real estate development projects if such projects lay within one kilometer of a state forest boundary; and issue and check documents of origin for timber harvested on public and private forestland (Government of Romania, 2000f; 1992a; Parliament of Romania, 2000a; 1996; 1993).

RNP's wide-ranging authority over forest management decisions continued until 1995 at which time some of its powers, and in particular, forest management auditing, were gradually transferred to a new office within the Ministry of Water Resources, Forest Resources, and Environmental Protection (and later still, the Ministry of Agriculture, Food and Forests). Parliament decided it was time for RNP to surrender some of its enforcement and policy appraisal functions to its parent ministry. As discussed in detail in the next section, this decision was precipitated by concern about RNP's ability to at once manage forestry operations and impartially audit its own performance. A new office in the ministry took over several key duties that had been RNP's, including random auditing of auction preparations (e.g., to verify that both RNP and timber companies complied with legal requirements); spot-checking documentation of origin for transported wood; and in conjunction with RNP and law enforcement officers, patrolling Romania's forests, including private forests (Government of Romania, 2000b; Romanian Ministry of Water Resources, Forest Resources, and Environmental Protection, 1995). However, the new unit in the ministry had no real presence in the field until 2000 with the opening of seven forest inspection and assessment offices.

Analysis of Forestry Institutions

Even with the transference of certain management functions to the Ministry of Agriculture, Food and Forests, RNP's administrative control over Romania's state forests and even private forests remained preeminent throughout the 1990s. The ministry's capacity to audit forest management operations was handicapped by a relatively small budget allocation, and ministry officials were hard-pressed to visit and audit each of RNP's forty-one county-level offices.[6]

Even after a second round of formal reforms were made for enforcement and auditing—changes meant to strip power from RNP—that agency remained the de facto forest manager and auditor as the overseeing ministry struggled to absorb its new duties. In this case, informal economic and social institutions proved hardier than formal interventions meant to replace Communist-era rules and procedures.

Through 1999, RNP continued to administer timber auctions while simultaneously assessing petitioners' eligibility to bid on and harvest trees in state forests. Since it was both chief auctioneer and chief arbiter of the integrity of the auctioning system, RNP was especially susceptible to bribes and other forms of graft.

In 1998, an inquiry commission was empanelled to evaluate the state's forest management performance, including its enforcement activities (Chamber of Deputies, 2000; 1998). According to the commission, there were 500,000 forestry-related offenses committed between 1990 and 1998 including approximately 1,540 instances of poaching. For the purposes of appraising the performance of RNP's and local police inspectorates' enforcement activities, these data are lacking in at least two respects. First, the tally of forestry-related offenses do not indicate whether violators were actually brought to justice, for example, whether fines were assessed and collected (Parliament of Romania, 1999e). Moreover, it is unclear what percentage of total illegal activities were actually discovered by law enforcement officials. Nevertheless, on this latter point, the data should give pause to forestry authorities as well as environmentalists in Romania. One-half million illegal acts in Romania's forests constitute only those violations that were detected by the police and RNP between 1990 and 1998—a great deal of deviance by any standard of law enforcement (Savaliuc, 2001a; 2001b; 2001c).

Moreover, and more troubling still, the inquiry commission and other investigators have linked a number of illegal activities to RNP itself. To illustrate, the managers of the Bucharest Forestry Office (Bucharest's local RNP office) failed to report, and indeed appear to have consented to, illegal harvests in 1996-1997 (Savaliuc, 1998b). Illegal felling also occurred in forests managed by the Sibiu County Forestry Office, with knowledge of a forest manager who was subsequently fired (Hoandră, 1998a; 1998b). Forestry offices in Maramures County were suspected of allowing logging above a legal harvest quota (Chima and Vidican, 1999). In counties Cluj and Sălaj, local officials facilitated illegal logging on municipally managed forest land. In this case, local RNP officials provided transportation equipment and issued false documents of origin (Poenaru, 2000).

Old, informal institutions of exchange and reciprocity helped actors circumvent formal prohibitions imposed during the 1990s. Bribery, which greased transactions in every economic sector in the Communist era survived intact in the new regime. In the forestry sector, the persistence of corruption could have been expected since the new system looked and behaved so much like the old one, namely, with a single government agency auditing its own monopolistic forest management operations.

Informal, personal networks of amity, exchange, and mutual obligation that helped raise individual and household-level living standards in the Communist era also abetted rent-seeking behavior in the post-Communist forest service. In the 1990s, RNP managers, local rangers, or familial relatives or close friends of forestry officials frequently owned private forestry companies supplied with wood from RNP-managed areas—a conflict of interest under Romanian forestry law (Savaliuc, 2001b).

Many other transgressions were violations of rules governing auctions. On more than one occasion, RNP officials failed to publicize upcoming auctions; instead, prospective bidders were invited to bid on a secret basis. At other times, certain stands of timber were sold to preferred companies outside of the mandated auctioning system. In yet other instances, RNP officials falsified official auctioning documents by deliberately undervaluing a timber stand to be auctioned. In the latter cases, both the opening and closing bids would tend to be artificially low (Savaliuc, 2001a; 2001b). Charges of favoritism and/or irregular auctioning were leveled against RNP offices in the counties of Harghita (Savaliuc, 2001b), Bucharest/Snagov (Savaliuc, 1998a; 1998b), Sibiu, Oradea, Neamt (Stanciu and Moroianu, 1998), Hunedoara (Stînan and Hoandră, 1998a), and Maramures (Chima and Vidican, 1999). Moreover, several of RNP's general directors have allegedly committed offenses during their time in public office, including alleged authorization of illegal fellings and kickbacks from private wood processing businesses (Szábo, 1998; Moroianu, 2000; 1998; Savaliuc, 2001b).

Corruption in forest management institutions in Romania was not confined to timber auctioning and illegal harvests. RNP also abused its responsibilities governing the transfer and exchange of forestlands. These functions were intended to allow forestry authorities to purchase or exchange land parcels on the borders of state forests so as to decrease fragmentation of forested areas. The system also provided RNP officials with additional opportunities to grant favors to family-owned and friend-owned businesses and to political elites. Under the pretense of transferring land to correct forest area perimeters, many transactions involved the exchange of land of lesser value for state-owned land located in or near prized resort areas. Recipients of the high quality land proceeded to clear-cut the plots, transforming them into built areas for tourism.

According to the report of the inquiry commission, RNP staff in more than two dozen RNP offices authorized over 1,500 illegal land transfers involving around 1,000 hectares of forest (Savaliuc, 2001a). One of the more infamous cases involved clear-cutting of old growth forest in the buffer zone of the nature reserve of the Bucegi Mountains (Ionică, 1998).

To deceive law enforcement, these unlawful transactions were accompanied by false records and reports (Savaliuc, 2001b; Hoandră, 1998b; Poenaru, 2000); the bribing of low-ranked RNP employees whose cooperation was needed

(Ionică, 1998); the illegal marking of trees for felling (Savaliuc, 2001b); and other deviant acts. Meanwhile, several managers involved directly in sweetheart land deals and/or illegal harvests allegedly embezzled proceeds from these transactions (Savaliuc, 2001a; Neamu, 1999; Moroianu, 2001a).

Regulations enacted after 2000 may ultimately prevent the kinds of abuses that occurred earlier in the decade when RNP was both chief manager of the forest and chief auditor of forest management policies (Government of Romania, 2000a; 2000b; 2000e; Romanian Ministry of Water Resources, Forest Resources, and Environmental Protection, 1999d). The Ministry of Agriculture, Food and Forests has assumed some auditing functions and more recently stepped up its own enforcement of rules governing forest cutting and other forestry policies. Also, in 1998, RNP was restructured such that some local RNP offices were closed (Government of Romania, 1998a). A year later, municipalities were authorized to establish their own forest management units, thereby diluting RNP's powers at the local level (Government of Romania, 1999). Also, a permanent national commission was created to monitor harvesting activities. However, even with these reforms, RNP remained the principal authority overseeing several forest management functions, including organizing timber auctions and wood sales in state-owned forests; marking trees to be harvested on both public and private lands; and, in conjunction with local law enforcement authorities, issuing and verifying documents of origin for wood felled on both public and private lands and inspecting wood cargo. All of these functions are susceptible to rent-seeking abuses; preventing corruption will depend on the effectiveness—and no less important—the integrity of the overseeing ministry and local authorities.

New incentives that make jobs in the forestry sector more attractive may stem corruption in the future (Government of Romania, 2000d). Benefits for state forest workers that were adopted by lawmakers in 2000 include: access to 1.25 acres of productive agricultural land or a quantity of firewood or construction wood equal in value to the harvest potential of said land; free firewood or construction wood for longtime workers or retirees of RNP; and guaranteed reinstatement of workers at RNP who complete advanced course work in forestry. These provisions resemble those recommended by institutional economists like Robert Klitgaard (1991: 115-138) who prescribe a variety of practical, positive incentives to discourage corruption in the public sector workplace.

Klitgaard also recommends strategic use of negative incentives, and Romanian legislators have followed that tack, as well. To illustrate, if a state forestry employee is fired for work-related offenses, he or she is barred from reemployment by a forest management agency. If recent history is a guide to the future, this particular punishment will be rarely applied. In the 1990s, RNP was authorized to discipline lawbreakers within the agency. Very few were fired; most received mild punishments. The threat of dismissal and expulsion from RNP will prove an effective deterrent against corruption only if an agency other than RNP performs this disciplinary function. Moreover, that agency itself must be clean and worthy of public trust.

On a positive note, there are some provisional indications that corrupt forestry practices are subsiding in Romania. In 2003, the U.S. Department of Agriculture reported that illegal timber removal had declined some 30 percent in 2002 compared to 2001 (from 139,733 cubic meters to 98,000 cubic meters) (USDA, 2003: 3).

The World Bank provided a similar assessment in late 2002. Among other indicators of diminishing forestry-related deviance, the Bank contended that forestry crimes perpetrated by RNP, or occurring with the knowledge of RNP, had dropped off steeply since the late 1990s (meeting with Peter Dewees, World Bank, 17 December 2002). The Bank's comments came amidst the final preparations of a US$25 million World Bank loan to "maintain and improve environmentally sustainable management of state and private forests" in Romania (World Bank, 2002: 2). Among other objectives, the loan aimed to improve RNP's ability to participate in the restitution of more than one-third of Romania's forestlands to pre-1948 owners.

Despite the Bank's assurances that corruption in the Romanian forestry administration was a thing of the past, five U.S. government agencies complained to a top U.S. official at the World Bank that, among other problems, the proposed loan lacked a serious anticorruption component, such as training for forestry inspectors in their auditing functions vis-à-vis RNP (private communication, Gwyn Koepke, U.S. Department of Treasury, 18 December 2002). When the proposed loan came before a quorum of World Bank executive directors (politically appointed executives from member states) for a procedural vote, the United States representative abstained, but all other participants voted in the affirmative, assuring an expedited approval process for the loan.

Conclusion

In many if not most CEE countries, after the collapse of Communism, institutions of totalitarian control over the economy and society were swept away and replaced by more open and pluralistic forms of government and governance. Nevertheless, we found a prominent example of an old, authoritarian form of policy making and administration in Romania that endured even into the twenty-first century, and with negative consequences for the environment and for public well-being.

In the case of Romania's principal state forestry agency, personalistic networks of exchange and reciprocity—remnants of Communist-era systems used alternatively for survival and for personal enrichment—provided the institutional rules for individuals to exchange valuable natural and capital assets. A high level of direct, official participation in illegal transactions were assured by the preservation of the forest service's formal monopoly powers, including unrestricted authority over auctioning, harvesting, and auditing functions.

It would be rushing to judgment to claim that post-Communist Romanian politicians intentionally perpetuated institutional structures of vice and corruption in the Romanian forestry sector. Lawmakers were convinced that maintaining old institutional arrangements was sensible, since state foresters as well as environmentalists warned that decentralizing forestry authorities and privatization of state forests would accelerate deforestation pressures. In some CEE countries, overharvesting following restitution of forests to private owners had already become apparent by the early 1990s. Romania's new leaders, perhaps naively, preserved monopolistic forms of state authority and central planning over forests, trusting these arrangements to be more environmentally sustainable than the alternatives adopted in neighboring states.

After repeated scandals and swelling public anger, lawmakers and ministerial officials were all but forced to reinvent the way Romania manages its forests and audits its forest managers. Many of the most significant changes, including the shifting of auditing and some enforcement functions away from RNP, were instituted in the late 1990s and the relative effectiveness of these new institutions remains to be seen. For many Romanians, more effective forest management will be evidenced by more transparency in forest policy making and policy execution. Meanwhile, the rehabilitation of state foresters' reputations will require the state to exhibit greater trust in the stewardship capabilities of nonstate forest actors, including both pro-development and conservation interests.

Notes

1. Tisa is the Romanian spelling; the Hungarian spelling (as used in chapter 4) is Tisza.

2. This is not to suggest that police and other law enforcers formally condoned corrupt acts. Occasionally, major corruption scandals would come to light, with the arrest and trial of prominent individuals, including high government officials. Those convicted were imprisoned or their private assets were seized. These enforcement actions served to remind the public that the state was vigilant and would deal swift punishments. Occasional bursts of anticorruption enforcement activity may have inspired some to reevaluate their desire to participate in networks of corrupt exchange and reciprocity.

3. The corporation, originally named ROMSILVA, changed to Regia National a Padurilor in 1996.

4. Since the collapse of Communism, forestry-related authorities in Romania have shifted between environmental and agricultural ministries, reflecting tension in forests' status as protected resources and as harvestable commodities. Since 2000, forest conservation and management are the responsibilities of the Ministry of Agriculture, Food and Forests. As in the United States and some European nations, a quasi-autonomous forest service operates under a larger department or ministry of agriculture. Early in the 1990s in Romania, forest policy was part of the Ministry of Environment's portfolio. A few years later, that ministry became the Ministry of Water Resources, Forest Resources and

Environmental Protection, and later still, the Ministry of Water Resources and Environmental Protection. The latter change affirmed the transfer of forestry authorities from the environmental ministry to the agricultural ministry.

5. While it is evident that annual revenue from forestry operations fell between 1990 and 1998, it is difficult to establish the precise decline in sales, based on official Romanian sources. Data on forest sector revenues for a particular year differ depending on which edition of official forest statistics one refers to. Moreover, year to year, it is unclear whether prices cited by the government are adjusted for inflation. Hence, caution should be exercised in interpreting the revenue trend described above.

6. By 1998, the number of county-level forest management offices had been consolidated to 25 from the original 41; 11 new offices were added in 2001. These fluctuations suggest a fairly high level of organizational indecision during the devolution process.

References

Bănăduc, Angela, Doru Bănăduc, Jozsef Feiler, Andrei Keleman, Ivona Malbasic, Radu Mititean, and Moisi Petruta. 2002. *Comments on the Romanian Forestry Development Program (Loan No. RO-P067367, World Bank)*. Prague: CEE Bankwatch Network.

Berend, Ivan T. 1996. *Central and Eastern Europe 1944-1993: Detour from the Periphery to the Periphery*. Cambridge: Cambridge University Press.

Carpathian Wildlife Foundation. 2002. *CLCP Project Description*. www.clcp.ro/proj/proj-desc.htm. Accessed 10 August 2002.

Chamber of Deputies/Parliament of Romania. 1998. "Decision #12 of 6 April 1998 Regarding the Appointment of an Inquiry Commission to Assess the State of Romanian Forestry Sector." *Monitorul Oficial* (Official Monitor) no. 144, 9 April.

———. 2000. "Decision #5 of 8 February 2000 Regarding the Report of the Inquiry Commission on the State of Romanian Forestry Sector." *Monitorul Oficial* (Official Monitor) no. 63, 14 February.

Chima, Florin, and Dorel Vidican. 1999. "Mafia lemnului înflorește cu acordul tacit al Poliției" (Wood Mafia Flourishes with the Tacit Support of the Police). *Ziua*, 15 November.

Food and Agriculture Organization. 1995. *FAO/Austria Seminar on the Economics and Management of Forest Operations for Countries in Transition to Market Economies*. Rome: FAO.

———. 1997. *Issues and Opportunities in the Evolution of Private Forestry and Forestry Extension in Several Countries with Economies in Transition in Central and Eastern Europe*. Rome: FAO.

Government of Romania. 1991a. "Decision #438 of 21 June 1991 Regarding Price Liberalization for Wood Stands." *Monitorul Oficial* (Official Monitor) no. 145, 12 July.

———. 1991b. "Decision #1364 of 29 December 1990 Regarding Prohibition of Exportation of Raw and Minimally Processed Wood." *Monitorul Oficial* (Official Monitor) no. 6, 14 January.

———. 1991c. "Decision #1335 of 21 December 1990 Regarding the Establishment of the National Forestry Corporation ROMASILVA." *Monitorul Oficial* (Official Monitor) no. 3, 10 January.

————. 1992a. "Ordinance #2 of 17 July 1992 on Rules for Determining the Value of Damages Caused to Forest Resources." *Monitorul Oficial* (Official Monitor) no. 185, 3 August (and subsequent modifications of the regulation to 2000).

————. 1992b. "Decision #784 of 8 December 1992 Regarding the Investment Project 'Increase of Re-use, Pretreatment, and Final Treatment of Wastewater at Sometra Company in Copşa Mică'." *Monitorul Oficial* (Official Monitor) no. 327, 18 December.

————. 1992c. "Decision #816 of 28 December 1992 Regarding Import Tax Exemption for Importation of Equipment Used in the Wood Processing Industry." *Monitorul Oficial* (Official Monitor) no. 8, 20 January.

————. 1994. "Decision #457 of 29 July 1994 Regarding the Organization and Operation of the Ministry for Water Resources, Forest Resources, and Environmental Protection." *Monitorul Oficial* (Official Monitor) no. 226, 19 August.

————. 1995a. "Decision #342 of 26 May 1995 Regarding the Organization of Auctions for the Sale of Wood to Business Agents." *Monitorul Oficial* (Official Monitor) no. 113, 5 June.

————. 1995b. "Decision #246 of 17 April 1995 Regarding Establishment of Wood Products Export Quotas and of Rules Regarding the Issuance of Export Permits for 1995." *Monitorul Oficial* (Official Monitor) no. 78, 28 April.

————. 1998a. "Decision #982 of 29 December 1998 Regarding the Restructuring of the National Forestry Corporation (RNP)." *Monitorul Oficial* (Official Monitor) no. 530, 31 December.

————. 1998b. "Ordinance #81 of 25 August 1998 Regarding Measures for Improving Eroded Areas through Afforestation." *Monitorul Oficial* (Official Monitor) no. 313, 27 August.

————. 1999. "Decision #997 of 2 December 1999 to Approve the Regulation for the Organization and Operation of Forestry Units for the Management of Forestland Administered/Owned by Local Government or Private Owners." *Monitorul Oficial* (Official Monitor) no. 597, 8 December.

————. 2000a. "Ordinance #226 of 24 November 2000 Regarding the Legal Transfer of Forested Areas." *Monitorul Oficial* (Official Monitor) no. 606, 25 November.

————. 2000b. "Regulation of 6 November 2000 Regarding the Organization of State Control on the Implementation of Forestry Regime Rules at National and Local Levels." *Monitorul Oficial* (Official Monitor) no. 604, 24 November.

————. 2000c. "Decision #1003 of 26 October 2000 Regarding the Maximum Allowable Quota of Wood to Be Harvested in Year 2001." *Monitorul Oficial* (Official Monitor) no. 540, 1 November.

————. 2000d. "Ordinance #59 of 26 May 2000 Regarding the Statute of Forestry Personnel." *Monitorul Oficial* (Official Monitor) no. 238, 30 May.

————. 2000e. "Decision #163 of 13 March 2000 to Approve Methodological Norms Regarding the Disbursement of Monies to Forest Owners in Support of Sustainable Forest Management Practices." *Monitorul Oficial* (Official Monitor) no. 128, 27 March.

————. 2000f. "Ordinance #96 of 27 August 1998—republished—Regarding the Regulation of the Forestry Regime and the Management of National Forestry Assets." *Monitorul Oficial* (Official Monitor) no. 23, 24 January.

————. 2001. "Decision #12 of 4 January 2001 Regarding the Organization and Operation of the Ministry of Agriculture, Food and Forest Resources." *Monitorul Oficial* (Official Monitor) no. 16, 10 January.

Hoandră, O. 1998a. "Directorul Romsilva Sibiu a fost eliberat din funcţie I" (Manager of Sibiu County Romsilva/RNP Office Was Dismissed I). *Ziua*, 9 August.
————. 1998b. "Directorul Romsilva Sibiu a fost eliberat din funcţie II" (Manager of Sibiu County Romsilva/RNP Office Was Dismissed II). *Ziua*, 10 August.
Institutul Naţional de Statistică. 2001. "Anuar. 2001: Agricultura; Silvicultura" (2001 Annual Data on Agriculture, Silviculture). www.insse.ro/. Accessed 16 July 2001.
Ionică, Eugen. 1998. "Barbarie in Rezervaţia Naţionala a Munţilor Bucegi" (Massacre in National Reserve of Bucegi Mountains). *Evenimentul Zilei*, 13 November.
Kaminski, Antoni. 1992. *An Institutional Theory of Communist Regimes*. San Francisco: ICS Press.
Klarer, Jürg, Patrick Francis, and Jim McNicholas. 1999. "Improving Environment and Economy—The Potential of Economic Incentives for Environmental Improvement and Sustainable Development in Countries with Economies in Transition." *Sofia Initiative on Economic Instruments*. Szentendre, Hungary: Regional Environmental Center.
Klitgaard, Robert. 1991. *Adjusting to Reality: Beyond "State Versus Market" in Economic Development*. San Francisco: International Center for Economic Growth.
Kornai, Janos. 1992. *The Socialist System: The Political Economy of Communism*. Princeton, NJ: Princeton University Press.
Leidig, Michael. 2002. "Wolf Boy Is Welcomed Home." *Sunday Telegraph*, 14 April: 26.
Los, Maria. 1990. *The Second Economy in Marxist States*. New York: St. Martin's Press.
Moroianu, Luminiţa. 1998. "PNTCD şi PD se războiesc pentru Romsilva" (PNTCD Party and PD Party Fight over Romsilva/RNP). *Ziua*, 3 August.
————. 2000. "Poveste cu defrişari şi trafic de influenta la Mediu" (Tale of Deforestation and Embezzlement at Ministry of Environment). *Ziua*, 16 August.
————. 2001a. "Fosta conducere a Romasilva a sărăcit regia" (Former Management Team of RNP Impoverished the Corporation). *Ziua*, 24 September.
————. 2001b. "Pădurea rentează oricum" (Forest Business Is Profitable No Matter What). *Ziua*, 22 September.
————. 2001c. "Romsilva a exportat de 14 milioane de dolari în 9 luni" (Romsilva/RNP's Exports over Nine Months Were Worth 14 Million USD). *Ziua*, 15 October.
Neamu, Daniel. 1999. "Din cauza defrişărilor masive, România riscă să devină o Sahară a Europei" (Due to Massive Deforestation, Romania Is at Risk of Becoming a European Desert). *Evenimentul Zilei*, 15 February.
Ognean T., and A. Vădineanu. 1992. "Quality of the Environment in Romania," in J. Alcamo (ed.), *Coping with Crisis in Eastern Europe's Environment*. London: Parthenon.
ÖKO Incorporated/Regional Environmental Center (REC). 2001. *Agriculture Water Management Policies in Bulgaria, Hungary, Romania, and Slovakia (Final Report)*. Regional Environment Center Working Papers. Budapest: Regional Environmental Center.
Organization for Economic Cooperation and Development. 1999. *Environment in the Transition to the Market Economy: Progress in Central and Eastern Europe and the Newly Independent States*. Paris: OECD.
Parliament of Romania. 1992. "Law #42 of 28 April 1992 Regarding the Maximum Allowable Quota of Wood to Be Harvested in Year 1992 and Measures for Protection of Forestry Assets." *Monitorul Oficial* (Official Monitor) no. 80, 30 April (and similar yearly regulations to 2000).

————. 1993. "Law #80 of 20 November 1993 on Determining Due Compensation for Damages Caused to Forest Resources." *Monitorul Oficial* (Official Monitor) no. 275, 29 November (and subsequent modifications of the law to 2000).

————. 1996. "Law #26 of 24 April 1996 'The Forestry Code.'" *Monitorul Oficial* (Official Monitor) no. 93, 8 May.

————. 1999a. "Law #107 of 16 June 1999 to Approve Government Ordinance #81/1998 Regarding Measures for Improving Eroded Areas through Afforestation." *Monitorul Oficial* (Official Monitor) no. 304, 29 June.

————. 1999b. Parliamentary Proceedings, Chamber of Deputies, 18 November 1999. www.cdep.ro/pls/steno/steno.home. Accessed 30 August 2002.

————. 1999c. Parliamentary Proceedings, Chamber of Deputies, 11 November 1999. www.cdep.ro/pls/steno/steno.home. Accessed 30 August 2002.

————. 1999d. Parliamentary Proceedings, Chamber of Deputies, 19 October 1999. www.cdep.ro/pls/steno/steno.home. Accessed 30 August 2002.

————. 1999e. Parliamentary Proceedings, Chamber of Deputies, 28 September 1999. www.cdep.ro/pls/steno/steno.home. Accessed 30 August 2002.

————. 1999f. Parliamentary Proceedings, Chamber of Deputies, 17 June 1999. www.cdep.ro/pls/steno/steno.home. Accessed 30 August 2002.

————. 2000a. "Law #31 of 3 April 2000 Regarding Estimation and Sanctioning of Forestry-Related Contraventions." *Monitorul Oficial* (Official Monitor) no. 144, 6 April.

————. 2000b. "Law #137 of 29 December 1995—republished—Regarding Environmental Protection." *Monitorul Oficial* (Official Monitor) no.70, 17 February.

Pavlínek, Petr, and John Pickles. 2000. *Environmental Transitions: Transformation and Ecological Defense in Central and Eastern Europe.* London: Routledge.

Poenaru, Călin. 2000. "Revoltă în Apuseni" (Unrest in Apuseni Mountains). *Ziua*, 21 September.

Romanian Ministry of Water Resources, Forest Resources, and Environmental Protection. 1995. "Order #171 of 11 April 1995 Regarding the Organization and Operation of State Control over the Management of Forest Resources, and Gaming and Fishing Resources." *Monitorul Oficial* (Official Monitor) no. 98, 28 May.

————. 1999a. "Order #264 of 26 March 1999 Approving Forestry Technical Norms Regarding Management of Woody Vegetation on Land Other Than National Forestland," *Monitorul Oficial* (Official Monitor) no. 233, 25 May.

————. 1999b. "Order #71 of 1 February 1 1999 Approving the Regulation for the Use of Wood Marking Devices." *Monitorul Oficial* (Official Monitor) no. 104, 11 March.

————. 1999c. "Order #70 of 1 February 1999 Approving the Regulation on the Organization and Operation of the National Committee for the Assessment of Forestry Operators." *Monitorul Oficial* (Official Monitor) no. 95, 5 March.

————. 1999d. "Order #109 of 10 February 1999 Regarding Privatization of Production Facilities for Subsidiary Activities of the National Forestry Corporation." *Monitorul Oficial* (Official Monitor) no. 80, 25 February.

Sampson, Steven L. 1984. *National Integration through Socialist Planning: An Anthropological Study of a Romanian New Town.* Boulder, Colo.: East European Monographs (distributed by Columbia University Press).

Savaliuc, Răzvan. 1998a. "Foştii directori ai Direcţiei silvice Bucureşti şi Ocolului Silvic Snagov sunt urmăriţi penal" (Former Managers of Forestry Offices Bucharest and Snagov under Penal Investigation). *Ziua*, 30 August.

————. 1998b. "Stejarii sunt tăiați și vânduți fraudulos de mafia lemnului" (Oak Trees Illegally Cut and Sold by Wood Mafia). *Ziua*, 17 July.

————. 2001a. "Mafia pădurilor I" (Forest Mafia I). *Ziua*, 5 January.

————. 2001b. "Mafia pădurilor II" (Forest Mafia II). *Ziua*, 6 January.

————. 2001c. "Mafia pădurilor III" (Forest Mafia III). *Ziua*, 8 January

Stanciu, Mirela, and L. Moroianu. 1998. "Romsilva e bună de restructurare de Sfânta Maria Mică" (Romsilva/RNP Ready to Be Restructured on September 8). *Ziua*, 27 August.

State Council of Romania. 1982. "Decree #320 of September 13, 1982 Regarding the Establishment and Operational Guidelines of the Ministry of Silviculture." *Buletinul Oficial* (Official Bulletin) no. 80, 14 September.

Stînan, Ofelia, and O. Hoandră. 1998. "'Aurul' e 'verde' doar pentru unii" ("Gold" Is "Green" Only for Some). *Ziua*, 28 October.

Szábo, Cristina. 1998. "Ministrul Romică Tomescu l-a destituit pe directorul Romsilva, Gheorghe Cahnița" (Minister Romică Tomescu Fires Romsilva Manager Gheorghe Cahnița). *Ziua*, 4 August.

Tomescu, Gabriel C. 1996. "Groundwater Resources and Pollution Effects in Romania," in E. A. McBean, J. Balek, and B. Clegg (eds.), *Remediation of Soil and Groundwater Opportunities in Eastern Europe*. Dordrecht, Netherlands: Kluwer Academic Publishers.

Turnock, David. 1996. "Romania," in Francis W. Carter and David Turnock (eds.), *Environmental Problems in Eastern Europe*. London: Routledge.

United Nations. 2001. *World Economic Situation and Prospects 2001*. New York: United Nations.

United Nations Economic Commission for Europe. 2001. *Trends in Europe and North America 2001: The Statistical Yearbook of the Economic Commission for Europe*. New York: UN.

UNECE/FAO. 1996a. *European Timber Trends and Prospects: Into the Twenty-First Century*. New York: UN.

————. 1996b. *UNECE/FAO Timber and Forest Discussion Paper ETTS V Working Paper Resources and Consumption of Forest Products in Countries in Transition, 1990-2020*. New York: UN.

————. 1997. *Forest and Forest Industries Country Fact Sheets, Geneva Timber and Forest Study Papers no.12*. New York: UN.

————. 2000. *Forest Resources of Europe, CIS, North America, Australia, Japan, and New Zealand, United Nations*. New York: UN.

USDA. 2003. *Romania Solid Wood Products Annual 2003*. Global Agriculture Information Network (GAIN) Report #RO3006. Washington, D.C.: UDSA.

Verdery, Katherine. 1983. *Transylvanian Villages: Three Centuries of Political, Economic and Ethnic Change*. Berkeley: University of California Press.

World Bank. 2002. *Project Appraisal Document on a Proposed Loan in the Amount of US$25.00 Million to Romania for a Forest Development Project*. Europe and Central Asia Region, ECSSD. Washington, D.C.: World Bank.

Chapter 5

Estonian Environmental Reforms: A Small Nation's Outsized Accomplishments

Matthew R. Auer

Environmental policy reforms have come further and faster in Estonia than virtually anywhere else in the former Soviet Union, including in the Baltic Republics to Estonia's south. This is a remarkable accomplishment considering that at the outset of the post-Communist transition period, Estonia's environmental problems seemed especially daunting, and by some measures, the cleanup challenge there was comparatively more formidable than in the other Baltic Republics of Latvia and Lithuania.

In 1991, when large delegations of Western environmental experts first visited Estonia, the broad contours of that country's environmental crisis were fairly well understood. In the first three decades after the Second World War, the Estonian economy was the envy of industrial planners in neighboring regions because of Estonia's valuable electricity export industry and its high level of energy self-reliance (around 85 percent) (US Bureau of the Census, 1992: 43). Estonia possessed a valuable natural resource that the other Baltic States lacked: oil shale. And Estonia's industrial northeast—a concentration of oil shale mining, processing, and ore conversion industries—has no equivalent in Latvia or Lithuania, measured by the value of the region's economic output or the size of its industrial footprint. Estonia also boasts some of the largest deposits of phosphorite ore in all of Europe. In the 1970s and 1980s, the latter was intensively mined as an ingredient for Soviet fertilizer, but at a grave environmental cost. A 1977 letter penned by a group of Estonian dissident naturalists spoke of the biological death of rivers in the mined "moonscape" of Estonia's northeast (Estonian Information Centre, 1977). Miners left pits of smoldering wastes at several sites; some of the waste contained natural radioactive compounds (Taagepera, 1989).

By the late 1980s, the environmental costs of being the Baltic States' richest repository of nonrenewable resources were obvious even to Moscow's hand-picked leaders in Tallinn and the all-Union industries that relied on these resources. Coupled with the toxic messes left by Russian army and air force units—security forces whose sprawling airfields, naval stations, and command and control centers occupied more than 2 percent of Estonian territory—Estonia confronted the most expensive environmental cleanup task of the newly independent Baltic Republics.

How Estonia overcame these man-made disadvantages is the primary concern of this chapter. Environmental institution-building in Estonia recorded a rate of success in the 1990s that impressed clipboard toting auditors from the European Union. This chapter examines the specific political and cultural determinants of this seemingly untroubled institution-building process.

On a day-to-day basis, Estonia's greatest environmental insults are generated by the oil shale industry. The economic geography of Estonian oil shale and the negative environmental impacts caused by its development and consumption are the subjects of the next section.

Latvia and Lithuania can also brag about the accomplishments of their respective environmental reforms. And yet, Estonian reforms outpaced those of its Baltic neighbors during the 1990s. Section three considers whether Estonia's triumphs in such contests as the race to transpose EU environmental laws into domestic legislation were preordained by Estonia's "head start" over its neighbors.

Language and culture as institutional dimensions of environmental protection are the subjects of section four. Estonia's environmental achievements can be traced, in part, to institutional connections forged by shared language and cultural ties to nearby Finland. Incentives created by EU membership are dealt with in section five and the key roles played by foreign aid and investment are considered in section six.

Not all policy reforms performed well during and after the transition period. Shortcomings in the pollution control and natural resource management arenas are the foci of sections seven and eight.

Work that lies ahead for Estonia's decision-making elites, its civic associations, and its citizens at large is addressed in the last section.

Background

Though Estonia was an independent nation in the period between the two world wars, planning ministers in Moscow spoke of a not-so-distant future when Estonia, by virtue of its hydrocarbon wealth, would be tethered to the energy-hungry industrial centers in Russia's northwest, and in particular, St. Petersburg. Estonia's oil shale presented a least-cost alternative to more distant fossil fuels in Russia's south. The plan called for ramping up mining in Estonia and building power stations there to be connected to the Russian power grid. The Second World War interrupted these designs but they were revived in 1945.

Before the end of the 1950s, oil shale energy and allied products became Estonia's dominant economic sectors—a radical transformation of what had been a primarily agrarian economy before the war. The heavy industrialization of Estonia in the 1950s and 1960s occurred in tandem with the equally rapid reshaping of the country's demographic map. Hundreds of thousands of ethnic Russians immigrated to Estonia during the postwar years to work in Estonia's oil shale mines, power plants, and derivative chemical industries. Meanwhile, during the 1940s, more than 250,000 ethnic Estonians were deported, emigrated, or perished because of political repression (Sakkeus, 1993: 7; Kahk, 1991: 42-43).

During those same years, Estonia's oil shale industry became the energy juggernaut of the northwest Soviet corridor, providing electricity from two huge power stations near the border town of Narva. The giant boilers and soaring smokestacks, visible from miles away, generated electricity for St. Petersburg, nearby Russian towns, and in later years, Estonia and parts of Latvia.

As suggested above, the demographic influx of Russian speakers and the intensive development of the oil shale industry were closely connected trends: in 1945, the USSR Defense Committee called for a westward migration of workers to Estonia "to restore and develop" the oil shale industry in the Estonian SSR and Leningrad region and to supply gas to Leningrad (Kahk, 1991: 42). It has been argued that importation of Russian workers was necessary since many Estonians "refused to participate" in the republic's industrial transformation (Pullat et al., 1985: 49-51). If that is the case, then many Estonians ended up working in the oil shale sector against their will (Auer, 1996: 370).

After operating for more than forty years, the oil shale-fired power plants left indelible marks not only on Estonia's environment but that of countries downwind of the Narva energy complex. By the end of the Soviet era, Estonia's power plants ranked among the top ten largest stationary source emitters of sulfur dioxide, nitrogen oxide, and dust in all of continental Europe (Auer, 1992: 379; Estonian Ministry of the Environment, 1992: 26). Coupled with phosphate ore mining to the west of Narva, oil shale extraction scarred many stretches of Estonian countryside and runoff from mines spoiled hundreds of kilometers of rivers, and thousands of acres of bogs, mires, and lakes.

Among the main beneficiaries of oil shale-fired electricity were Soviet army and air force detachments in Estonia. The military needed energy to power hundreds of generators at command and control centers, listening posts, military airstrips, and at a giant Soviet naval training center which housed a mock-up of a nuclear submarine, equipped with an atomic-powered engine. The military left their own expensive and dangerous environmental mess in Estonia, the full extent of which remained a mystery until Soviet forces retreated in 1994—a full three years after Estonia's independence. Groundwater in and near ex-military bases, some adjacent to major population centers, were either threatened or were already contaminated by a variety of toxic chemicals, including kerosene and rocket propellants. In the early 1990s, the Estonian government estimated cleanup costs at abandoned military sites at approximately US$4 billion (Estonian Ministry of Environment, 1999: 118).

These and other environmental problems confronted a resource-poor, thinly staffed Ministry of Environment and local authorities with little or no experience in environmental management. Yet by 2000, Estonians could point not only to measurable improvements in environmental conditions, but could directly sense these improvements. Inhabitants of the gritty industrial towns of Kunda and Kohtla-Järve breathed easier because the air was cleaner. The smelly, murky waters of Soviet-era Tallinn harbor were comparatively odorless and transparent by the mid-1990s. At century's end, officials in the old university town of Tartu drew property lines on what had been an abandoned, polluted military base; townspeople contemplated building summer homes and making other uses for the site.

Certainly, the deep economic recession of the early 1990s and the many pollution-intensive primary industries that succumbed during this period explain much of Estonia's environmental rebound. For example, oil shale consumption in Estonia fell by nearly 50 percent between 1990 and 1998 (Estonian Ministry of Environment, 2001: 24). Russian and other former Soviet markets for Estonian energy, minerals, and low value heavy industrial goods collapsed after Estonia's independence and producers found no replacement markets in the West.

But Estonia's economy largely recovered in the 1990s, even without a rebound in the heavy industry sector which had dominated the economy during the Soviet era. New environmental problems emerged in the wake of this economic revival, including, for example, the growing dilemma of urban air pollution from automobiles and a spike in illegal logging. But some very serious environmental problems were largely conquered, and these successes cannot be understood as a by-product of the decline of dirty industry, alone. The most important and consequential examples of policy-driven environmental reform in Estonia included: vigorous cleanup of ex-military sites, which began early in the decade; the overhauling of Tallinn's obsolete sewerage system; and investments in pollution abatement in primary industries that survived the recession.

Based on these and other accomplishments, Estonia's environmental restoration constitutes a genuine institutional success story. But some of the key institutions that helped restore the environment did not originate with Western-style reforms in the 1990s. The seeds of Estonia's environmental recovery were sown decades before Estonia's restored independence in 1991.

Estonia's Head Start?

In June of 2001, authorities in Tallinn received anxiously awaited news from Brussels, and that news was good: Estonia's environmental law chapter had been provisionally closed—part of the lengthy process of transposing the EU's legislation into Estonia's own. At that point, Hungary and the Czech Republic were the only other CEE accession countries to have successfully incorporated EU environmental directives into national legislation (European Report, 2001). The process lagged behind in Latvia and Lithuania, though Latvia had received otherwise positive reviews from external experts on the quality of its environment and its efforts to promote sustainable development (Hill, 2002). In Lithuania, the obsolete Ignalina nuclear power station posed an obstacle to that nation's early entry to the EU. Lithuania had earlier promised to shut down one of the power plant's two reactors, but the EU called for the complete closure of the facility before 2010 (*City Paper,* 2002b).[1]

The early provisional closure of Estonia's environmental chapter reinforced its front-runner status among the Baltic States for EU membership, consistent with the pace it set in 1998. That year, it was invited by Brussels to commence formal ministerial-level negotiations on accession. Latvia's and Lithuania's invitations to negotiate arrived later, as did the bids to other "second tier" candidates for accession, namely Bulgaria, Malta, Romania, and Slovakia (Vilpišauskas and Steponavičiene, 2000: 57).

Other indicators showed Estonia leading its Baltic peers in the late 1990s, measured by such trends as the rate of annual economic growth; national exports of goods and services as a percentage of gross domestic product; net foreign direct investment flows as a percentage of GDP; per capita electricity consumption; per capita ownership of cars; and per capita ownership of computers (UNDP, 2001: 56; 61; 70; Hughes and Lovei, 1999: 8; 49; 51; World Bank, 2001: 306-307). By the end of the 1990s, and compared to the other Baltic Republics, Estonia boasted the highest human development index—a statistical measure of human well-being that combines data on purchasing power parity adjusted per capita GDP; life expectancy at birth; adult literacy rates; and combined primary, secondary, and tertiary school enrollment (UNDP, 2001: 141). Its per capita income, alone, exceeded that of Latvia's by more than 33 percent.

What explains Estonia's rapid economic transformation, the relatively swift overhaul of its environmental legal institutions, and its winning ways with the European Union? Data in the previous paragraph show Estonia outpacing other Baltic Republics at the end of the 1990s. But was Estonia destined to lead the Baltic pack from the first days of post-Soviet independence?

Comparing basic indicators of economic and social well-being, it cannot be said that Estonia enjoyed a significant head start over its Baltic neighbors at the beginning of the transition period. Income per capita, price inflation, life expectancy, and other economic and social indicators suggest relative parity between

TABLE 5.1
Socioeconomic Indicators for the Baltic States, circa 1992

Country	Per Capita Gross Domestic Product, 1992 (purchasing power parity-adjusted, US $)[*]	Average Annual Rate of Inflation, 1992 (%)[†]	Life Expec-tancy at Birth, 1992 (years)[†]	Infant Mortality Rate, 1992 (per 1,000 live births)[††]	Adult Liter-acy Rate, 1992 (%)[†]
Estonia	6,326	1,009	69.3	13	99.0
Latvia	6,891	1,032	69.1	17	99.0
Lithuania	5,025	1,194	70.4	16	98.4

Sources: [*]World Resources Institute, 1996: 166; [†]United Nations Development Programme, 1995: 155-156; 197; [††]World Bank, 1994: 214-215.

the Baltic States in the early 1990s (table 5.1). But the divergence between Estonia's performance and that of its neighbors began shortly thereafter.

All three Baltic Republics embraced market reforms and redirected their trade toward EU countries and away from Russia during the early 1990s. But Estonia built trade ties with Europe more quickly and in more sectors. In the late 1990s, commerce with the EU constituted a larger percentage of Estonia's total trade than did trade with the EU for either Latvia or Lithuania (Vilpišauskas and Steponavičiene, 2000: 72). Moreover, the Latvian and Lithuanian economies were relatively less economically integrated with the Nordic economies. By 1997, some 47 percent of Estonian exports to Europe were destined for Finland and Sweden. Less than 19 percent of Latvian and 8 percent of Lithuanian exports bound for Europe flowed to these Nordic countries (UN, 1999: 317; 561; 580; Statistikaamet, 2002). Several Estonian companies, particularly financial institutions, merged or were purchased by larger, Nordic companies during the 1990s (Huang, 2000). These business relationships allowed Estonia to achieve one of the highest levels of foreign direct investment per capita in all of Central and Eastern Europe (Behr, 2002b: 6; Ilves, 1997) as well as one of the highest rates of per capita GDP growth in CEE during the late 1990s (World Bank, 1998: 190-191; World Bank, 2002: 232-233).

In 1998, before a public forum in Tallinn, Estonia's Foreign Minister described Estonia's Nordic-focused trade orientation not simply as an economic survival strategy, but as a way to distinguish it from the other Baltic Republics generally.

> To be frank, my goal as foreign minister was to separate Estonia from being a Baltic state . . . I don't think Estonia is a Baltic state . . . I've seen Estonia suffer through the years because of misguided policies in other Baltic countries.

My line has been all along, and remains to this day, that Estonia pursued its reforms, and if they were not pursued elsewhere, why should Estonia suffer as a result? . . . When it comes to economics and how integrated Estonia is with the Finnish and Swedish economies, it shows this country is much more like a post-Communist Nordic country. Its behavioral patterns, the way people act, the way the economy has gone, it's strictly Nordic. Lithuania is a completely different place. (Ilves quoted in *City Paper*, 1998)

Ilves's Nordic-centric conception of Estonia was deemed arrogant by Latvians and Lithuanians. After being rebuked by Estonia's prime minister, Ilves modified his views, observing, "Relations with Latvia and Lithuania, thanks to their proximity and common interests in many spheres, are actually much closer and deeper than with most other nations" (Gunter, 2001: 4).

Nevertheless, the foreign minister's comments merely articulated for an international audience what many ordinary Estonians have long held true: Estonia *is* different from its Baltic neighbors and the differences are not just a matter of economics. Estonia, and the institutions that make Estonia's economy relatively more vibrant than that of Latvia and Lithuania; its relatively early invitation to join the EU; the early provisional closure of its environmental chapter in the accession process; its citizens high level of computer literacy; its high per capita mobile phone use—all point to cultural and linguistic factors that Ilves invoked in answering his own rhetorical question: "Why should Finland be more of a Scandinavian country than Estonia? We're all the same Finno-Ugric sort of swamp people" (*City Paper*, 1998).

By "swamp people" the minister was referring to the Finnish and Estonian words for swamp (suo and soo, respectively). "Finland" in Finnish is "Suomi," or literally, swampy land. More importantly, Ilves alluded to Estonia's cultural and linguistic affiliations with its neighbor to the north. The inference is that Finnish-Estonian social and cultural connections partly explain Estonia's affinity for—and ability to replicate—Finland's export-oriented economic policies, outward-looking political orientation, and even its high cell phone usage. As argued in the next section, Estonia's cultural and language ties to Finland also elucidate the process of environmental institution-building in Estonia.

Culture, Language, and Environmental Institution-Building

In the 1980s, well before the collapse of the Soviet Union, Finnish environmental authorities occasionally met their Estonian Soviet Socialist Republic counterparts in Tallinn or in Helsinki, ostensibly for the purpose of building environmental management skills among the Estonians, but more broadly, as a means to strengthen ties between like-minded professionals in the two regions (interview, Kristiina Isokallio, Finnish Ministry of Foreign Affairs, 9 June 2000; *The Economist*, 1989: 49). These contacts were not just early forms of environmental cooperation. They paved the way for Finnish foreign aid and investment in post-Soviet Estonia. By early 1991, Finland knew the priority environmental concerns of their Estonian counterparts and already had conducted studies of Estonian-borne environmental hazards affecting Finland (including, for example, acid rain caused by Estonia's oil shale-fired power stations) (Finnish Ministry of Foreign Affairs, 1991). But concern about pollution imported from Estonia was not the only factor motivating Finnish-Estonian environmental détente. Finns were reaching out to their cultural and linguistic cousins across the gulf, and Estonians were reciprocating.

"Institutions," Douglass North writes (1990: 3), "are the humanly devised constraints that shape human interactions." Defined this way, mutually recognized words and symbols are the building blocks of institutions, especially when the speaker and the listener are engaged in some collective endeavor. As per North's key notion of institutions as "constraints" on human interaction, persons engaged in verbal interaction deliberately constrain the world of possible meanings that their speech can take. If Person A wants Person B to do something, Person A will use particular words in particular ways, hoping to provoke the desired response from Person B. Of course, Person A's objective is greatly facilitated when both Person A and Person B speak the same or similar languages. The efforts of Estonians and Finns to manage regional environmental problems, and in particular, to stem transboundary hazards from Estonia were enabled by language ties; this advantage was comparatively lacking between other pairings of CEE and Western European states.

Estonian and Finnish are two languages of the Finno-Ugric family of languages. Basic vocabulary in Finnish and Estonian is similar, including for example numbers, generic names of family members, verbs for common activities, and many adjectives. There *are* differences in grammar and syntax between standard Finnish and standard Estonian (Keerdoja, 1966). Moreover, spoken Estonian tends to be less easily comprehended by Finns than is spoken Finnish by Estonians. Many Estonian words are shortened versions of Finnish words. For example, whole syllables of Finnish nouns are missing in their Estonian equivalent. So much of the original is lost that Finns have relatively more difficulty grasping spoken Estonian. In contrast, to the Estonian ear, the longer Finnish words resemble familiar parts of speech in Estonian folklore or in certain Estonian dialects and are relatively easily understood (Holman, 1995). Despite these differences, patient Estonian and Finnish speakers are capable of understanding one another even when they speak their respective languages.

The advantages of shared language in promoting cooperation should not be underestimated. An Estonian who has never heard a word of Finnish or English (an exceptional individual indeed in contemporary Estonia) would have considerably more ease communicating with a Finnish speaker than with an English speaker. Hence, in the 1990s, Finnish advisers who trained Estonians to operate modern, fee-based wastewater treatment and water delivery services spoke Finnish with their Estonian trainees. Moreover, in Tallinn, where the first international loan was authorized to rehabilitate a Soviet-era sewerage system, Finns helped Estonian counterparts negotiate the loan with London-based creditors. The languages used in training sessions were Finnish and/or broken Finnish and Estonian. In contrast, in other CEE countries and in Russia, English was the principal language of communication between Western aid donors and CEE and Russian aid recipients, and for some recipients, it was their third language.

One important caveat to the institution-building functions of language ties between Estonians and Finns is that similarities between the two languages are not uniform across the two countries. Northern, coastal Estonian dialects and southwestern Finnish dialects bear the strongest similarities, a legacy of the many waves of ancient migrations of Estonians from northern Estonia to southern Finland, as well as regular contacts between Estonian and Finnish traders and fishermen along the Gulf of Finland (Holman, 1995). However, Estonian dialects in southeast Estonia are significantly different phonologically, grammatically, and syntactically from the standard Finnish spoken in Helsinki, not to mention from the Finnish dialects spoken north and east of Helsinki.

Differences in regional dialects have ramifications for the uniformity of environmental reforms and the pace of economic development in Estonia, to the extent that language ties between Finns and Estonians abet collective action between the two peoples. Versus Estonians in the south, northern Estonians tend to benefit relatively more greatly from institutional contacts with Finns. Indeed, there are indications of growing gaps in the standard of living of northern versus southern Estonians, and the vicissitudes of cultural and language ties to Finns play a role in these disparities. This problem and other obstacles to sustainable development in Estonia are considered in a later section.

The Disciplining Effect of EU Accession Rules

Estonia and Finland share another distinction—both are relative newcomers to the most important regional intergovernmental organization in Europe. Finland was among the last nations to join the EU in the 1990s. Before its accession in 1995, Brussels demanded that Finland rein in its domestic agricultural subsidies—provisions that riled Finnish farmers and made for lengthy negotiations between Helsinki and the European Commission (Agri Service International Newsletter, 1995; *The Economist*, 1993). But Finland's preparations for EU membership were painstaking primarily in one sector. The challenge is much greater for former Eastern bloc nations like Estonia, beginning with the epic task of transposing all EU legislation into national laws and regulations. Through 2003, Estonia was well along with this task, including in the area of environmental legal reforms.

The transposition of EU environmental legislation began early in post-Soviet Estonia. The government created a special unit of environmental legal experts in the Estonian Ministry of Environment whose main duty was the transposition task. All in all, the provisional closure of Estonia's environmental chapter required the adapting of preexisting domestic rules as well as the drafting of new regulations to conform to EU standards in areas as diverse as biodiversity protection, hazardous waste management, nuclear safety, wetlands protection, regulation of biotechnologies, and automobile emissions testing.

It could be argued that Estonia's rapid transformation of its environmental laws was motivated by its single-minded zeal for EU membership. From this perspective, transposition was a means to an end, though the end was EU membership rather than an effort to enhance and secure public and environmental wellbeing.

At best, this interpretation oversimplifies Estonians' attitudes toward EU membership and misconstrues Estonia's impetuses for protecting the environment. First, it suggests that all Estonians were keen on EU membership, which was not the case. While support for EU accession was nearly universal among major political parties in Estonia, public attitudes were more mixed. In the early years of the twenty-first century, popular support for accession barely exceeded one-third of Estonians (Auvinen, 2001). Polls conducted by the European Commission in 2001 indicated that, versus the citizens of other EU accession countries, Estonians were the most skeptical about EU membership. Only 33 percent of Estonians polled by the EU's own polling organization said that EU membership was a "good thing" and less than 40 percent said they would vote yes in a referendum on membership (European Commission, 2001: 5-6).

Pro-EU Estonian politicians knew well the public's ambivalence toward Brussels. Rather than cajole EU skeptics, Estonia's leaders quietly promoted the purported advantages of EU membership that were espoused by EU optimists in other European countries, including, for example, citizens' freedom to live and work anywhere in the EU; the portability of social security rights within the EU; businesses' unfettered access to the EU internal market; and other social and economic advantages (Auvinen, 2001).

But the very fact that Estonians were divided on the merits of EU membership suggested that Estonia's self-confidence was growing—a sentiment comparatively lacking among its Eastern European neighbors. Among Latvians and Lithuanians, for example, EU membership was more strongly embraced by ordinary citizens (EC, 2001: 5-6). The more southerly Baltic Republics regarded EU membership as economic and political succor. Membership promised security and stability that could not be achieved by going it alone. The attitude of ordinary Estonians, in contrast, more nearly resembled that of Danes in the early 1990s or of the Irish in the late 1990s—decidedly noncommittal about the advantages of EU passports and the common currency. A sizable portion of the population was willing to contemplate political life untethered to Brussels.

The contention that Estonia's rapid transposition of EU directives was merely a means toward an EU membership end also underestimates the strong desire among Estonian lawmakers and civic groups to promote meaningful domestic environmental reforms. In some cases, advocates sought to preserve Estonian environmental norms that, from the Estonian perspective, were superior to the EU's.

While it is true that Estonia's aspirations for EU membership expedited the transposition of European laws, the myriad EU directives covered most of the disparate problem areas that Estonia needed to tackle—and intended to address—in any case. The EU's environmental legal agenda did not interfere with an Estonia-led environmental lawmaking process as it did help guide that process.

In 1997, Estonia adopted its first National Environmental Strategy which, according to the United Nations, conformed with a key 1995 EU paper detailing a policy framework for accession to the EU, and moreover, incorporated the recommendations made by the United Nations in its first environmental performance review of Estonia in 1995 (UNECE, 2001: 11). Through its national environmental fund and other centrally allocated funds, the Ministry of Environment spent several hundred million dollars to advance ten policy goals identified in the three-year strategy, including promoting environmental awareness; improving air quality; installing clean technologies in industries; groundwater protection; maintenance of landscapes and biodiversity; and other priorities (UNECE, 2001: 11).

EU environmental directives amounted to more than just a checklist that Estonians referred to in the rush for EU membership. The task of transposing EU environmental laws simplified another, almost equally grand task, namely, reconciling Estonia's desire to remediate many large and varied environmental problems with the reality of the country's human and financial resource constraints. Accession requirements forced Estonian politicians and administrators to focus on core sets of environmental problems; set up legal and administrative structures to address these core problems; and set targets and timetables for satisfactory environmental improvements. Hence, the directives offered a distinct advantage to Estonian environmental authorities: they bounded a monumental policy-making task, creating "humanly devised constraints" for policy reform. And critically important for Estonia: the EU's main priorities for environmental protection (as prescribed in the EU directives and in consultations between the European Commission and Estonian leaders) were consistent with many areas deemed priorities by the Estonian government, and in particular, improvement and extension of sewerage services, energy efficiency, clean industrial production, and habitat protection (UNECE, 2001; Estonian Ministry of Environment, 1997).

Though EU environmental directives offered organizational and substantive guidance for strengthening formal environmental institutions in Estonia, European rules were not adopted without debate nor were all directives automatically assumed to be superior to rules, conventions, and procedures already in place in Estonia.

In some areas of environmental protection, Estonia strenuously argued that its extant legal and policy institutions were best suited to the Estonian environmental context and that the EU's were less appropriate or even irrelevant. To illustrate, the EU's main directive on species protection creates strict prohibitions on hunting of large animals such as wolves, elk, lynx, and black bears (European Council, 1992). However, in Estonia, these species are relatively abundant despite having been hunted for hundreds of years; moreover, Estonian farmers and ranchers insist that their numbers must be controlled. In 2001, the EU agreed to allow hunting of certain large game animals in Estonia. Estonian environmental authorities convinced EU counterparts that the nation's Nature Preservation Act—a statute developed even before the Soviet Union's all-Union act of the same title—had protected generations of large breeding populations of black bears, wolves, and other predators—and indeed, that Estonia's rules for conserving large game animals should be studied in countries where these species are relatively scarce, namely, in most of Western Europe.

The transposition of EU laws in Estonia, then, was not a one-way street with Estonian environmental authorities passively copying the norms and conventions of the club they hoped to join. Certain time-tested, well-functioning domestic institutions were preserved in the transposition process. That the EU granted Estonia a partial waiver to the European prohibition on hunting large game evidences the EU's own adroitness as institution-builders. As Ostrom asserts (1999: 49), flexibility in institutional arrangements allows institutions to cope with unique conditions and to prosper. Rather than asserting a one-size-fits-all formula for prospective members, in the Estonian case, the EU demonstrated a well-reasoned pliancy without affecting the legitimacy nor weakening the authority of EU laws and regulations.[2]

Foreign Aid, Foreign Investment, and Estonian Environmental Institutions

No less important than EU norms in guiding Estonia's environmental restoration were EU grants and technical assistance. Indeed, without help from its European neighbors and various international financial institutions, many of Estonia's most impressive environmental accomplishments in the 1990s would not have been realized.

Five countries in CEE (Poland, the Czech Republic, Russia, Hungary, and Romania) received 45 percent of foreign government-sponsored technical assistance and 56 percent of bilateral and multilateral investments during the mid-1990s. But on a per capita basis, Estonia, Latvia, and Lithuania received the largest outlays of government-to-government financing, multilateral credit, and technical assistance among CEE nations (OECD, 1999: 134). Virtually all EU environment-related funds to Estonia in the 1990s and early twenty-first century were grants. Between 1990 and 2003, the EU's PHARE (originally set up to facilitate economic and political transition in Poland and Hungary) and ISPA (the Instrument for Structural Policies for Pre-Accession) programs spent nearly US$52 million on environmental projects in Estonia with the peak year in 2001 at around US$15.2 million (UNECE, 2001: 84). Nordic countries, and in particular, Finland, provided millions more for a variety of projects. Finnish largess was greatest for activities that reined in transboundary air and water pollution affecting Finland's own environment; for example, Tallinn's sewerage upgrade and the cleanup of Kehra Pulp and Paper Mill and Kunda Cement (Finnish Ministry of the Environment, 1999: 16-17; 36).

Some Finnish grants helped leverage generous lines of credit from the European Bank for Reconstruction and Development (EBRD), the Nordic Investment Bank, and other international financial institutions. Most of the international bank loans were engineered under a multilateral program that Estonia joined in 1992: the Joint Comprehensive Environmental Action Programme (JCP). The objective of the JCP was to remediate the most seriously polluted sites (or "hot spots") in the Baltic Sea drainage basin. Of 132 hot spots identified by program participants, thirteen resided in Estonia, including the Tallinn Sewage Treatment Plant (hereinafter, Tallinn Sewerage) and two major air pollution sources, Kunda Cement and Kehra Pulp and Paper Mill. These three sites, along with most other JCP hot spots in Estonia, were beneficiaries of either bilateral aid, loans from international financial institutions, or externally sponsored private investment during the 1990s (Helsinki Commission, 1999: 92; FMOE, 1999: 44; Auer and Raukas, 2002).

An assessment of progress in cleaning up seriously contaminated industrial, municipal, and ex-military sites in Estonia reveals that JCP hot spots were remediated more quickly and thoroughly than were non-JCP hot spots (Auer and Raukas, 2002). In contrast, many non-JCP hot spots languished, and generally, these sites received less attention from major lenders or from foreign investors during the 1990s.

Large, externally funded environmental projects in Estonia shared an essential element: their backers had strong confidence in the creditworthiness of the borrower. For example, Estonia's steady economy, stable currency, and Tallinn municipality's sound financial condition were important considerations preceding EBRD's loan for the Tallinn Sewerage project in 1994—the first environmental loan by any of the international lending institutions in the Baltic Sea region. Biochemical oxygen demand (BOD) from Tallinn treatment works declined from 100 milligrams per liter in 1991 to 4 milligrams per liter in 1998. Moreover, a smoothly operating, fee-for-service, water/wastewater company was established as a condition of the loan, ensuring a steady revenue stream to the enterprise and uninterrupted payments to creditors.

Two other JCP hot spots with impressive environmental results, Kunda Cement and Kehra Pulp and Paper Mill, were retrofitted by private investors from Europe, North America, and Asia. Dust emissions from Kunda dropped more than 99 percent during the 1990s and by decade's end, sulfur dioxide emissions from Kehra were reduced by more than 90 percent over 1991 levels (Auer and Raukas, 2002).

The positive environmental results at these and other JCP hot spots contrast with ex-military sites in Estonia. None of the latter were entries in the JCP list. The Estonian government, Finland, Sweden, Germany, the United States, and the EU invested in the cleanup of several ex-military sites. But none of these sites attracted large loans from international financial institutions or significant foreign private investment. Environmental recovery at these sites greatly lagged the nearly complete environmental turnaround of Tallinn Sewerage, Kunda Cement, and Kehra Pulp and Paper (Auer and Raukas, 2002).

The forms of aid and investment that performed best in Estonia in the 1990s were sponsored by income-seeking actors like the EBRD and by European and North American entrepreneurs. The guidelines for the Joint Comprehensive Environmental Action Programme, which was developed by national governments in the Baltic Sea region and five multilateral investment banks, exhibit the influence of the banks, in particular. The guidelines call for a "least cost approach" to investment and assert that

> funding for projects which have been partially completed or involve the reha-
> bilitation of existing facilities will be given priority where the incremental in-
> vestment can be shown to be economically viable. (Helsinki Commission,
> 1992)

The JCP's list of 132 hot spots included many sites where rehabilitation activities had already begun or that were otherwise promising investments, on a least-cost basis; for example, Tallinn Sewerage and Kunda Cement were on this special list.

The JCP had no central funding of its own; individual countries, donors, and entrepreneurs were the program's main investors, with the JCP secretariat in Helsinki serving more as a listing agent than a coordinating or decision-making body. Nevertheless, the list of hot spots served a key function because for each site, prefeasibility studies were performed by the very countries and international organizations that were most likely to invest in the program: namely, by Nordic governments and the multilateral banks. As per North's (1990) and Krasner's (1983) conception of "institution," actors in the JCP developed rules and procedures to reduce uncertainty in their joint endeavor and to achieve preferred outcomes. JCP actors used preinvestment studies, the principle of least-cost financing, and the list of hot spots itself to narrow the range of possible projects, to increase the probability of successful cleanup outcomes, and to secure respectable returns on investments. The comparatively good environmental end states of listed hot spots and the less impressive results at nonlisted hot spots (e.g., most ex-military sites) suggest that the JCP, as an institution, made an important, positive contribution to Estonian environmental efforts in the 1990s.

Shortcomings of Antipollution Efforts

Having made great strides in cleaning up some of its most troublesome pollution hot spots, Estonian environmental officials are turning to new or heretofore lower priority environmental problems. That Estonia can afford to shift away from the major pollution crises of the immediate post-Soviet era is a coming of age that some Estonian environmental officials quietly, but proudly, acknowledge. Indeed, among some, there is even a sort of guilty pleasure in knowing that new and emerging problems, such as controlling toxic emissions from automobiles, finding new space for landfills, and stopping encroachment on fragile coastal environs are by-products of "high living" that Estonians could only dream about under Communism.

Pollution from automobiles is an especially urgent concern. As described in the Czech case (chapter 2) and as is true in most CEE countries, cars and trucks are replacing factory smokestacks as the major emitters of sulfur dioxide and nitrogen oxide. On the other hand, the obsolescence of leaded gasoline and diesel-fueled Soviet-era vehicles has helped reduce certain types of urban air pollution, such as soot and carbon monoxide, even as other auto emissions increase.

Much as Estonia faces a formidable mobile source air pollution problem, stationary source pollution remains a vexing concern. For even as contaminants such as sulfur dioxide and dust have sharply declined from many enterprises, dirty factories of yesteryear in Estonia remain major polluters in the new century. The Estonian and Baltic oil shale-fired power plants near Narva are members of this ignominious club; both facilities are Estonia's largest emitters of carbon dioxide and neither power plant is equipped to stanch these emissions. Switching fuels away from oil shale to natural gas would dramatically decrease carbon pollution and other contaminants, but in doing so, Estonia would give up its comparative advantage in oil shale combustion, becoming reliant on imported gas.

Even if Estonia finds an alternative to fuel switching, the cleanup of the Narva power stations will likely involve substantial imports of capital and expertise. This would be consistent with the nation's heavy reliance on foreigners to help redress its most serious environmental dilemmas. Indeed, in the late 1990s, an American company promised to invest more than US$320 million (of which US$253 million were to be loans) to modernize the power plants and other oil shale enterprises in exchange for long-term electrical power sales to Estonian customers (Kurm, 2001: 13). The American firm also agreed to invest several million dollars in an environmental upgrade of the plants. More than five years after the announcement of the modernization plan, the Narva plants remained largely unremediated and, not coincidentally, in state hands. The deal to sell the plants fell through in 2002 when the American would-be buyer failed to raise capital for the purchase (Behr, 2002a). As of that year, the Estonian government was not forging ahead on its own to clean up the power stations because, quite simply, it could not. As in the Kehra Pulp and Paper, Kunda Cement, and other cases where old Estonian factories were modernized, investments by foreign actors will prove decisive in revitalizing the Narva power plants.

But the benefits of large capital inputs and know-how from abroad are accompanied by the risk of dependency. When the investment comes via the sale of Estonian assets to foreign companies, the latter's promises to protect the environment are generally only as reliable as the duties specified in the terms of sale. Ordinary Estonians might not expect foreigners to share the same level of affection for the country's natural resources nor the same degree of concern about Estonian public health. From the foreign investor's perspective, environmental management is mostly a cost of doing business. It is a worthy undertaking to the extent that it yields public relations dividends to the firm, that is, the firm can promote its environmental good deeds to customers and to regulators.

Estonia was fortunate in that on most occasions in the 1990s, foreign assistance and investments pledged for environmental cleanup arrived when promised and were put to good use. Nevertheless, Estonian political elites do express unease about relying on foreign investment and aid; they are nervous about not having sufficient control of the process nor an ability to assure favorable environmental outcomes.

In the language of institutional economics, this is a "moral hazard" problem, that is, one where the principal surrenders control over key decisions to the agent, and in the process, loses some or all of the ability to ensure that the agent fulfills his or her promises. When foreign investors in Estonia are purchasing companies that are embroiled in both financial and environmental messes, the principal (in this case, the Estonian state) typically relinquishes some or all control to the agent (the foreign investor) to decide how and when to make environmental improvements. In the case of the aborted deal to sell the Narva power stations to an American company, details concerning the environmental retrofit, including the timetable for clean up, were contractable items. Nevertheless, the Estonian state, which was at once the seller of the asset and the country's chief environmental authority, was relying on the good faith of an outsider who was motivated more by earnings than environmental altruism.

Assume for analytical purposes that the deal was completed and the American company became the new owner. Had the company failed to abide by a contractual promise to clean up the power stations, the Estonian government's efforts to seek remedy might have entailed costly legal action and no certainty of a satisfactory outcome. Moreover, the unremediated power stations would continue to emit pollution.

This brand of moral hazard is different from that identified by other scholars of East-West environmental affairs. For example, Darst (2001: 170-171) identified a moral hazard to Western donors who provided aid to Ukraine, Lithuania, and Russia to shut down or add safety features to old, Chernobyl-style nuclear power plants. In the Estonian case, the Estonian government and citizens bear moral hazard risk when they sell dirty factories to foreigners who may or may not make good on pledges to clean up these enterprises.

As mentioned earlier in this section, long negotiations over the sale of Estonia's largest stationary sources of air pollution—the Narva power plants—collapsed in early 2002 when creditors lost faith in the prospective buyer. In this case, large commercial banks refused to lend to an American company already saddled with debts from earlier purchases. Ordinary Estonians and several Estonian politicians were relieved by this outcome. Terms of the prospective sale which were published in 2001 had received mixed reviews; some prominent Estonians complained about the low sale price (Kurm, 2001). Environmentalists, meanwhile, quizzed government officials about the would-be owners' environmental responsibilities.

A larger lesson can be extracted from the Narva case. As multinational corporations—the captains of the global economy—come to own Estonia's most valuable assets, the state must become increasingly savvy in contract negotiations, particularly when more is at stake than the property sale price. In the case of the Narva power stations, public and environmental health in Estonia and in nations downwind of Estonia are important facets of the transaction.

Shortcomings of Natural Resource Management Efforts

Even as Estonian environmental officials express quiet satisfaction about recent efforts to stanch pollution and are ambivalent about outsiders' major role in this endeavor, they are more concerned than ever about the future of the nation's forestlands and wilderness areas.

Some forestry experts in Estonia believe that the Ministry of Environment, the agency that oversees both protected and harvested forestlands, maintained timber harvest levels that were unsustainably high during the late 1990s (Ahas, 1998; interview, Heino Luik, Institute of National Development and Cooperation, 1 August 2001). Overharvesting of trees is a dilemma in many parts of Estonia, but official, sanctioned harvests are only a part—and perhaps only a small part—of the problem. A more serious headache is illegal logging. According to the director of Estonia's largest environmental advocacy group, some 50 percent of trees harvested in Estonia are illegally logged (interview, Peep Maardiste, Estonian Green Movement, 31 July 2001). Another environmentalist estimates that during the 1990s around 50,000 cubic meters of wood were illegally logged in Estonian forests (Ahas, 1998). The main drivers of this unlawful activity are different in Estonia than in, say, Brazil or Malaysia, where harvesting pressures from large domestic and multinational timber companies, landless migrants, and corrupt forestry officials are key factors. In Estonia, most of the illegal harvesters actually own title to forested land. But they spurn local- and national-level rules requiring each landowner to obtain an approved forest management plan and they rarely seek the obligatory permits for tree felling (interview, Peep Maardiste, Estonian Green Movement, 31 July 2001).

Aggravating the overharvesting problem is the rapid reversion of previously state-owned forestland to citizens and their families who held legal title to said lands in pre-Soviet times. Forestry authorities have not adapted to the enforcement challenges posed by Estonia's new patchwork of private small-holder, company-owned, communally owned, and central state-owned forestlands. Moreover, according to environmentalists and Estonian forestry experts, forest management authorities are overwhelmed by the wide-scale transgression of forestry regulations—lawbreaking that occurs daily, throughout the country. Enforcement has deteriorated since the Soviet era. Understaffing partly explains this trend: during the 1970s and 1980s, more than 1,000 local-level foresters managed the Estonian Soviet Socialist Republic's forests, each with purview over 1,000 hectares of land. In the 1990s, Estonia's forest service maintained 105 district offices but many of these units were poorly managed and enforcement duties were not rigorously executed (Ahas, 1998; interview, Heino Luik, Institute of National Development and Cooperation, 1 August 2001). Even environmentalists agree that forest management under the Soviets was preferable to the post-Soviet system of fragmented property rights, accelerated harvesting pressure, and spotty enforcement (interview, Peep Maardiste, Estonian Green Movement, 31 July 2001).

Illegal logging is unlikely to diminish in the midst of a growing rural-urban income gap. Disparities in wealth and well-being between agrarians and urbanites are unwanted outcomes of ten years of relatively harsh agrarian reforms by center and center-right governments in Estonia. These reforms include a virtual embargo on agricultural subsidies—a policy that other CEE governments rejected under pressure from domestic agricultural interests. Employment in the Estonian farming and livestock sectors has contracted sharply, though farms that survived the economic transition have grown more efficient. However, unemployment, and in some districts, persistent economic recession, have had negative indirect effects on the environment, including on the country's small-holder forestlands. For many economically stressed farmers, time spent illegally harvesting trees is more profitably spent, at least in the short term, than is legally harvesting row crops.

Through 2002, the government made little progress to discourage illegal logging. While forestry inspectorates and local law enforcement agencies were too thinly staffed to catch farmers and other small-scale forest harvesters in the act of poaching, there was little political will to prevent illegal logging in the first place owing to persistent economic hard times in rural areas.

Strikingly, some private landowners claim they are compelled to cut trees on their land for fear that poachers will strike first (interview, Peep Maardiste, Estonian Green Movement, 31 July 2001). If these fears are genuine, then landowners are casting doubt on the integrity of a vital institution, namely, that of private property. Lurking beneath the system of private title to forestland is the "commons" problem. Farmers and landowners are pressured to illegally harvest their own resources because excluding poachers is difficult and expensive to do, and law enforcement officials are on the sidelines.

Conservative governments in Tallinn, determined to please the EU, took a tough line on agricultural subsidies in the 1990s. But in the early years of the twenty-first century, they made some amends to agrarians in response to demands from a remarkable alliance of farmers, environmentalists, and state agencies in Estonia. This alliance evidences the enduring importance of environmentalism in Estonian politics. It is also an unusual instance where environmentalists and agriculturalists find common cause.

The partnership originates with the decline of a unique natural treasure in Estonia: meadows. The nation boasts some of the largest, intact tracts of meadowland in all of continental Europe, and on a per capita basis, has more hectares of meadows than any other European nation. Four major types of meadowland exist: wooded, coastal, floodplain, and alvar, and all are in decline due, ironically, to the decline of agriculture (Estonian Environment Information Centre, 2001: 74). These ecosystems are highly complex and rich in plant species diversity; are habitats for millions of animals; serve as key stopping-over grounds for migratory species; and are vital organs for groundwater recharge. But to subsist, they require regular physical disturbance—namely, from the grazing pressure of cattle and sheep—which prevents nonmeadow vegetation from gaining a foothold. In the absence of grazing or other interventions, meadows tend to revert to other ecosystem types, such as scrubland forest or marsh.

Naturalists raised the alarm about disappearing meadows in Estonia in the mid-1990s. Later in the decade, "nature-friendly" land use subsidies were made available to farmers who promised to manage pasture lands to revitalize meadows. 2001 marked a turning point for these special subsides as meadow-maintenance funds were authorized in the sum of 19 million kronor (approximately US$1.1 million)—a more than 100 percent increase from previous years (interview, Mari Lahtmets, Estonian Ministry of Environment, 1 August 2001). In the case of Estonia's meadows, a governmental initiative satisfied a variety of actors whose own interests were not always complementary. And the policy was instituted without appearing to contradict previous rules and procedures, namely, the state's hard line against agricultural subsidies.

Clouds on the Horizon:
Disparities in Wealth and Well-Being

Tallinn's support for meadow preservation was an implicit subsidy to farmers, but it was a small victory for agrarians in a decade marked by constant setbacks. Poverty was much more prevalent in rural than in urban areas. Approximately one-quarter of all Estonians employed in agriculture and forestry were classified as poor (i.e., they had average expenditure levels that were 45 percent below the minimum pension) (Valdes, 2000: 29). Agricultural production of main farm staples such as cereals and livestock shrank by 40 percent between 1990 and 2000; during that same period, production of beef contracted by more than 45 percent (Statistikaamet, 1997: 225; 228; Statistikaamet, 2001: 67; 70).

In contrast, urban economies, and especially Tallinn's, thrived during the decade. The capital's economic output grew exponentially as Estonian entrepreneurs and many foreign investors made Tallinn their headquarters, and found residence in the city's picturesque old town. Within a short time, Tallinnites were enjoying benefits, including environmental benefits like clean drinking water, that were found in few other Estonian towns and cities. In comparison, public service delivery in rural areas struggled to keep up with Soviet-era standards.

Estonia's small size does not necessarily simplify the problem of providing environmental services to its population, especially its rural population. Serving densely populated urban areas, where more than 70 percent of Estonians reside, is relatively easy to do; and during the 1990s, Estonian authorities added thousands of city residences to urban sewer and water networks. A bigger conundrum is finding cost-effective wastewater treatment and drinking water solutions for Estonia's small rural towns and hamlets. In years to come, 20 percent of the Estonian population—the portion living relatively far away from urban water/sewer lines—will account for some 80 percent of the nation's new sanitary infrastructure expenditures (interview, Mari Lahtmets, Estonian Ministry of Environment, 1 August 2001). In large part because of the steep costs for hooking up rural residents to urban sewers or providing alternative sewerage solutions, Estonia won a reprieve from the European Union, which initially demanded nationwide sewerage coverage preceding Estonia's entry to the EU. With the compromise, Estonia has until 2010 to meet this standard.

But the problem of water/wastewater coverage in Estonia's rural areas belies a larger problem that is of increasing concern to political elites and ordinary citizens alike: growing disparities between urban and rural Estonians, measured by income, educational and health status, and as illustrated above, access to public services. Indeed, a pecking order has emerged even among Estonian urban centers. Tallinn is pulling away from the rest of the country.

Estonia's capital is nearly four times as large as the next largest city and it generates the lion's share of the nation's economic output, particularly in the value-added industrial and service sectors. It also attracts the vast majority of the nation's incoming foreign investment. Its harbor is the country's main commercial port, and in the 1990s, a key export facility for Russian oil. Estonian politicians have mixed feelings about Tallinn's soaring fortunes, especially to the extent that Tallinn benefits while the economies of other Estonian cities and towns stumble. In 2000, Estonia's prime minister quietly proposed moving the seat of national government to Estonia's second largest (and economically quiescent) city of Tartu (Sindrich, 2000: 1). While the proposal instilled little enthusiasm among Tallinnites and members of government, it underscored anxiety over growing political and economic imbalances in a country that, based on its territorial area alone, seems far too small to suffer from inequities born of geography.

Estonia's otherwise providential legacy of close cultural and language connections to Finland actually widens the gap between Tallinn and the rest of the country. Much Finnish public and private investment has been channeled to Tallinn with relatively less arriving in secondary cities not to mention rural areas. Consider, for example, Finnish investments in real estate. In the 1990s, upwardly mobile Finnish urbanites eschewed pricy properties in Helsinki, instead renovating apartments and homes in Tallinn's Hanseatic-era old town, sending real estate prices soaring. In the late 1990s, rapid ferry service between Helsinki and Tallinn reduced what had been a three- to six-hour round-trip to ninety minutes (those preferring travel by helicopter make the round-trip in less than an hour), rendering the distance between the two capitals a reasonable daily commute for white-collar workers, and especially for Tallinn's growing clique of transplants from Finland (Maheshwari, 2000: 11).

As the capital's old town flourished, real estate prices in other parts of the city lagged behind, but property values in other Estonian urban markets declined further still (Baltic News Service, 2000). The high real estate prices and large residential and commercial tax bases in Tallinn help the city pay for the extension and improvement of physical infrastructure including its drinking water and sewerage systems. With the exception of major secondary cities like Tartu and Parnu, most small municipalities cannot contemplate the large capital investments that make Tallinn's sanitary services the envy of other Estonian towns and of urbanites in other parts of the former Soviet Union.

The Finland-Estonia connection, then, partly explains the privileged conditions that Estonians in Tallinn enjoy, including the capital's state-of-the-art sewer and water services. But Estonia's links to Finland have not reaped comparable benefits for other urban areas in Estonia.

The trend whereby Tallinn benefits disproportionately from its connections to Finland is not of recent origin. If Estonia was a window to the West during the Soviet times, then Tallinn was the transparent part of that window where there was regular, direct contact between Estonians, Finns, and other foreigners.

Moreover, in Tallinn and its suburbs, there was "virtual" contact with Finns and other Westerners via the voices from Nordic radio and television broadcasts—transmissions that were relatively difficult to pick up in Estonia's south or were ignored in Estonian towns where Russian speakers dominated.

For foreigners, Tallinn was always the most familiar, accessible, and most cosmopolitan part of Estonia—reputations that developed well before the collapse of the Soviet Union. For investors, would-be commuters, and vacationers, it was an obvious destination: a regional capital with worldly people; a city of commerce even in Soviet times; a communication center for the republic; and for virtually everyone traveling from across the Baltic Sea to Estonia, the main port of entry. For professionals who travel frequently to Estonia as well as for the one-time visitor, Tallinn is the first, and often the last, Estonian port of call. Understanding Tallinn's elevated position among Estonian towns in the twenty-first century is to appreciate the informal institutions built and nurtured jointly by thousands of Finns and Estonians every day—networks of learning, commerce, and affection that long predate the formal friendship pacts, Western-style commercial codes, joint venture agreements, and other formal legal provisions that affirmed Estonia's close connections to the West, and especially to Finland.

But the potential downsides of Tallinn's continued ascendance are the withering of the country's other cities and towns and the disappearance of Estonia's proud agrarian past. From a narrowly conceived environmental perspective, one might be sanguine about the emergence of one or two great urban centers in Estonia, with much of the rest of the country abandoned and reverting to forestland. But, this situation is *not* favored by Estonians. Most citizens prefer to bridge gaps between urban "haves" and rural "have-nots" and to protect one of that country's rarest and most revered ecosystems—its meadows. Moreover, growing disparities between urbanites and agrarians is not promoting forest protection. Rural peoples, increasingly desperate to make a living, are overharvesting trees, and forest authorities lack resources and the will to stop it.

Estonians' concerns with the growing income and welfare gaps between urban and rural residents came to a head in the country's presidential elections of 2001. The constitution dictates that Estonia's parliament chooses the nation's president. But when the first ballot failed to produce a majority among four leading candidates, the decision reverted to a special electoral college. To the surprise of many urbanites—and to the delight of agrarians—neither of the two popular center-right candidates prevailed. With strong support from electoral delegates in rural districts, the mantle passed to a Soviet-era leader and one of the country's most outspoken critics of policies that inadvertently punish or neglect Estonia's rural citizens. The new president is also aware of the unsustainable drain on Estonia's forests, among other environmental problems (interview, Arnold Rüütel, Institute of National Development and Cooperation, 1 August 2001). The Estonian constitution affords the president with relatively few formal powers. Nevertheless, environmentalists hope the new leader will help the nation negotiate trade-offs between economic development and environmental protection, including raising rural peoples' standard of living while strengthening environmental enforcement in the countryside.

Conclusion

In years to come, Estonia's efforts to redress social and economic inequities will require the same commitment to institutional reforms that buoyed that country's region-leading economic performance in the 1990s. However, the state will need to reorient its institution-building role. In the 1990s, the government intentionally minimized its role in business regulatory affairs and it cut state support for lagging economic sectors. Becoming more active in economic affairs does not require the state to jettison its Nordic-focused export strategies, nor does it call for major resource transfers to rural areas where fewer and fewer Estonians live and work.

However, the state can jump-start the institution-building effort in Estonia's rural areas through the use of incentives to stimulate economic growth and environmental protection. Some of these incentives, such as job training, the creation of economic empowerment zones, or tax incentives for relocating businesses or for protecting forests, are not cost free in the short run. But like many of Estonia's most successful environmental remediation projects, such as the overhaul of Tallinn's sewerage system and the cleanup of Kunda Cement, well-conceived short-term investments to promote rural economic recovery will produce long-term benefits and returns on investment.

Estonia has already demonstrated it can improve both economic and environmental conditions for its citizens. Few former Soviet republics are better poised to flourish in the twenty-first century, what with its close connections to continental Europe and the Nordic countries (and especially Finland), its dynamic economy, and its good reputation for environmental protection. Indeed, Estonia's relatively blessed economic and environmental conditions and the strategies Estonians deployed to achieve them offer lessons in institution-building for Russia and for CEE countries profiled in other chapters of this book.

Notes

1. Rejecting a firm date for closing Ignalina, Lithuania's President Valdas Adamkus (a former regional U.S. Environmental Protection Agency administrator) commented, "I view nuclear energy as a clean energy source, the energy source of the future . . . I don't in any way accept this pressure [from Brussels]" (City Paper, 2002a).

2. However, the EU may have conceded the hunting prohibition issue too early as official statistics from Estonia suggest that hunting of some predators may endanger

breeding populations in that country. For example, in 2000, 150 wolves were counted in Estonia while five years earlier, the number was 700. In 2000, hunters shot 56 wolves in Estonia (*Baltic Times*, 12-18 July 2001: 13). At least one prominent Estonian environmental expert contends that the tally quoted by the *Baltic Times* exaggerated the total number of large prey animals killed in the country in 2000 (interview, Jaan Punning, Ökoloogia Instituut, 3 August 2001).

References

Agri Service International Newsletter. 1995. "EU Enlargement: Finnish and Austrian Farmers Voice Discontent," 1 September. Lexis Nexis News/World News/European News Sources. Accessed 23 March 2002.

Ahas, Rein. 1998. "Underlying Causes of Deforestation and Forest Degradation in Estonia: A Local Level Case Study in Põlva County." Unpublished report prepared for the Estonian Green Movement. Tartu: EGM.

Auer, Matthew. 1992. "Environmental Restoration, Economic Transition, and Nationalism in Estonia." *Journal of Baltic Studies*, vol. 23, no. 4: 377-386.

———. 1996. "The Historical Roots of Environmental Conflict in Estonia. *East European Quarterly*, vol. 30, no. 3: 353-380.

Auer, Matthew, and Anto Raukas. 2002. "Determinants of Environmental Cleanup in Estonia." *Environment and Planning C: Government and Policy*, vol. 20, no. 5: 679-698.

Auvinen. 2001. "Report on Estonia's Progress toward EU Accession: UNICE Task Force on Enlargement." www.baltictrade-information.fi/estonia/news.php?lang=fin. Accessed 15 February 2002.

Baltic News Service. 2000. "Differences in Prices of Apartments in Central Tallinn Is Growing." *Baltic News Service*, 12 January. Lexis Nexis News/World News/European News Sources. Accessed 18 March 2002.

Baltic Times. 2001. Untitled article on abundance of large game in Estonia. 12-18 July: 13.

Behr, Rafael. 2002a. "Estonia Pulls out of Power Deal with NRG." *Financial Times*, 8 January. Lexis Nexis News/World News/European News Sources. Accessed 18 March 2002.

———. 2002b. "Tallinn Aims to Reassure over Rapid Pace of Economic Reform." *Financial Times*, 29 January: 6.

City Paper. 1998. "Selling Estonia: Part II." www.balticsww.com/news/features/selling_estonia2.htm. Accessed 8 August 2002).

———. 2002a. "Lithuanian President Valdas Adamkus Said Tuesday That the Country Shouldn't Commit to a Firm Date for the Complete Shutdown of Its Sole Nuclear Power Station—as the European Union Asked It to Do, BNS Reported." 26 February. www.balticsww.com/wkcrier/archive_links.htm. Accessed 4 June 2002.

———. 2002b. "The European Union Said on March 23 That Lithuania Must Close Its Sole Atomic Power Station by 2009, Warning That a Failure to Commit to That Date Could Jeopardize Lithuania's Bid for EU Membership." 24 May. www.balticsww.com/wkcrier/archive_links.htm. Accessed 4 June 2002.

Darst, Robert G. 2001. *Smokestack Diplomacy: Cooperation and Conflict in East-West Environmental Politics*. Cambridge, MA: MIT Press.

The Economist. 1989. "The Pleasures of Estophilia." 3 June: 49.
————. 1993. "European Union: Expansio Ad Absurdum." 4 December: 58.
Estonian Environment Information Center. 2001. *State of the Environment in Estonia: On the Threshold of XXI Century.* Tallinn: Estonian Environment Information Center.
Estonian Information Centre. 1977. "The Letter of Eighteen Estonian Naturalists to Colleagues in Finland, Sweden, Denmark and the Federal Republic of Germany." Documents from Estonia on the Violation of Human Rights. Stockholm: Estonian Information Centre.
Estonian Ministry of Environment. 1992. *National Report of Estonia to UNCED 1992.* Tallinn: Estonian Ministry of Environment.
————. 1997. *Estonian National Environmental Strategy.* Tallinn: Estonian Ministry of Environment.
————. 1999. *Endise Nõukogude Liidu Sõjaväe Jääkreostus Ja Selle Likvideerimine* (Past Pollution of the Soviet Army in Estonia and Its Liquidation). Tallinn: Estonian Ministry of Environment.
————. 2001. *State of Environment in Estonia: On the Threshold of XXI Century.* Tallinn: Estonian Ministry of Environment.
European Commission. 2001. *Applicant Countries Eurobarometer 2001: Public Opinion in the Countries Applying for European Union Membership.* Brussels: EC.
European Council. 1992. *European Council Directive 92/43/EEC of 21 May 1992 on the Conservation of Natural Habitats and of Wild Fauna and Flora, Article 12 and Annex IV.* www.ecnc.nl/doc/europe/legislat/habidire.html. Accessed 3 February 2002.
European Report. 2001. "EU Enlargement: Sweden Closes 12 More Negotiating Chapters," 6 June. Lexis/Nexis News/World/Europe Library.
Finnish Ministry of the Environment. 1999. *Environmental Cooperation in Central and Eastern Europe 1998.* Helsinki: FMOE.
Finnish Ministry of Foreign Affairs. 1991. *Environmental Priority Action Programme for Leningrad, Leningrad Region, Karelia and Estonia: Summary Report* (prepared by IVO International, Vesi-Hydro Consulting Ltd, Enviro Data Ltd, and Outokumpu EcoEnergy Ltd.). Helsinki: FMFA.
Gunter, Aleksei. 2001. "Ilves Admits Being Baltic Is Not So Bad." *Baltic Times,* 10-16 May: 4.
Helsinki Commission. 1992. *The Baltic Sea Joint Comprehensive Environmental Action Programme (Preliminary Version),* Conference Document no. 5/3, Agenda Item 5 of the Diplomatic Conference on the Protection of the Marine Environment of the Baltic Sea Area. Helsinki: HELCOM.
————. 1999. *The Baltic Sea Joint Comprehensive Environmental Action Programme (JCP) Annual Report 1999.* Helsinki: HELCOM.
Hill, Don. 2002. "A Group of U.S. Environmental Scholars Says Latvia Leads Eastern and Central Europe in What It Calls 'Environmental Sustainability'—That Is, Maintaining or Improving Its Environment." *Radio Free Europe/Radio Liberty,* 8 February. www.rferl.org/nca/features/2002/02/08022002102010.asp. Accessed 4 June 2002.
Holman, Eugene. 1995. "Estonian and Finnish." Unpublished listserve communication: soc.culture.baltics newsgroup, 21 April.
Huang, Mel. 2000. "Estonia for Sale." *Central Europe Review,* vol. 2, no. 40: 1.

Hughes, Gordon, and Magda Lovei. 1999. *Economic Reform and Environmental Performance in Transition Economies.* World Bank Technical Paper No. 446. Washington, D.C.: World Bank.

Ilves, Toomas Hendrik. 1997. "Opening Remarks by Mr. Toomas Hendrik Ilves, Estonian Ministry of Foreign Affairs." *Proceedings of the AIESEC Nordic Management Seminar, Pirita Hotel.* Tallinn, Estonia, 27 January.

Kahk, Juhan. 1991. *World War II and Soviet Occupation in Estonia: A Damages Report.* Tallinn: Perioodika Publishers.

Keerdoja, Liina. 1966. *Some Characteristic Differences in the Use of Finnish and Estonian Verbs and Cases.* A.M. thesis dissertation (Department of Central Eurasian Studies, Indiana University).

Krasner, Stephen D. 1983. "Structural Causes and Regime Consequences: Regimes as Intervening Variables," in Stephen D. Krasner (ed.), *International Regimes.* Ithaca, NY: Cornell University Press, 1-21.

Kurm, Kairi. 2001. "Anger at Power Plants Deal Set to Explode." *Baltic Times,* 12-18 July: 13.

Maheshwari, Vijai. 2000. "Baltic Kith and Kin Revive Family Ties." *Financial Times,* 28 October: 11.

North, Douglass. 1990. *Institutions, Institutional Change and Economic Performance.* Cambridge: Cambridge University Press.

Organization for Economic Cooperation and Development. 1999. *Environment in the Transition to a Market Economy: Progress in Central and Eastern Europe and the New Independent States.* Paris: OECD.

Ostrom, Elinor. 1999. "Institutional Rational Choice: An Assessment of the Institutional Analysis and Development Framework," in Paul Sabatier (ed.), *Theories of the Policy Process.* Boulder, CO: Westview Press, 35-71.

Pullat, P., B. A. Ejov, Yu Truuvyali, K. Siylivask, A. Keerna, K. Kala, and P. Yuursoo. 1985. *Istori Rabouego Klassa Covetskoi Astonii* (History of the Working Class of Soviet Estonia). Tallinn: Estonia Book, 1985.

Sakkeus, Luule. 1993. "Post-War Migration Trends in the Baltic States." *RU Series B No 20,* Tallinn: Estonian Interuniversity Population Research Centre.

Sindrich, Jaclyn M. 2000. "Moving the Capital to Tartu?" *Baltic Times,* 15-21 June: 1.

Statistikaamet. 1997. *Eesti Statistika Aastaraamat 1997* (Statistical Yearbook of Estonia 1997). Tallinn: Statistikaamet.

———. 2001. *Estonian Statistics 2001: Monthly No. 5 (113).* Tallinn: Statistikaamet.

———. 2002. "Annual Turnover of Foreign Trade Increased." Press release of the Statistical Office of Estonia, Tallinn, 3 March. www.stat.ee/index.aw/section=27933/set_lang_id=2. Accessed 5 June 2002.

Taagepera, Mare. 1989. "The Ecological and Political Problems of Phosphorite Mining in Estonia." *Journal of Baltic Studies,* vol. 20, no. 2: 165-174.

United Nations. 1999. *International Trade Statistics Yearbook 1998: Volume I, Trade by Country.* New York: UN (Department of Economic and Social Affairs).

United Nations Development Programme. 1995. *Human Development Report 1995.* New York: Oxford University Press: 155-156; 197.

———. 2001. *Human Development Report 2001.* New York: UNDP.

United Nations Economic Commission for Europe. 2001. *Environmental Performance Reviews: Estonia.* Geneva: UNECE.

U.S. Bureau of the Census. 1992. *Estonia*. Washington, D.C.: U.S. Bureau of the Census (Center for International Research).

Valdes, Alberto. 2000. "Estonia: Challenges of EU Accession," in L. Alexander Norsworthy, (ed.), *Rural Development, Natural Resources and the Environment: Lessons of Experience in Eastern Europe and Central Asia*. Washington, D.C.: World Bank, 29-31.

Vilpišauskas, Ramūnas, and Guoda Steponavičiené. 2000. "The Baltic States: The Economic Dimension," in Helena Tang (ed.), *Winners and Losers of EU Integration: Policy Issues for Central and Eastern Europe*. Washington, D.C.: World Bank, 52-96.

World Bank. 1994. *World Development Report 1994*. New York: Oxford University Press.

————. 1998. *World Development Report 1998/99*. New York: Oxford University Press.

————. 2001. *World Development Indicators 2001*. Washington, D.C.: World Bank.

————. 2002. *World Development Indicators 2002*. Washington, D.C.: World Bank.

World Resources Institute. 1996. *World Resources Report 1996-97*. New York: Oxford University Press.

Chapter 6

The Disappearance of Popular Environmental Activism in Post-Soviet Russia

Joshua E. Abrams and Matthew R. Auer

Beginning in the mid-1980s, environmental sustainability and human health became high-profile political issues, gaining the attention of both world leaders and average citizens. Around that same time, the Soviet political system began slowing opening up, giving entrée to grassroots movements, including a popular environmental movement. Political transformation and environmental quality in Russia were inextricably linked in those years, for it was the Chernobyl nuclear disaster in April of 1986 that shook the Soviet political establishment and galvanized citizens in the USSR and beyond.

After 1991, Western aid agencies and nonprofit organizations poured into Russia to assist in the transition to a market-based democracy. Among the programs introduced by these donors were high-profile "civil society" initiatives, intended to institutionalize the civic organizational activity that had emerged during the previous decade. If successful, such aid would improve the capacity of nongovernmental actors and ordinary citizens to engage and influence the state. Yet, more than ten years after the first aid programs were initiated, indicators of the relative statuses of environmental and public health, of popular political activism, and of the accomplishments of official policy making reveal mostly failure by the civil society paradigm to advance environmental protection in Russia. Moreover, the environmental policy reform movement as it existed in the 1980s has all but vanished.

This chapter analyzes why that movement disappeared, and why an influx of international assistance programs under more liberal political conditions has been unable to resuscitate it. It addresses the disjunction between civil society as the idealization of the advanced, liberal democratic state and civil society as an explicit strategy for promoting policy reforms, and in particular, environmental policy reforms. "Civil society development" has been the key organizing principle for the West's (and especially, the United States') noneconomic aid to the former Soviet Union (FSU); it has been promoted as the best guarantor of a robust and participatory democracy. Despite more than a decade of effort, the civil society-nurturing model of policy reform has wrought, at best, marginal improvements to peoples' material conditions and environmental well-being.

For three key reasons, any consideration of post-Soviet environmental institutional change must take Western aid policies into account. First, Western assistance has shaped many of Russia's formal environmental institutional reforms since 1991, whether due to the demands made by donors or by the examples created by aid programs and projects themselves. Second, the West made explicit use of the civil society development paradigm to shape the organizational forms, missions, and strategies of Russia's environmental NGOs and private voluntary associations—all with the intention of adapting Western-style, liberal democratic civic institutions. Third, civic initiatives were more conspicuous than were state initiatives in promoting environmental reforms in the late Soviet era. The West recognized this trend and channeled much of its post-Soviet environment-related aid to nonstate actors.

The prominence of Western or Western-supported civic organizations in Russia raises questions about the prospects for homegrown, sustainable environmental policy reforms in that nation. Institutions and organizations influence one another through the symbiotic interplay of their respective functions. To borrow Douglass North's analogy (1990: 4), if institutions are the (formal and informal)[1] rules of the game, organizations are teams of actors who play by those rules, or who seek to challenge and change them. The interplay between rules and actors is thus dynamic and reflexive, with each reacting and adjusting to the other. Incremental adjustments over time lead to institutional changes that in turn effect the ordering of society.

In this vein, Western civil society programs in Russia affect the interplay between indigenous institutions and organizational actors. Many Russian NGOs, including the most prominent national environmental associations, are either subsidiaries of organizations that are chartered in other countries; are affiliates of foreign entities; or are recipients of major grants from foreign actors such as governments, private foundations, or international NGOs. As such they tend to promote interests and focus on issues that are not necessarily priority concerns of local actors, employ strategies alien to local sensibilities, or are ignored or mistrusted by citizens or Russian authorities (Henry, 2001). From the skeptic's perspective, Western-sponsored NGOs are not organic parts of Russian society, yet they are trying to influence institutional change as if they were.

In the early 1990s, bilateral aid agencies quickly assembled and administered democratic initiatives in Russia; many such programs were geared to raise the profile and political effectiveness of nonstate actors. European and North American governments were confident about the need for such programs but overconfident about the malleability of a society with no historical memory of democracy. In the environmental aid arena, the now mythologized legacy of late Soviet "green" activism determined the forms and functions of Western aid programs, and at the expense of thorough needs assessments and feasibility studies performed collaboratively by donors and recipients.[2] Such collaboration was requisite for environment-related aid to have any real effect but was often sacrificed in the rush to seed and make flourish civil society in Russia.

This chapter considers the challenges of turning the civil society model into an effective instrument for environmental policy reform in Russia. Case material highlights problems that plague international assistance programs, from donors' unrealistic expectations about the pace with which social capital is constructed in Russia, to the economic and political constraints activists face, to the extent of the ecological and health problems that the Green movement confronts.

Chernobyl as Stimulus for Institutional Reform

In the last decade of the Soviet regime, less than twelve months after General Secretary Mikhail Gorbachev introduced his new program of political reforms, the worst nuclear disaster in history took place in Chernobyl, Ukraine. The explosion of Reactor Four on 26 April 1986 spread a cloud of radiation over much of the western Soviet republics—Ukraine and Belarus in particular—and northeastern Europe. Dozens died from acute radiation exposure after the explosion, and hundreds more, mostly emergency workers, took ill in the days and months after the accident. No less affected was the Soviet regime itself.

It has been said that, without Gorbachev, there would have been no glasnost or perestroika; likewise, without Chernobyl, the reforms would not have evolved as they did. As Davison (1991) wrote:

> the Chernobyl disaster is perhaps the one event that made glasnost an operative principle in Soviet political reform. . . . In acknowledging the accident . . . Chernobyl became a jarring example of the regime's—and of its ideology's—vulnerability.

The authorities' tardiness first in acknowledging and then addressing the disaster exposed the operational weaknesses and moral callousness of Soviet policy institutions. Gorbachev used the accident (and the poorly managed response to it) as an opportunity to justify political liberalization, and in particular, to give a wider berth to unauthorized political opinions.

Environmental advocacy groups began to form immediately after the disaster. Some organizations, such as the Socio-Ecological Union which was formed in Moscow in 1987, were still active more than ten years later (Socio-Ecological Union, 2001). Another group, Nevada-Semipalatinsk, formed in Almaty in 1989, was particularly successful in mobilizing Kazakhs against nuclear testing in that republic. The peak years of the Green movement were 1989 and 1990, when millions of people joined political organizations and parties, formed scientific associations, or took part in direct-action and mass-demonstration movements throughout the country.

According to official data for 1990, 6.4 million people participated in environmental activities across the country in January and February alone (Shlapentokh, 2001). During the 1989 Congress of People's Deputies, the first parliament in Soviet history for which freely contested elections were held, "[almost] nine-tenths of the speakers mentioned the vital issues of pollution in their statements and press releases . . . and called for new legislation and additional financing" (Wolfson and Butenko, 1992: 49). Surveys conducted between 1989 and 1991 found that throughout the USSR, environmental problems were deemed priority concerns, and that "informal" environmental groups were believed more trustworthy than the Communist Party or the Soviet government (Peterson, 1993: 195). Between 1986 and 1991, the Soviet Union became more assertive in international environmental policy making. Wolfson and Butenko (1992: 52) even suggest that

> decisive measures to save the ozone layer and many of the cooperative programs [in the global ecological field], particularly those involving industrialized countries, only became feasible after ecological pressure was brought to bear by the Soviet leadership.

The Chernobyl crisis sparked public interest in environmental affairs in the Soviet Union, and the bungled response caused a political firestorm domestically and abroad, putting both party apparatchiks and government bureaucrats on notice. But to what extent, if any, did Chernobyl jump-start new and more effective institutions for environmental protection?

In their influential edited volume, *Institutions for the Earth*, Robert Keohane, Peter Haas, and Marc Levy (1993: 19-20) offer three conditions for the formation and successful operation of institutions for environmental protection: sufficient *concern* to prompt action about the problem at hand; a *contractual environment* in which agreements to address the problem can be made and kept; and institutional *capacity* to successfully redress the problem. In the Soviet case, the shock of the Chernobyl disaster, and in particular, authorities' flawed response, stimulated both popular and governmental *concern* over environmental problems. Governmental efforts to create *contracts* to remedy environmental problems were initiated, notably in the deliberations of the 1989 Congress of People's Deputies. But a variety of constraints, both formal (ineffective administrative reforms) and informal (growing, popular nationalist sentiment and suspicion of government), impeded the government's *capacity* to address these and other environmental crises.

To a limited extent, Soviet authorities *did* manage to engage the public in a dialogue on environmental policy. A number of controversial development plans were postponed or scrapped—such as a scheme to divert Siberian waters to Central Asia. Moreover, in 1989, the State Committee for Environmental Protection (Goskompriroda), a monitoring and regulatory commission, was created by presidential decree. Gorbachev himself won plaudits from the international environmental community for his contributions to global environmental policy making (Wolfson and Butenko, 1992: 53), work he continues as the founder and president of Green Cross International. All the same, most positive environmental outcomes during the late Soviet era were the results of political instability or financial insolvency rather than constructive policy reforms. For example, Gorbachev declared a moratorium on nuclear testing in Kazakhstan only after the attempted anti-Gorbachev coup in 1991, when authorities' capacity to conduct tests was already severely eroded (Janco, 1991). Moreover, and as was true throughout the CEE region, the Soviet economy's downturn in the early 1990s was accompanied by reduced stresses on the environment in Russia and in other FSU republics.

Environmentalists in the Glasnost Vanguard

For a brief few years in the late 1980s and early 1990s, a nascent form of participatory politics emerged in an unexpected place, characterized by mass demonstrations, the formation of popular interest groups and political parties, and the use of mass media as a forum for debate. Previously forbidden forms of political speech were spoken, transmitted, and diffused throughout Soviet society; and though only in embryonic form, a dialogue began between state, civic actors, and Soviet peoples at large. The Soviet Union would appear to have been taking the first tentative steps toward "civil society."

Progress toward more open and democratic forms of politics and policy making in Russia and other Soviet republics was greeted with enthusiasm in the West. And while glasnost's flowering took by surprise many American and European intellectuals, there was a prevailing sense that the Soviet Union was somehow ready for democracy—that Soviet citizens were dormant democrats merely waiting for a thaw.

The anticommunist and antitotalitarian prose of East European and Soviet dissidents from the 1970s and 1980s greatly influenced Western perceptions of glasnost-era political developments. The writings of Vaclav Havel and Adam Michnik in particular stressed the need for popular opposition to oppression. Soviet intellectual dissidents such as Andrei Sakharov and Alexander Solzhenitsyn were highly influential, though more for what they symbolized than what they actually thought.[3] They were not conventional advocates for democracy, but the dissidents' appeals to freedom reminded Americans and others of their own political heritage and inferred the Eastern bloc's untapped potential for democratic pluralism. The political successes of popular activism in Central and Eastern Europe and the USSR in the late 1980s, often achieved without bloodshed, reinforced the idea of civil society as the basis for democratic nation-building.

These charismatic, anti-Soviet voices inspired many donors in the West to imagine great, bottled-up demand for open markets and open society among the Soviet masses. This mind-set formed a backdrop for noneconomic aid programs to the Soviet Union and its successor states.[4] For a variety of reasons, environmental organizations in Russia and elsewhere in the Soviet Union benefited greatly from this perspective.

First, environmentalism had the prestige of being among the first political issues in the late Soviet period to galvanize popular activism. Grassroots organizations' success in challenging the Soviet regime was as much an ideological victory for environmentalists and other activists in the West as it was for cold warriors.

Second, compared to the nationalist and chauvinist movements that by 1990 had come to dominate political discourse in the USSR, environmentalism represented a "safe" or "apolitical" democratic forum that external actors could support. Sponsoring green organizations was a way to promote anticommunist forces (real or imagined) under a general rubric of concern for public well-being and universal rights, without overtly challenging state legitimacy.

Third, the magnitude of Soviet environmental problems was deemed threatening to human health and nature within the Soviet Union and beyond. Chernobyl was a symptom of a much more pervasive problem, as scientists and journalists unveiled acute ecological and health crises throughout the Eastern bloc. The enormity and variety of these problems shocked world leaders and ordinary citizens alike, and the negative implications for regional and even global environmental quality were manifest.

Fourth, the prominence of environmental agendas in mainstream Soviet political discourse and the vibrancy of popular activism merited the West's attention. The dissident writers' sureness about Eastern bloc citizenries' democratic potential were being borne out as "the democratic opposition [became] . . . incessantly visible in public life, [created] political facts by organizing mass actions, [and formulated] alternative programs" (Sargent, 1999: 7). Furthermore, environmental activists were using the media to reach out to the international environmental community for cooperation and support. The growth of environmental movements was a worldwide phenomenon in the late 1980s and early 1990s, with environmental organizations actively seeking partners from all parts of the world (Institute mirovoi ekonomiki, 1998: 195). Pleas from Soviet environmentalists fell on receptive ears.

In the context of late Soviet politics, environmentalism was a prominent feature of a seemingly democratic revolution from below, with provisional and unreliable support from above. Because the form, if not the content, of Soviet activism resembled Western models (more on that content below), many in the

West assumed that glasnost-era civic spiritedness represented the early stages in the evolution of a liberal civic culture.

Ten Years On

American support for economic reforms and civil society initiatives increased after the collapse of the Soviet Union in 1991. Between 1992 and 1999, the United States provided nearly $16 billion in aid to the former Soviet Union. Russia alone received close to $8 billion (U.S. Department of State, 2000). Approximately $25 million of the aid to Russia was spent under the Freedom Support Act, the main legislative vehicle for democracy-building assistance to the FSU (U.S. Department of State, 2000). Freedom Support Act funds supported a variety of programs, from institution-building initiatives for the media and political parties to scholarships for former Soviet scholars. USAID contractors, such as the Institute for Social Renewal and Action in Eurasia (ISAR) and Counterpart International, administered many of these programs, working directly with beneficiaries in various Russian civic organizations. Other bilateral aid agencies and various international and intergovernmental organizations participated in the "transition to democracy" as well, and nearly all of them supported environmental initiatives in one way or another.

The number of nongovernmental organizations in Russia exploded in the 1990s. As of 2001, there were approximately 300,000 registered public organizations involving about 2.5 million citizens in charitable work affecting another 30 million Russians (Domrin, 2001). The Socio-Ecological Union, an umbrella group for environmental NGOs, boasted 293 member organizations throughout Russia, as well as another 43 outside of its borders, including the other former Soviet republics, the United States, and Europe (Socio-Ecological Union, 2001).

Press releases and reports from Western sponsors frequently announce successes in the strengthening of civil society. A 1998 article from ISAR pronounced, "there [has] been growth in both the number and sophistication of NGOs, especially in countries like . . . Russia . . . where NGOs can register, hold travel accounts and have been granted special tax status" (Klose, 1998). Local NGOs' capacities to administer programs have also improved. USAID's 2000 annual report on assistance to the New Independent States (NIS) (U.S. Department of State, 2000: 84) reported helping 6,000 NGOs to:

> [build] up their institutional capacity and their ability to provide services and advocate on behalf of their clients. In FY 2000, these NGOs formed over 200 coalitions . . . and submitted 181 expert commentaries to government officials on policy matters.

Ceteris paribus, the growth of "green" NGOs in Russia shows that environmental activism is a viable possibility there. There are activists working to expose and to oppose policies and practices that injure Russia's environment and to promote positive environmental changes. But a tally of registered environmental NGOs is a crude measure of the salience of these organizations in Russian public life. Henry observes:

> The primary focus of civil society programs thus far has been to increase the total number of NGOs in a transitional society. In this task, donors have been guided by the firm belief that "more NGOs meant more democracy" (Sampson, 1996: 128). In spite of donors' efforts, however, many Russian organizations resemble their Western brethren only superficially, on their business cards and brochures. Many are simply "NGIs," or "nongovernmental individuals"— organizations based on family networks or a charismatic leader. (2001: 10)

A trend indicating growing numbers of Russian NGOs reveals less about these organizations' impact on public life than do verifiable outcomes of NGO activity. As Sievers observes,

> The substantive value of NGOs and other parts of civil society . . . arises neither from their rights as codified nor from their current or prospective existence per se, but from what they actually do in the system in which they exist. (2001: 394)

Essential questions, then, are whether environmental NGOs are facilitating substantive ecological improvements in Russia or are bringing about substantive institutional changes that will lead to such improvements.

The answers are stark: more than ten years of civil society programs have had little effect either on the state of Russia's environment or on domestic environmental or public health policy. This is not to say that Russian environment-oriented civic organizations are not active, or that their efforts are wasted. Rather, they are still too politically weak and the nation's environmental and health problems too overwhelming for these actors to make significant impacts. Moreover, to the extent that certain environmental pressures diminished during the 1990s—such as the decline of emissions of sulfur dioxide and carbon monoxide—these benefits were wrought by economic contraction and not NGO action.

Approximately 30 percent of the population of Russia is exposed to unhealthy levels of polluted air, mostly in the country's urban areas. Respiratory problems caused or exacerbated by air pollution affect thousands of Russians; these same citizens are exposed to abnormally high levels of lead in air, water, and soils. All of Russia's major rivers are classified as polluted, and nearly 40 percent of all water resources in the country are severely contaminated by industrial or domestic wastes (Gosudarstvennyi komitet Rossisskoi Federatsiia po okhrane okruzhaiuschei sredy, 1999).

In addition to peoples' high level of exposure to conventional contaminants like airborne dust and organic pollutants and pathogens in water, Russians are exposed to old pollution risks left by the Soviet military as well as persistent industrial wastes in soils, water, and in the food supply. Among the most worrisome problems are hazards from nuclear wastes. Radioactive materials from the country's military-related nuclear programs contaminate land and water in the Arctic and Pacific Rim regions (Bodrov, 2001; Turnock, 2002). Russians living near military-industrial sites face higher cancer risks, due to their exposure to ionizing radiation (Hertzman, 1995: 45).

According to an environmental update following the Chernobyl accident,

> Children [in the Tula region of Russia] have been diagnosed with fatigue, listlessness, headaches and joint pain, as well as a failure to develop normally. Pregnant women in the region often fail to gain weight properly, and birth defects are more and more frequent. Every tenth child has been diagnosed with thyroid gland abnormalities and official forecasts for the frequency of thyroid cancer have risen; the rise is not expected to peak until 2020. (Cherkasova, 2002: 13)

A 1999 State Committee for Environmental Protection report states blandly, "The decreases in living standards and ecological adversity have a negative influence on public health, especially among children" (Gosudarstvennyi komitet Rossisskoi Federatsiia po okhrane okruzhaiuschei sredy, 1999). Referring to the state of the Russian environment and public health, one scholar concludes, "In our country the ecological situation may be called threatening; to be more correct, it is catastrophic" (Kogai, 2000: 107).

It is unrealistic to expect environmental organizations in Russia to conquer such formidable ecological and epidemiological problems. There are too many other proximate determinants of environmental quality and many of them are beyond the control of grassroots organizations. Russian civic organizations' greatest contributions would presumably come upstream in the policy process, in knowledge-building, consciousness-raising, advocacy, and policy advising roles. More telling indicators of success for the Green movement should therefore be its effects on Russian environmental politics and policy making and the extent it has made Russia's economic development more environmentally friendly.

In the political realm, there is perhaps no more striking example of Russian NGOs' relative powerlessness than in President Vladimir Putin's 2000 decision to dissolve the State Committee for Environmental Protection and the Forest Service and to move these authorities into the Ministry of Natural Resources. The ministry is charged with developing but not conserving the nation's natural resources (Blagov, 2000). Preceding this decision, the country's main environmental authority had already been downsized from a full ministry to a state committee (in 1996). Following the president's action, Russia's minister of natural resources, himself, cast doubt on his agency's ability to take on new environmental regulatory duties (Blagov, 2000).

Environmental NGOs opposed the president's move; more than fifty such groups signed a letter of protest. But the executive order remained intact. Observers contend that intense lobbying by Russian oil and gas interests helped seal the fate of the country's environmental committee (Blagov, 2000). Environmentalists had complained that prospective development of petroleum reserves in the Caspian Sea threatened water quality and rare habitats and sea life. But environmental NGOs were no match for representatives of Russia's most important economic sector.

Douglas Blum (1998: 255) comments on the vast influence that Russian hydrocarbon interests have in the Caspian Sea context. By the late 1990s,

> it had become clear that financial-industrial elites had captured the levers of power, either by acting within approved government channels or by working outside state agencies to thwart uncongenial [environmental] initiatives.

Most of the NGOs' key demands, such as prohibitions on drilling in certain sensitive areas of the sea, were unheeded by state regulators, even when NGOs received strong support from international environmental organizations and private foundations. Leslie Powell (2001: 14) neatly summarizes the constraints on the effectiveness of the latter:

> The weakness of the state with respect to powerful industrial and commercial lobbies, the continual instability and flux of state institutions and elites, and the link between environmental and economic issues all have a limiting effect on the influence of foreign foundations seeking to impact the state of the environment in Russia.

In the early years of the twenty-first century, Russian NGOs came up short in other battles pitting environmentalists against oil and gas interests. A Russian oil company received approval to drill near pristine coastal wetlands off Russia's Curonian Spit—an isthmus of sand along the Baltic Sea and an important habitat for migratory birds and other animals. Though NGOs were allowed to present their case at public hearings, the state ultimately awarded a drilling permit to Russia's partly state-owned oil company, Lukoil (Weir, 2002: 6). On the other hand, NGOs were heartened by having been allowed to participate in an open hearing. Regarding that accomplishment, a Russian lawyer for the region's largest environmental NGO commented, "The legal basis for public input is very new. While we don't think it was used fairly in this case, the process certainly opens opportunities we couldn't have dreamed about before" (Weir, 2002: 6).

Nevertheless, industry received a go-ahead to drill—the same outcome for a much larger and more controversial project involving the development of up to 13 billion barrels of oil off the Russian Pacific island of Sakhalin. Studies by environmentalists, petitions, and testimony from Russian and American scientists did not dissuade authorities in Moscow nor the State Committee of Natural Resources on Sakhalin from issuing drilling permits to a consortium of multinational companies. Environmentalists condemned the developers' plans to transport oil by tanker through the seasonally ice-choked waters near Sakhalin. Scientists produced evidence that seismic blasts used for oil exploration were harming migratory pods of endangered Pacific gray whales, and activists claimed that toxic drilling muds dumped off Sakhalin were responsible for large kills of herring. But regional environmental authorities and regulators in Moscow found another study, funded by industry, to be more persuasive.

In 2001, Russia's State Committee on Fisheries rescinded its rules protecting fisheries in drilling zones off the island's northwestern coast, after research—funded by the oil companies—found the oil-rich area wasn't as valuable a fishery as previously thought. Officials of the federally chartered State Committee of Natural Resources on Sakhalin say they accepted the study results because no other research had been done (Carlton, 2002: A1).[5]

Applying Keohane et al.'s (1993) "three Cs" criteria for institutional effectiveness (i.e., concern, contractability, and capacity), NGOs, scientists, and other civic actors clearly evinced a high level of *concern* about the Sakhalin project's potential hazards. But in this case as well as in the Curonian Spit and Caspian Sea cases, NGOs lacked the *capacity* to seriously affect the industrial permitting process. Moreover, *contractable* arrangements between government and society did not allow NGOs to function effectively. Regarding this latter "C," consider the Sakhalin case, where environmentalists were able to persuade the ministry of Natural Resources in Moscow to declare a moratorium on seismic explosions off Sakhalin, but local authorities on the island rebuffed the ministry and refused to suspend private licenses for such tests (Carlton, 2002: A1).

In all of these cases, NGOs were able to disseminate environment-oriented information to broader audiences in Russia. But in no instance was public concern great enough to make state regulators pause. Indeed, it may be relatively easy for powerful state and economic actors in Russia to ignore environmental NGOs and civic organizations because many ordinary citizens have lost faith in these organizations' effectiveness and are apathetic about public service and volunteerism, generally. According to responses to surveys administered in fourteen regions throughout Russia, public confidence in the efficacy of civic actors' lobbying efforts decreased from 15 percent of respondents in 1995 to 3.5 percent in 1998. Conversely, the percentage of respondents who believed that "effective means to influence the government in Russia do not exist" increased from 42 percent in 1995 to 51.5 percent in 1998 (Petukhov, 1999: 205). Similarly, in response to the question "What [civic] activities have you participated in during the past year?" only 3.1 percent claimed to have taken part in "protests, meetings, or demonstrations" while 65.5 percent claimed they did not participate in any civic activity whatsoever. Another survey revealed that only 1 to 1.5 percent of the population "[were] members of voluntary associations dealing with social welfare services, environment, human rights . . . etc . . . . [It] is evident that Russians demonstrate a very low interest in public self-organization" (Bashkirova, 2001).

These trends do not necessarily mean that public concern about environmental problems has disappeared. Rather, the contract zone between state and society has shrunk since the heady days of the late glasnost era, as policy elites make only halfhearted attempts to invite and incorporate public participation in policy-making institutions. Moreover, the shock of the environmental crisis that galvanized people in the 1980s has been eclipsed by other, more pressing concerns, whether nationalist militarism in Russian border regions or worries about job security and personal safety.

Many environmentalists would concur with Keohane et al.'s assertion that meaningful environmental policy reforms do not occur in the absence of substantial public agitation (1993: 14). If that is the case, then Russia's ongoing environmental malaise is unsurprising. For all of the Western donors' involvement, Russian activists have been unable to sustain popular demands for environmental quality even as the government itself has given the go-ahead for controversial development projects (such as the Caspian, Curonian, and Sakhalin projects) and have abolished the country's main environmental regulatory agency.

Environmental Activism in Russia's New Democracy

Russia's environmental reforms are sluggish and most Russians are indifferent to environmental issues—paradoxical tendencies for a nation whose founding legal document affords environmental rights and privileges not found in most European constitutions.

Article 30 of the Russian Constitution unequivocally states that "Everyone will have the right to association. . . . The freedom of public associations' activities is guaranteed." Article 31 guarantees the right of citizens to "gather peacefully, without weapons, in order to hold rallies, meetings, demonstrations, marches, and pickets." Strikingly, Article 42 guarantees each citizen "the right to a decent environment, reliable information about the state of the environment, and compensation for damage caused to one's health or property by ecological offenses." Finally, Article 58 explicitly obliges each citizen to "protect nature and the environment" (Konstitutsiia Rossiiskoi Federatsii).

The Law on Environmental Protection, passed in 2001 and put in force in 2002, accords similar rights and responsibilities. Article 12 outlines a fairly broad mandate for environmental organizations, including the right to hold public demonstrations and advise and petition the government on matters of environmental concern (Ministerstvo prirodnyx resursov Rossiisskoi Federatsii, 2002).

Russian NGOs' legal protections are more precarious in practice. What NGO activities are allowed is not only prescribed (and proscribed) by the government, but even spontaneous social gatherings—no matter the impetus for such assemblies or the substance of the meetings—must be preauthorized by the state or organizers could be subject to prosecution.

Russian law distinguishes between different types of organization, each of which is governed by specific rules. The 1995 Law on Public Associations pertains to secular, not-for-profit organizations such as environmental advocacy groups. Although reaffirming citizens' right to "voluntarily establish public associations," the law prescribes cumbersome registration procedures for politically oriented nongovernmental organizations and there are clauses empowering the state to dissolve such organizations under particular circumstances (Human Rights Online, 1995). Moreover, politically oriented NGOs lack tax exempt status in Russia.

Government actions against free speech have created other hazards for environmental causes. The trials of Alexander Nikitin and Grigory Pasko are two widely publicized examples of the state's use of coercive power against perceived threats to state interests (which also happen to be public and environmental interests). Nikitin is a scientist and environmentalist, Pasko an investigative journalist. Both were arrested in the mid-1990s on treason and espionage charges, Nikitin for his efforts to publicize the mishandling of nuclear wastes by the Soviet Northern Fleet, Pasko for publishing similar reports on the Russian Pacific Fleet. The Russian Supreme Court threw out the charges against Nikitin in 2000 (Gauslaa, 2001).

Though many hoped that the outcome in Nikitin's case would set a legal precedent, it apparently had little influence on Pasko's fate. On 25 December 2001, a military court sentenced the latter to a four-year jail term for international espionage. Domestic and international human rights groups assert that the trial and the court's finding were political vendettas against a journalist who embarrassed the Russian military. The verdict itself relied on a secret decree issued by the Ministry of Defense. Pasko's punishment served to warn not only investigative journalists and environmentalists, but all politically oriented individuals and organizations of the perils of private enquiry into closely guarded state secrets.

The government's seeming insensitivity to free speech and citizens' right to know in the Nikitin and Pasko cases and its determination to keep secret the military's potential environmental misdeeds suggest that under certain circumstances Russian constitutional rights are largely paper rights. Nikitin and Pasko tested newly enacted constitutional guarantees, and their actions elicited an old-fashioned, Soviet-era response: they were arrested and accused of spying. If there is a recognizable pattern in these cases, it is that civil society is allowed to subsist under conditions agreeable to the state. But this formula trivializes the Western notion of civil society, namely, that there are arenas of political action, public enquiry, cultural activity, and economic affairs outside of the direct control of the state.

The Case of the Civil Forum

On 21-22 November 2001 President Vladimir Putin convened the first conference of the Civil Forum, a civil society support organization sponsored directly
by his office. Representatives of more than 4,000 civic associations from
throughout Russia attended, including many that were, to some degree, antago-
nistic toward the federal government. The Civil Forum's mission was to "com-
bine the strengths and opportunities of Russian non-commercial organizations to
form a permanently active civic chamber" (Grazhdanskii Forum, 2001). The
forum promised to support the country's many civic organizations and to facilitate coordination between them and between the groups and the government to
redress societal ills. It also declared that:

> If the result of this discussion will be constructive solutions facilitating the dia-
> logue between the government and society, then the Forum will become an im-
> portant step in the development of civic initiatives, civic institutions, civic
> thinking, and the securing of civil peace in the country. (Grazhdanskii Forum,
> 2001)

The inauguration of the forum was something of a wonder. At a preliminary
June meeting, in which the framework for the organization was developed, representatives from only twenty-eight civic associations attended, among them the
Union of Philatelists, the "Virtuosi of Moscow" chamber orchestra, the Union of
Beekeepers, and the vice president of Alfa Bank. Other attendees were a mixture
of charitable, scientific, advocacy, and professional groups—including the Russian Red Cross/Red Crescent and Interlegal, a Western-sponsored legal research
and aid group. No environmental organizations were present (Grazhdanskii Forum, 2001). A press release from the Socio-Ecological Union declared that,
"They invited those who cannot say anything unpleasant to the President," and
that many of the more established or prominent advocacy organizations were
intentionally "not invited," including the Russian Union of Journalists, the Moscow Helsinki Group, the Glasnost Defense Foundation, and the Socio-
Ecological Union itself (Zabelin, 2001).

Then something happened between June and November. The "tasks of the
Forum were in principle changed; real civic associations were included in its
plans" (Arkhangelsky, 2001). The conspicuously overlooked NGOs were invited, and by opening day of the forum's convention, all of the most prestigious
Russian organizations were allowed to participate. A series of conference round-
tables were dedicated to environmental issues including one on the creation of
an "Environmental Doctrine for Russia" (Grazhdanskii Forum, 2001). Putin
himself declared:

> I understand—representatives of the government do too, believe me—that civil
> society cannot be established at the state's initiative, at the state's will, much
> less in accordance with the state's plans. Moreover, I consider attempts to form

civil society in this manner unproductive, impossible, and even dangerous. . . . Civil society should have its own foundation, it should feed on the spirit of freedom. (Putin, 2001)

This is among the most unambiguous statements about civil society by any leader of a Soviet successor state. It suggests that the president recognizes the importance of civic organizations' autonomy vis-à-vis the state. It also infers that NGOs make an impact on politics in Russia, and that their roles may be evolving into something different from what Western aid practitioners had conceived.

Rather than functioning as completely independent and autonomous organizations, Putin's conception is that nongovernmental organizations are involved in the collective act of nation-building and that the state is obliged to provide financial and moral support to this cause. And while NGOs benefit from state largess, they do not surrender their freedom to petition and cajole the government.

Taken at face value, the Civil Forum promises greater possibilities for horizontal integration between NGOs (or "noncommercial organizations" as it translates from Russian), and greater vertical communication between them and the government. This could benefit many civic actors who endured a decade of nonrecognition by the administration of former president Yeltsin and who had virtually no constructive engagement with national governmental agencies.

One Russian observer had a more cynical view of the president's intentions for the forum:

Kremlin officials say that if anyone wants to raise controversial issues at the forum, they're free to do so and can speak their minds. The main thing is that by the end of the forum, the president should have a loyal, organized civil society ready to give all his policies its full support. (Pinsker, 2001)

A St. Petersburg-based human rights activist echoed this opinion, warning, "The real fear is that the state will seek to implement the dream of a 'civil society' that does not permit itself to criticize the government" (Pustintsev, 2001).

Skepticism is warranted. In principle, a state-sponsored program like the Civil Forum could be an efficient conduit of governmental support to the country's many civic associations and a means to promote civil society's institutionalization without dependence on foreign support. But the government's "big tent" approach to constituting the Civil Forum—it is an eclectic group that includes service providers, political activists, professional associations, and hobbyists—combines organizations with very different missions, interests, and societal functions. If the forum becomes the primary—or sole—avenue whereby members access and obtain support from the state, then policy reform-oriented organizations, including many environmental groups, will be competing with myriad other actors for attention. Lumping together every kind of civic organization dilutes the collective voice of like-minded associations and ignores the different aims, purposes, and modes of operating that make a Socio-Ecological Union very different from a chamber orchestra. Moreover, cases like Nikitin's and Pasko's, which have sullied the government's reputation among human rights groups, journalists, and environmentalists, have also increased doubts about the credibility of and confidence in the Civil Forum.

Opportunities for popular activism in Russia are relatively abundant compared to the small arenas for civic activity permitted in most other parts of the FSU. But in Russia, the pieces are coming into place for the establishment of a vertical state hierarchy to regulate civic associations. A Russian activist commented on the situation as of 2002,

> In the past few years the state has grown much stronger and has managed to return to its traditional position at the head of everything . . . the scope for public involvement in decision-making is narrowing. In fact, it's being locked into limited and formal mechanisms . . . which are totally under control [by the state]. (Weir, 2002)

Perhaps the Nikitin and Pasko court cases describe the real measure of civil society's progress in Russia, and not formal, organizational milestones, like the creation of the Civil Forum.

It is still too early to gauge the impact that the Civil Forum will have on Russian public affairs and civic life, nor at this early stage is it possible to fully understand the president's motives in creating such a congregation. Even assuming his intentions are noble, it is unclear what civil society actors can actually accomplish in Russia, especially as "civil society" is a Western concept only recently transplanted into Russian society.

Civil Society in Theory and Practice

Civil society is a centuries-old concept with origins in the writings of Enlightenment philosophers. The modern understanding of civil society—or the interpretations most familiar to contemporary Western intellectuals—rely partly on John Locke, who argued for the primacy of individual liberty over state power and a balance of power between government and the governed. Hegel later located civil society as the political space between the family (the most basic unit of human organization) and the state (the highest) (Petrova, 1999: 138). The American formulation is based in large part on the observations of Alexis de Tocqueville in his *Democracy in America*. Tocqueville observed causal connections between civic vitality and the shape, substance, and quality of public life. He attested,

> In their political associations the Americans, of all conditions, minds, and ages, daily acquire a general taste for association and grow accustomed to the use of

it. . . . They afterwards transfer to civil life the notions they have thus acquired and make them subservient to a thousand purposes. (Tocqueville, 1990: 119)

Associational life is, to Tocqueville, an organic outgrowth of the way Americans think and act. Americans' appetite for association permeates everything they do, from mixing with their neighbors to relating to their government.

Civil society as a development aid paradigm came to the fore only within the last twenty years. Premised on the notion that vigorous civic association is requisite for a healthy democracy, it advocates promotion and protection of indigenous civic initiatives, and the free and open exchange of ideas both within and between associations of civic-minded actors and the state. It is foremost

> an ideal-typical category . . . that both describes and envisages a complex and dynamic ensemble of legally protected nongovernmental institutions that tend to be non-violent, self-organizing, self-reflexive, and permanently in tension with each other and with the state institutions that frame, constrict and enable their activities. (Keane, 1998: 6)

There is no consensus among experts about how civil society should be nurtured and sustained in an advanced democracy. Fostering civil society becomes more complicated still when the context is a nascent democracy on the outskirts of Europe. At a superficial level, the notion that civil society actors are somehow different from state actors is appreciated by both Western donors and Russian aid recipients, and this common understanding may persuade them that they are speaking the same language. But as per the specific functions of civil society, for example, regarding civic actors' relations with the state, Western and Russian participants in aid institutions tend to conceive of different things. Thus, for example, Russian authorities tend to conceptualize civil society in statist terms while donors view it as the nurturing of nonstate bases of power.

Western donors' and Russian recipients' perspectives diverge on fundamental notions of civil society, such as the organizational features and functions of NGOs.[6] Russian NGOs' organizational missions, structures, and policy strategies have baffled many of their counterparts in the West. The confusion begins with the different ways that Russians and Westerners define "nongovernmental organization."

The expression nongovernmental organization dates back to the founding of the United Nations. According to Article 71 of the UN Charter and subsequent rules of procedure, NGOs are "consultative bodies" to certain UN organizations and councils, rather than advocacy or agenda-setting bodies, per se. In practice, this definition went by the wayside many years ago, since from almost the beginning, NGOs *were* advocates for particular interests or policies.

Experts' notions of what NGOs are and what they do depart from the United Nation's more circumscribed definitions. NGOs, according to Anna Vakil, are "self-governing, not-for-profit organizations that are geared toward improving the quality of life of the disadvantaged people" (Jordan and Van Tuijl, 2000:

2052). Robert Putnam (1993: 91) defines them as citizen initiatives that instill habits of "cooperation, solidarity, and public spiritedness" and that constitute coherent interest groups.

According to the Federal Law on Non-Commercial Organizations, passed by the Russian Duma in 1995,

> Non-commercial organizations may be organized to carry out social, charitable, cultural, educational, scientific and administrative purposes, with such missions as the protection of public health, development of physical training and sports, satisfaction of spiritual and other non-material civic needs, protection of citizens' and organizations' legal rights and interests, the resolution of disputes and conflicts, rendering of legal aid, as well as other purposes dedicated to the public good. (Human Rights Online, 1995)

Unlike Vakil's or other Western conceptions, Russian law distinguishes "noncommercial organizations" from "policy-oriented" and "religious" groups, with different sets of laws regulating each of these classes of organizations. Russian law also blurs the line between state and nonstate organizations, which is at odds with the Western notion of nongovernmental organizations as interlocutors between the individual and the state. For example, almost one-fourth of the Russian environmental NGOs listed on Priroda.ru, the Russian Ministry of Natural Resources' Internet website, are directly affiliated with the state; the rest consist of "children's," "international," "civic" (obschestvenie) and other organizations (Ministerstvo prirodnyx resursov Rossiisskoi Federatsii, 2002). Most of the organizations with ties to the government boast no more than a handful of members and have little funding.[7] Some have received assistance from external donors, but most are struggling experiments in civic self-reliance. Even organizations with similar missions (teachers' associations in different schools) rarely network with one another, and most do not outlive the early enthusiasm of their founders (Richter, 1999). Laura Henry attributes some of this noncooperation to competition for donor resources. She writes:

> The way in which the first grant competitions were administered led to the proliferation of small groups and a competitive environment among green organizations. Groups were reluctant to cooperate for fear that in sharing information and projects they would lose their comparative advantage or devalue their contribution. Under the conditions of those programs, it made sense for activists in a medium-sized Russian organization with two project ideas to splinter into two smaller groups in order to maximize their funding potential. Another common strategy was for one activist to found several organizations, each with a slightly different name, so that each organization could apply to the same grant program. (2001: 7)

Competition for scarce grant resources undoubtedly discourages cooperation among environmental NGOs in Russia. A related determinant of noncooperation is that NGO actors often do not trust one another. Mistrust is shaped as much by competition for grants as it is by Russian cultural norms. This variable of trust has not been adequately investigated by Russian development experts; failure to understand it is a serious liability for sponsors of civil society aid in Russia since trust would appear to be vital to the construction of social capital. We explore trust and mistrust in Russian civic organizations in the next section.

Trust as a Scarce Resource

Trust is lacking between state and society in post-Soviet Russia; the Pasko and Nikitin cases are archetypes of mistrust. But trust is also in short supply between Russian NGOs, which greatly complicates the adaptation of an idealized Western civil society to Russian society.[8]

In the United States and many Western European countries, a sort of "impersonal trust" is an accepted norm—it is almost presumed that very different people from disparate backgrounds can come together for a common purpose and trust one another to cooperate on specific organizational and work-related tasks. Trust is central to collective action, according to a well-established literature (Fukuyama, 1995; Bowles and Gintis, 1998; Putnam, 1993).

However, Western accounts describe the difficulty of establishing trusting professional relationships in the post-Soviet NGO community. A report by Ruth Greenspan Bell on the results of an American-Russian environmental NGO workshop in Moscow noted that "personal trust is a condition precedent to establishing a working relationship" between civil society actors; yet many Russian participants were skeptical of American claims to have "cooperated successfully with people of diverse political opinions, lifestyles and tastes who they didn't know at all" (Bell, 2001: 9). In assessing the lack of cooperation between civic actors in Central and Eastern Europe, Wedel observed (2001: 11) that "Central and Eastern European groups often were unwilling to share information or otherwise cooperate with anyone who had not reached the status of personal friend."

Findings from a survey published in 2000 describe the ways in which Russians value and express trust. Respondents deemed socialization or "informal human communication" to be very important; but most expressed "very little trust in fellow-citizens" and consequently, "it makes the formation of social ties more difficult" (Bashkirova, 2001).[8] Trust in the Soviet era was typically nurtured in small circles of close acquaintances who helped each other both professionally and personally—practices not unlike those propagated by many NGOs in Russia.

Between 1993 and 1998, Abrams, coauthor of this chapter, worked professionally and collaboratively with NGOs in Russia and Kazakhstan. Many of these organizations were either outgrowths of school or university faculties, research institutes, or other professional groupings, in which nearly all the members already worked with one another.[9] NGOs tend to be small in Russia and other FSU republics; at times, their collective voice is more valuable than their individual voices. Nevertheless, Abrams encountered difficulty in developing trusting relations between like-minded organizations; trust generally required a period of intense socialization. Moreover, on an anecdotal basis, Abrams observed that the degree of socialization within individual organizations, that is, the extent to which association members socialized outside of business hours, was much greater than among U.S. organizations.

A synonym of trust is confidence, and evidence suggests that Russian activists have little confidence in ordinary Russians' abilities to effectively participate in environmental affairs. Western observers have reported a "technocratic disdain" among environmentalists that prevents them from reaching out to their constituents and customers for political and economic cooperation. With reference to the U.S.-Russian NGO workshop, Bell observed that very few Russian environmentalists "really seemed to take citizen participation seriously" (Bell, 2001: 12). As opposed to the American participants, who emphasized the democratic process as a tool for environmental decision making, the "emphasis on process and interest groups was not satisfying for the Russians. [Scientific solutions] appeared to them more reliable than the uncertainties of process and interest group engagement" (Bell, 2001: 11). Henry's research on Russian NGOs' attitudes toward public outreach and membership drives are instructive. Drawing on her own interviews with NGO officials and summarizing the work of other researchers, she writes:

> When asked about his organization's relations with the local community, one St. Petersburg environmentalist answered with this proverb: "To make a deal with a Russian man, beat him with money or a big stick." In other words, motivating people with ideas is futile; only economic incentives or punishment gets the public's attention. Other groups have reported that the public relates to them with suspicion or simply is not interested. . . . A St. Petersburg activist and a Russian scholar, through their own survey research, received responses from environmentalists such as: "We do not know what to say to people and what to call them for"; "We do not know where to find interested people, nor do we know what to suggest to them"; "We do not know how to mobilize people for constructive action and are afraid of misunderstandings"; "We do not have experience talking to people" (Tysiachniouk and Karpov, 1998). Considering this lack of a social base for NGOs, one longtime environmental activist from southern Russia goes so far as to say that there is no environmental movement in Russia today. She states that as new organizations have sprung up, they have "formed what they called the third sector and they work without, or almost without, connections with the population" (Luneva, 1998). (2001: 14-16)

Part of the problem, Bell proposes (2001: 8), is that the Western notion of "compromise" which "is the core of U.S. decision-making" has a negative connotation in Russian. "There is a belief in Russia . . . that there is one Truth, and that you are supposed to try and achieve it, not compromise it." She adds, "[Russians] had great difficulty believing that government agencies and NGOs would work together voluntarily" because they saw "local NGOs primarily as protestors, not constructive participants" (Bell, 2001: 8). The public's narrow view of what NGOs stand for and what they do serves to close the triangle of mistrust between state, civic organizations, and the public at large. The West's failure to understand this context of mutual misgiving goes some distance in explaining the failure of Western civil society aid programs in Russia. Donors and other sponsors discovered that the spirit of mistrust, so palpable in Dostoevsky's *Crime and Punishment*, more accurately described the Russian context for aid programs than did depictions of a Russian nation ready and eager to create social capital.

Reappraising Civil Society in the Russian Context

Percy B. Lehning (1998: 27) cites three "general prerequisites" for the development of civil society: a liberal constitutional democracy; socioeconomic factors that include a market economy; and sociocultural factors, including an inclination toward public spiritedness. Of the three, the last condition is especially lacking in contemporary Russia and hence, it is unsurprising that the fortunes of civil society actors have followed a mostly downward trend since the late Soviet period. Without a history of political liberalism; without a cultural predisposition toward civic activism; and with legacies of patriarchal decision making in most arenas of public and private life, there is mostly sterile ground for the cultivation of civil society in post-Soviet Russia.

Much as Adam Michnik and other dissident intellectuals had intended, Russian civil society as it emerged in the late 1980s was an antistate movement. This is crucial for understanding the phenomenon of Soviet popular activism under Gorbachev and its subsequent demise. Western sponsors of local NGOs assumed they were providing moral and financial support for a budding liberal civic culture. However, it was not civil society or liberalism that defeated Soviet power, but nationalist separatism, combined with the political opportunism of various party and state elites (Artyomova, 2002).

Soviet environmentalism in nearly all regions was informed by a rejection of state authority in favor of local autonomy or independence (Wolfson and Butenko, 1992: 44-50). Soviet ideology and policies failed to deliver promised economic improvements, the government proved unable to manage crises such as Chernobyl, and glasnost could not keep pace with citizens' pent-up demands for political reforms. Even in the late Soviet period, citizens had few safe and reliable political or legal instruments to challenge governmental policies. Environmental agitation became one of the few default options. "Organizing traditional mass demonstrations . . . [became] the most visible popular tactic . . . [and]

served to send the most potent messages to the authorities" (Peterson, 1993: 208).

The economic collapse that rumbled through the former Soviet Union beginning in the early 1990s, and the disruption of political and economic ties between the former republics—in some cases sparking violence between and within them—marginalized environmental activism as citizens became preoccupied with meeting immediate needs. More broadly, grassroots political activism stalled in the 1990s before it had a chance to become an organic feature of Russian politics, and civic associations lost both members and a central place in the public's imagination. Some NGOs survived the early years of post-Soviet transition, only to be distrusted by ordinary Russians and misunderstood by sponsors and ostensible allies in the NGO and donor communities in the West.

Though many in number, Russian NGOs, including environmental NGOs, are marginal actors in official policy-making arenas, and their activities are nearly invisible to ordinary Russians. For NGOs to prosper, and to become more effective in Russian environmental policy institutions, they must persuade Russian rank and file about the primacy of a healthy environment (Keohane et al.'s notion of *concern*); make the case to citizens, the state, and economic actors that environmental interests must be enrolled in public policy-making (*contracting*); and demonstrate the intellectual, moral, and organizational wherewithal to effectively participate in policy institutions (*capacity*).

Moreover, if civic organizations are to succeed, they will most likely do so by relying on their own resources and will, sustained by local demand for their work, and not because foreign donors believe NGOs are a good idea. Research on the performance of civic organizations finds that "[the] most successful local organizations represent indigenous participatory initiatives in relatively cohesive local communities," while organizations "implanted" from the outside had a "high failure rate" (Putnam, 1993: 91).

Anecdotal evidence suggests that, indeed, "homegrown" experiments in self-reliant environmental activism are among the most promising bases for diffusing environmental norms in Russia. In the context of the Caspian Sea, for example, Douglas Blum notes the relatively successful efforts of conservationist forces in Astrakhan—a Caspian port city that is a center for both the commercial fishing and petroleum industries. In the drive to ramp up oil production in the region, local fishers and environmentalists were on the defensive. However, "Fishing interests represent a large constituency, and there is widespread recognition that the Oblast depends on the ecological well-being of the basin" (Blum, 1998: 257). In this case, local government officials mediated between environmentalists, fishers, and oil development interests. While cooperation did not always proceed smoothly nor were the results equally satisfactory to all parties, the Astrakhan context represents a rare instance where Russian environmentalists' concerns resonated with other resource-based interests (namely, fishers) and inspired action by local government. Moreover, foreign aid played little or no role in the formation of problem-solving institutions.

It may be in the long-term interest of Russia's NGOs to hold at arm's length the political agendas and nonessential project aid of certain donors, foundations, and international NGOs. In the 1990s, Russian activists all but internalized the role of supplicant to Western aid sponsors, and as a consequence, struggled to create self-sustaining organizations. The appearance that Russian NGOs were dependent on the West and beholden to Western interests diminished NGOs' standing among the Russian state and society at large. Henry suggests (2001: 13) that Russian NGOs' reliance on Western aid dampened these organizations' incentives to reach out to local communities and develop membership bases.

Whether or not "homegrown" environmental initiatives are more viable than those sponsored by Western donors, even the most well-managed environmental organizations, including those with vast popular support, will be handicapped by bad laws or by government agencies that fail to enforce good laws. President Putin and other Russian leaders have called for the "rule of law" in Russia, but it remains to be seen whether the government can foster a "civic-friendly" rule of law, and whether public and private external actors can help advance such a complex and multifaceted endeavor. The answer to the latter question depends partly on whether donors and other sponsors of Russian NGOs have learned from their mistakes.

Conclusion

Barbara Connolly writes:

> [We] need to recognize the possibility that donor governments or some elements within them sometimes care more about the *appearance* of doing something to solve an important international environmental problem than they care about finding viable solutions to the problem itself. (1996: 333)

The Soviet Green movement thrived in the 1980s because people were angry and frustrated—for more reasons than ecology alone—and were demanding attention from the government in the narrow political space available to them. Over the past decade, the West has sponsored the remnants of that movement, indulging the donors' aspirations to construct a civil society in Russia that had never before existed. As Connolly suggests, some of the aid sent to NGOs and other civic actors was symbolic, since flows of noneconomic aid to Russia were relatively small, planning was rushed, and objectives often lacked precision.

Despite its failings, the impetuses for civil society-oriented aid were laudable, particularly the idea that citizens' participation in Russian public affairs should involve much more than just elections and economic reforms. But inadvertently, Western aid may be fostering what President Putin's Civil Forum has been accused of propagating—a class of bland NGO "professionals" who lack popular support, who are marginalized by genuinely powerful political actors in Russia, but who are dependent on the latter for support and approbation.

Neither the United States nor any other Western donor is primarily responsible for Russia's environmental well-being. That this chapter has focused on external influences on Russian environmental policy-making institutions is itself an indication of Russia's domestic environmental policy vacuum. Russian policymakers have attended primarily to economic development priorities with only token concern for the country's long-term environmental condition (Blagov, 2000). At the same time, the authorities treated environmental activists and whistleblowers with paranoia-tinged contempt. At best, environmental activists were ignored; at worst, they were deemed threats to national security. The results were the compromising of environmental quality, the democratic process, and public faith in the political system.

It is conceivable that international environmental norms will help persuade the Russian state to take environmental concerns more seriously. Russia's neighbors to the immediate west, for example, must clean up their environments and strengthen domestic environmental institutions to gain entry to the European Union. Russia is not an EU candidate. However, Russia *has* developed a long-term protocol of cooperation with the EU known as the EU-Russia Partnership and Cooperation Agreement. Part of that accord obliges both Russia and the EU to "improve" Russian environmental laws to "Community standards" (European Commission, 1997: title VII, article 69, para. 3).

Russia has other public relations-oriented incentives to become more environmentally responsible. It seeks recognition and respect as a leader in world affairs, and presumably, aspires to have self-reliant, independent, professional environmental organizations enrolled in the formidable task of cleaning up Russia's environment. Pessimists might retort that Russia already enjoys an ill-begotten public relations advantage, considering that the international community is more reluctant to condemn the environmentally problematic policies of the post–Soviet Russian regime than of its Communist predecessor (Blagov, 2002).

The many shortcomings of the civil society institution-building experience in Russia should not overshadow real accomplishments made by Western-sponsored civic organizations in that country. In the environmental arena, some programs have made an impact in public affairs. Educational and professional exchanges are notable examples. Exchanges help forge personal and professional links between participants and their sponsors, and between the participants themselves. Russian alumni of the Tahoe-Baikal Institute, for example, have gone on to assume leadership posts in a variety of environment-related organizations in Russia. No less important, most alumni, both American and Russian,

> remain in touch with TBI headquarters, as well as each other, forming a vital support network that serves to enhance the TBI program, as well as providing

venues for TBI participants to investigate career opportunities. (Tahoe-Baikal Institute, 2002)

For Russia, a country in which professional cooperation is often forged in networks of families, friends, and coworkers, and where NGOs are often small groupings of like-minded specialists, collaborative programs like those of the Tahoe-Baikal Institute have obvious benefits.

One positive outcome of the past ten-plus years of development assistance to Russian NGOs is that Western sponsors have a clearer conception of the "winners" and "losers" among their recipients. The winners are those that, like the Tahoe-Baikal Institute and Socio-Economic Union, have been genuine participants in Russian policy-making arenas, have trained participants to assume leadership positions in the public, private, and not-for-profit sectors, and have reached out to other civic organizations and to the public at large.

Western-sponsored educational and knowledge-building programs do have important roles to play, especially as they raise public awareness, counter ignorance, and counterbalance information disseminated by media outlets owned or controlled by powerful special interests.[10] All the same, education- and awareness-oriented aid is of limited value if it fails to induce and sustain public demands for institutional reforms. It is one thing to learn about environmental problems and another thing to do something about them. As was true in the late 1980s, activists are the best candidates to add intensity to public demands and organize and channel those demands to politicians and lawmakers.

Nevertheless, for the most part, NGOs remain marginal actors in Russian politics and policy making. External aid programs intended to raise the political profile and improve the effectiveness of civil society actors often missed their marks in the 1990s. Reengineering noneconomic aid for the region, whether it is aid for environmentalists or other societal actors, will require not merely technical fixes, but a wholesale reexamination of Russian recipients' interests, values, modes of operating, their perceptions of their roles as agents of change, and their views of state-society relations. This reexamination will reveal that values as basic as trust and strategies as commonplace as compromise mean very different things to Russian and Western civic actors. Working constructively with Russian NGOs requires that Western advisers and donors appreciate Russians' more personalistic notions of trust and their almost instinctive doubt about the merits of compromise. Western partners must also recognize environmentalists' and other activists' deep skepticism about collaboration between state and societal actors.

Add to this list Russian NGOs' tendencies to "go it alone," to avoid networking, to eschew outreach to ordinary citizens, and to perceive Western organizational allies as providers of funds, first, and as programmatic partners, second. These might be deemed daunting initial "field conditions" for any prospective donor, foundation, or transnational NGO. But they *do* describe the Russian context, and the West's failure to understand that context in the 1990s partly explains the very modest accomplishments of environmentalists and other societal actors in the early years of the new century.

Notes

1. We distinguish between formal and informal institutions, as per North (1990: 4-5). Formal institutions are the "official" rules that humans devise; informal institutions are "unofficial" codes of conduct and social conventions.

2. After the failed coup d'état in Moscow in August 1991, donors quickly mobilized aid resources for Russia and other FSU republics. Very often, routine policy analysis and program preassessments were waived in the rush. At USAID, for example, aid officers in the agency's NIS and Europe Bureaus were authorized to use an accelerated project review process. These efforts to expedite aid flows, however well-intentioned, occurred at a cost to thorough planning and preparation, led to overlapping programs and rivalry among aid implementers, and confusion among Russian and other former Eastern bloc aid recipients (Wedel, 2001: 34; U.S. General Accounting Office, 2000; U.S. General Accounting Office, 1995).

3. Sakharov did not so much advocate popular dissent as he did individual conscience and the rule of law. Solzhenitsyn is a Russian neotraditionalist whose periodic xenophobic harangues and disdain for American materialist values are nearly as well known as are his classic anti-Soviet tracts.

4. "Open Markets, Open Societies" was the universal theme (and pervasive slogan) adopted by the United States Agency for International Development for its CEE and NIS aid programs in the early 1990s.

5. Scientists and some government officials condemned the industry-sponsored study, calling it biased. Among other problems, the study allegedly considered prospective impacts on permanent fish populations found near proposed drilling sites, but not on migratory fish, including commercially important species like salmon. Also, the study focused on likely impacts on fish without examining effects on other parts of the Sakhalin coastal ecosystem, critics alleged (Carlton, 2002: A1).

6. Aid participants' conflicting perceptions of NGOs and their societal roles have been discussed elsewhere in the development literature (e.g., UN, 1998). Consider this anecdote from Africa: "A young man thrusts his crudely printed calling card at the visitor. After his name are printed three letters: NGO. 'What do you do?' the visitor asks. 'I have formed an NGO.' 'Yes, but what does it do?' 'Whatever they want. I am waiting for some funds and then I will make a project'" (Economist, 2000: 25).

7. St. Petersburg, for example, is host city to hundreds of NGOs; yet most have only a few active members. Relatively large membership rolls usually list no more than one or two hundred names (Negosudarstvennie ekologicheskie organizatsii Sankt-Peterburga, 2002).

8. Much as Bashkirova documented bad rapport between NGOs and ordinary Russians, she also detected citizens' potent mistrust of organs of the state, skepticism of most news outlets, and apathy toward grassroots public participation. In Russia, "Such democratic institutions as parliament and mass media are generally distrusted" and most citizens "do not believe their membership in political parties or movements can change anything" (Bashkirova, 2001).

9. A review of the St. Petersburg Nongovernmental Organizations list (Negosu-darstvennie ekologicheskie organizatsii Sankt-Peterburga, 2002) verifies the close affilia-tions that most of that city's NGOs have with extant scholarly, business, or research insti-tutions.

10. In the early twenty-first century, independent media outlets in Russia, especially those that reached a wide audience, were increasingly rare. In 2001, the government forced the takeover of Russia's only nationwide independent television network and closed two leading print publications (Csongos, 2001).

References

Arkhangelsky, Alexander. 2001. "Dogovor na ponyatiyakh." *Izvestia*. 21 November. www.izvestia.ru/rubr.cgi?idr=522&idbl=&id=9919. Accessed 22 November 2001.

Artyomova, T. 2002. "Eko-dvizheniia Rossii na vzglyad eko-zhurnalista." Bulletin *Eko-logiia i prava cheloveka*, no. 637, 23 February. www.index.org.ru/othproj/eco/637.html. Accessed 10 March 2002.

Bashkirova, Elena. 2001. "Value Change and Survival of Democracy in Russia (1995-2000)." ROMIR Consulting and PR. www.romir.ru/eng/value-change.htm. Accessed 10 November 2001.

Bell, Ruth Greenspan. 2001. *Reaching across the Communication Gulf: Reflections on the Challenges of Environmental Assistance Programs*. Discussion Paper 01-05. Washington, D.C.: Resources for the Future.

Blagov, Sergei. 2000. "Environment-Russia: Environmental Protection Agency Gets Axe." *Global Information Network*, 29 May. Lexis-Nexis News/World News Li-brary. Accessed 30 August 2002.

———. 2002. "WSSD-Russia: NGOs Challenge Development Claims." *Inter Press Ser-vice*, 21 August. Lexis-Nexis News/World News Library. Accessed 30 August 2002.

Blum, Douglas. 1998. "The Russian Trade-Off: Environment and Development in the Caspian Sea." *Journal of Environment and Development*, vol. 7, no. 3: 248-277.

Bodrov, Oleg. 2001. "Kakie iaderniie otkhody strashnee—chuzhie ili svoi?" Bulletin *Ekologiia i prava cheloveka*, no. 537, 9 November. www.index.org.ru/othproj/eco/537.html. Accessed 20 November 2001.

Bowles, Samuel, and Herbert Gintis. 1998. "The Moral Economy of Communities: Struc-tured Populations and the Evolution of Pro-Social Norms." *Evolution and Human Behavior*, vol. 19, no. 1: 3-25.

Carlton, Jim. 2002. "Stymied in Alaska, Oil Producers Flock to a Newer Frontier." *Wall Street Journal*, 4 September: A1.

Cherkasova, Maria. 2002. "Environmental Effects on Children's Health: An Adult Re-sponsibility." *Give and Take Quarterly*, vol. 5, no. 1: 13.

Connolly, Barbara. 1996. "Increments for the Earth: The Politics of Environmental Aid," in Robert O. Keohane and Marc A. Levy (eds.), *Institutions for Environmental Aid: Pitfalls and Promise*. Cambridge, MA: MIT Press: 327-365.

Csongos, Frank T. 2001. "Russia: U.S. Voices Concern over Media Freedom." *Radio Free Europe/Radio Liberty*, 19 April. truthnews.net/media/2001_04_russian_media.html Accessed 1 February 2004.

Davison, Ronald N. 1991. "Natural Change: Soviet Environmental Groups and the Roots of Reform," in *USCAR Reports: Cleaning Up the Environment in the Soviet Union* and *Eastern Europe*, vol. 1, no. 4. Washington, D.C.: The Center for American-Eurasian Studies and Relations. www.eurasiacenter.org/archive.html. Accessed 25 September 2001.

Domrin, Alexander N. 2001. *Civil Society in Russia: A Historic Necessity or a New Round of Social Engineering?* Paper prepared for the conference "Ten Years Later: The Development of Russian Civil Society," Wittenburg University, Springfield, OH, 3 November.

Economist. 2000. "Sins of the Secular Missionaries." *The Economist*, vol. 354, no. 8155, 29 January: 25-27.

———. 2001. *Pocket World in Figures 2001 Edition*. London: The Economist.

European Commission. 1997. *Agreement on Partnership and Cooperation between the European Union and Russia, 27 November 1997*. europa.eu.int/comm/external_relations/russia/pca_legal/. Accessed 4 September 2002.

Fukuyama, Francis. 1995. *Trust: Social Virtues and the Creation of Prosperity*. New York: Free Press.

Gauslaa, Jon. 2001. "Aleksander Nikitin Wins in Supreme Court," Bellona Foundation, 14 September. www.bellona.no/imaker?id=21867&sub=1. Accessed 10 January 2002.

Gosudarstvennyi komitet Rossisskoi Federatsiia po okhrane okruzhaiuschei sredy. 1999. *Gosudarstvennyi doklad o sostoyanii okruzhaiuschei prirodnoi sredy rossiiskoi federatsii v 1999 godu*. Rossiisskoye Ekologicheskoye Federalnoye Informatsionnoye Agestvo. www.mnr.gov.ru/text/4/Gosdoklad99/show_doc.php?gid=4&file=Contents.htm. Accessed 3 March 2002.

Grazhdanskii Forum (Civil Forum). 2001. *Grazhdanskii Forum* 25 November 2001. www.civilforum.ru. Accessed 25 January 2002. Website could not be accessed on 5 September 2002.

Henry, Laura. 2001. "The Greening of Grassroots Democracy? The Russian Environmental Movement, Foreign Aid, and Democratization." *Berkeley Program in Soviet and Post-Soviet Studies*. Paper 2001_03-henr. Berkeley: University of California at Berkeley, Institute of Slavic, East European, and Eurasian Studies.

Hertzman, Clyde. 1995. *Environment and Health in Central and Eastern Europe: A Report for the Environmental Action Program for Central and Eastern Europe*. Washington, D.C.: World Bank.

Human Rights Online. 1995. Federalny Zakon "O nekomercheskikh organizatsiyakh," 8 January. www.hro.org/docs/rlex/nco/index.htm. Accessed 1 November 2001.

Institute mirovoi ekonomiki i mezhdunarodnykh otnoshenii Rossiiskoi akademii nauk. 1998. *Grazhdanskoye obschestvo: Mirovoi opyt i problemy Rossii*. Moscow: Editorial URSS.

Janco, Gerard. 1991. "Nevada-Semipalatinsk—The Soviet Union's Anti-Nuclear Movement: An Interview with Almaz Estekov," in *USCAR Reports: Cleaning Up the Environment in the Soviet Union and Eastern Europe*, vol. 1, no. 4. Washington, D.C.: The Center for American-Eurasian Studies and Relations. www.eurasiacenter.org/archive.html. Accessed 25 September 2001.

Jordan, Lisa, and Peter Van Tuijl. 2000. "Political Responsibility in Transnational NGO Advocacy." *World Development*, vol. 28, no. 12: 2052-2065.

Keane, John. 1998. *Civil Society: Old Images, New Visions*. Stanford, CA: Stanford University Press.

Keohane, Robert O., Peter M. Haas, and Marc A. Levy. 1993. "The Effectiveness of International Environmental Institutions," in Robert O. Keohane, Peter M. Haas, and

Marc A. Levy (eds.), *Institutions for the Earth: Sources of Effective International Environmental Protection*. Cambridge, MA: MIT Press: 3-26.

Klose, Eliza K. 1998. "US Foundations Find Civil Society Is Taking Root: A Survey of Funders on Third Sector Development." *Give and Take Quarterly*, vol. 1, no. 1. www.isar.org/isar/archive/GT/GT1eliza.html. Accessed 1 October 2001.

Kogai, E. A. 2000. "Ekolgiia i zdorovie cheloveka." *Sotsial'no-gumanitarnie znaniia*, no. 3: 107-125.

Konstitutsiia Rossiiskoi Federatsii. 1993. www.hro.org/docs/rlex/index.htm. Accessed 10 October 2001.

Lehning, Percy B. 1998. "Towards a Multi-cultural Civil Society: The Role of Social Capital and Democratic Citizenship," in Amanda Bernard, Henry Helmich, and Percy B. Lehning (eds.), *Civil Society and International Development*. Paris: OECD.

Luneva, L. 1998. "Obshchestvennoye Dvizheniye ili Tretii Sektor?" *Byulleten' Moskovskogo ISAR*, no. 7: 24-25.

Ministerstvo prirodnyx resursov Rossiisskoi Federatsii. 2002. Federalny Zakon "Ob okhrane okruzhayuschei sredi," 10 January. www.priroda.ru/index.php?32+1+&txt=zacon.html. Accessed 6 July 2002.

Negosudarstvennie ekologicheskie organizatsii Sankt-Peterburga. 2002. St. Petersburg Nongovernmental Organizations. www.ecoart.net.ru/eco/list.htm. Accessed 1 March 2002.

North, Douglass C. 1990. *Institutions, Institutional Change and Economic Performance*. Cambridge: Cambridge University Press.

Peterson, D. J. 1993. *Troubled Lands: The Legacy of Soviet Environmental Destruction*. Boulder, CO: Westview Press.

Petrova, V. F. 1999. *Demokratiia posttolitarnogo mira: istoriia i sovremennost*. Almaty, Kazakhstan: Atamura.

Petukhov, Vladimir. 1999. "Politicheskoe uchastie Rossiyan: Kharakter, Formy, osnovnye tendentsii," in Michael McFaul and Andrei Ryabov (eds.), *Rossiiskoe obschestvo: stanovlenie demokraticheskikh tsennostei?* Moscow: Carnegie Center for International Peace: 198-228.

Pinsker, Dmitry. 2001. "The Kremlin Tames Civil Society." *Russia Journal*, 16-22 November. www.russiajournal.com/weekly/article.shtml?ad=5430. Accessed 25 November 2001.

Powell, Leslie. 2001. *Evaluating Strategies: Foreign Foundations and Russian Environmental NGOs*. Report prepared for the Columbia University Project on Evaluating Western NGO Strategies for Democratization and the Reduction of Ethnic Conflict in the Former Communist States. Washington, D.C.: Carnegie Endowment for International Peace.

Pustintsev, Boris. 2001. "The Kremlin and Civil Society." *Moscow Times*, 22 October: 10.

Putin, Vladimir. 2001. "States Are Judged by the Level of Individual Liberty: Excerpts from President Vladimir Putin's Speech at the Civil Forum." *Johnson's Russia List*, 22 November. www.cdi.org/russia/johnson/5561-4.cfm. Accessed 1 July 2002.

Putnam, Robert. 1993. *Making Democracy Work: Civic Traditions in Modern Italy*. Princeton, NJ: Princeton University Press.

Richter, James. 1999. "NGO Image in the FSU: What's the Public View?" *Give and Take Quarterly*, spring. www.isar.org/isar/archive/GT/GT4Richter.html. Accessed 15 March 2001.

Sampson, Steve. 1996. "The Social Life of Projects: Importing Civil Society to Albania," in Chris Hann and Elizabeth Dunn (eds.), *Civil Society: Challenging Western Models.* London: Routledge, 121-142.

Sargent, Daniel. 1999. Community Foundation Development in Poland: Building Cooperation in Support of Philanthropy. Paper in partial fulfillment for the requirements of Master of Arts Degree, Russian and East European Institute, Bloomington, IN: Indiana University.

Shlapentokh, Vladimir. 2001. "Hobbes and Locke at Odds in Putin's Russia." Paper prepared for the Conference "Ten Years Later: The Development of Russian Civil Society," Wittenburg University, Springfield, OH, 3 November.

Sievers, Eric W. 2001. "The Caspian, Regional Seas, and the Case for a Cultural Study of Law." *Georgetown International Law Review,* vol. 13: 361-415.

Socio-Ecological Union. 2001. SEU Member List. www.seu.ru/members/list.htm. Accessed 9 January 2004.

Tahoe-Baikal Institute. 2002. Tahoe-Baikal Institute, 15 January. www.tahoebaikal.org. Accessed 1 March 2002.

Tocqueville, Alexis de. 1990. *Democracy in America.* Vol. 2. New York: Vintage Books.

Turnock, David. 2002. "The Soviet Union and Successor States," in *Environmental Problems of East Central Europe.* London: Routledge, 92-116.

Tysiachniouk, Maria, and Alexander Karpov. 1998. "Development of Environmental Nongovernmental Organizations in Russia," Presented at the Third International Conference of the International Society for Third Sector Research, 8-11 July, Geneva, Switzerland: ISTSR.

United Nations. 1998. "NGOs—Losing the Moral High Ground?" *UN Chronicle,* vol. 35, no. 1: 93-94.

U.S. Department of State. 2000. *U.S. Government Assistance to and Cooperative Activities with the New Independent States of the Former Soviet Union: FY 1999 Annual Report.* Washington, D.C.: U.S. Department of State.

U.S. General Accounting Office. 1995. *Former Soviet Union—U.S. Bilateral Program Lacks Effective Coordination.* Letter Report, 02/07/95, GAO/NSIAD-95-10. Washington, D.C.: United States General Accounting Office.

———. 2000. *Foreign Assistance: International Efforts to Aid Russia's Transition Have Had Mixed Results.* Chapter Report, 11/01/2000, GAO/GAO-01-8. Washington, D.C.: United States General Accounting Office.

Wedel, Janine. 2001. *Collision and Collusion: The Strange Case of Western Aid to Eastern Europe.* New York: Palgrave Macmillan.

Weir, Fred. 2002. "Russia's Fledgling Civil Society." *Christian Science Monitor.* 30 July: 6.

Wolfson, Ze'ev, and Vladimir Butenko. 1992. "The Green Movement in the USSR and Eastern Europe," in Matthias Finger (ed.), *Research in Social Movements, Conflicts and Change.* Greenwich, CT: JAI Press, 42-50.

Zabelin, S. 2001. "Vstrecha Presidenta RF c obschestvennost'iu," Bulletin *Ekologiia i prava cheloveka,* no. 401, 16 June. www.index.org.ru/othproj/eco/401.html. Accessed 10 September 2001.

Chapter 7

Conclusion: Lessons Learned for the Road Forward

Matthew R. Auer

The preceding chapters infer that there are many elements common to the environmental reform experiences of post-Communist CEE countries and Russia. Foremost among them is the profound influence of external actors in shaping domestic environmental institutions. Foreign governments, intergovernmental institutions, and international financial institutions (IFIs) will loom large in CEE and Russian environmental affairs for the foreseeable future.

First, external actors are key enablers of environmental reforms through environment-oriented aid. In the 1990s, all nations in the region were environmental aid beneficiaries, though aid was distributed unevenly. Poland, Hungary, the Czech Republic, Russia, and Romania absorbed more than 50 percent of the total, environment-oriented aid to CEE and the New Independent States through the mid-1990s. Recipients' dependence on this aid for environmental investments varied from country to country. Foreign-sponsored grants and loans amounted to less than 10 percent of investment expenditures in Poland, around 25 percent in Hungary, 80 percent in Lithuania, and nearly 100 percent in Georgia (OECD, 1999: 134).

Second, high quality, domestic environmental institutions are necessary credentials for joining Europe's most important political club. For countries seeking EU membership, acceding to European environmental norms became nothing less than an obsession in the early years of the new century. For most EU candidates, transposing EU environmental legislation and developing credible domestic environmental legislation were one and the same.

Foreign Actors as Key Players in CEE and Russian Environmental Affairs

Returning to the three primary questions this book sets out to answer, consider question number two which addresses the role of external actors, specifically. (To what extent have external actors helped or hindered environmental reforms in CEE and Russia?) The Estonian and Russian cases presented in the last two chapters accent the pluses and minuses of external actors' influences in especially vivid and contrasting ways. Estonia's remarkable achievements in remediating dirty, heavy industries and cleaning up contaminated, ex-military sites could not have occurred without generous aid and technical assistance from the European Union and Estonia's neighbor, Finland. The latter extended far less capital assistance to Estonia than did either the EU or IFIs, but the relative importance of Finland's contributions was vast. Estonians look north to their ethnic cousins for models of economic and social development. Finnish aid found Finns and Estonians working side by side with Finns delivering the "soft assistance" that enabled the more costly "hard assistance" to function. To illustrate, when an IFI provided loans to upgrade Tallinn's sewage treatment plant, water treatment experts from Helsinki moved into the Estonian capital and lived there year-round, training dozens of Estonian industrial managers and engineers to run a modern water company.

The Russian experience with environment-oriented aid could hardly be more different. Though some foreign aid was pivotal for environmental protection in Russia—for example, the overhaul of St. Petersburg's wastewater treatment systems[1]—other contributions languished, including the many millions of dollars spent to raise public consciousness of environmental problems and to assist advocacy-oriented NGOs. The aid was well-intentioned. But in many cases, it built only the shells of institutions or more accurately, built organizations *without* institutions. Some grants covered the costs of salaries and kept office equipment running—critical functions for any organization—but rules and incentives to encourage the recipients' good performance were soft-pedaled or simply were never instituted. Those rules could have included, for example, making continued funding contingent on verifiable progress in reaching program goals or in moving recipients toward financial independence. But to attract and keep donors interested, polished interviewing and English-language communication skills were more valuable to recipients than were clear mission statements or serious business plans.

It was not as though private foundations and bilateral aid agencies were unfamiliar with the pitfalls of institution-building through foreign aid. Experts in development know well the risks of fostering dependency and the imperative of creating a sense of "ownership" among grantees. Nevertheless, even when donors were diligent in sponsoring only the most selfless and serious-minded NGOs, both the grantors and the grantees failed to win the confidence of essential domestic actors, including ordinary Russians. When average citizens became convinced that Russian NGOs were lackeys of the West, the NGOs could only founder. Donors failed to do sufficient homework on the larger, political institutional arena where NGO programs were deployed. Understanding and being able to counter citizens' misgivings (not to mention politicians' doubts) about NGOs was just as important—if not more crucial—than getting right the technical facets of sponsored programs themselves.

Donors also failed to create institutional incentives to build bridges between civic actors in Russia. Russian political elites mistrust NGOs and vice versa, but NGOs also mistrust one another. This helps the preservers of the status quo who prosper when resource-deprived and politically marginalized opponents are divided. Donor resources are scarce and competition for these resources is fierce, intensifying noncooperation among NGOs. These problems are apparent even in relatively wealthy CEE countries, like the Czech Republic. The latter has "graduated" from the rolls of most bilateral aid programs and has bid farewell to several private donors who closed out their programs. Grant programs sponsored by Czech ministries help fill some of the funding gaps for NGOs. These grants are available mostly on a competitive basis, and in selecting grant recipients some critics insist that the government favors organizations that refrain from forcefully challenging official policies.

Lack of trust between key actors not only undermines participatory environmental policy making in CEE and Russia; it risks injuring environmental protection efforts in Europe, generally. However vigorous and thorough are Brussels's attempts to ensure complete transposition of EU environmental norms by CEE countries, moral hazard remains. Bell's chapter, perhaps more than any other in this volume, considers the various measures that the EU relies on to assure accession countries' *implementation* of EU laws, and not merely the approximation of those laws in domestic legislation. Nevertheless, the earnestness of CEE governments' efforts to administer and enforce these laws and regulations will not be fully known for years to come. In determining if CEE countries are playing by the rules, EU auditors are relying primarily on process-oriented performance indicators, such as milestones reached in adapting domestic laws and regulations. Ex post facto examinations of environmental conditions are true tests of institutional reforms, but decisive, natural environmental measures of institutional performance may be unavailable until well into the decade or beyond.

Of grave concern to environmentalists is that the domestic implementation of EU norms will stumble because regulated actors and society at large in CEE lack "ownership" of the norms and the processes to institutionalize them. The transposition process is distinctly top-down. Public hearings on EU environment-related projects tend to be quiet affairs and public comment on new, draft environmental laws is often dominated by a few, elite national NGOs or international NGOs with local affiliates. On occasions when NGOs are shut out of governmental meetings dealing with environmental aspects of EU development projects (see chapter 2), very few citizens hear the NGOs' complaints.

This contrasts with the more spontaneous, at times unruly, and often conse-quential participation of NGOs and citizens in environmental institutional pro-cesses in the United States and some Western European countries.[2] Strict rules governing liability for hazardous waste contamination in the United States, such as those embodied in Superfund, are prominent examples of laws spurred from the bottom-up rather than the top-down. The worry is that absent a similar fo-mentation of grassroots demands for environmental protection, EU norms will not resonate with ordinary citizens and might be willfully ignored by polluters.

This is not simply a matter of whether or not externally generated ideas and initiatives can take deep root in CEE and Russia. Historical examples of foreign institutions that created revolutionary changes in societies that imported those institutions are too numerous to mention. But it is difficult to find a historical analogy for the enormously complex and subtle process of EU approximation—a multinational endeavor characterized by a sense of urgency, and by simultane-ous political, administrative, and societal consent to and comprehension of highly specific norms dealing with issue arenas as disparate as free movement of persons; customs duties; corporate law; wildlife protection; agricultural policy; health policy; and information sharing. It is fair to query whether CEE and other accession countries, and perhaps even Russia someday,[3] can fairly digest such a rich meal.

Sustainable Development in Europe as an Exercise in Problem Definition

As mentioned previously, EU auditors may not know for years whether CEE governments' promises to step up environmental protection are yielding satis-factory environmental dividends. The approximation process represents an elaborate honor system whereby EU members rely on indicators of policy change in CEE as a proxy for policy-driven outcomes.

Indicators of policy change can be valuable nonetheless. Decision makers can hone in and harvest strategies that have worked well in analogous con-texts— all in an effort to replicate preferred policy outcomes (Brunner and Klein, 1999). In a sense, this is precisely the tack adopted by the EU as it re-quires candidates to adopt the entire body of EU legislation (the *acquis*).

A larger question remains (indeed, it is question 3 in this book) whether the EU's environmental directives and related legislation are appropriate bases for protecting the environment. The EU is keeping score of a complicated game; it is tracking candidates' progress to internalize community norms. Less frequently contemplated is whether EU environmental norms, themselves, are adequate to ensure a clean environment and ample, high quality natural resources for present and future generations.

Querying about the ultimate adequacy of EU environmental institutions is different than worrying about whether EU norms will take root in CEE countries. It is still possible for CEE environmentalists and citizens at large to lend vigorous support to the EU accession process, yet Europeans end up losers because the rules themselves failed to secure community aims.

In 2001, the OECD published its *Environmental Outlook*—a survey of environmental trends and a forecast for environmental quality to 2020 for member countries, including several CEE countries. The authors used traffic lights to signal key findings in the report: green indicated that environmentally deleterious pressures were decreasing. A yellow light signaled areas of uncertainty or potential problems. Serious problems or problems expected to worsen were marked red. Results from the OECD survey corroborate several of the findings of this book and provide a basis for answering the book's first question, namely, What are the accomplishments and shortcomings of nearly fifteen years of environmental policy reforms in CEE and Russia?

Environmental trends earning green lights included steep declines in ambient lead levels; diminishing emissions of various pollutants to the atmosphere, including sulfur oxides, carbon monoxide, and some particulates; and increased rates of waste recycling, among other improvements (OECD, 2001: 17-20). Yellow warning lights underscored many regions' declining per capita water supply; the paucity of countries meeting basic water quality objectives; and uncertainties about the health and environmental effects of toxins and certain biotechnologies. But the red traffic light headed the longest list of parameters; several culprits are problems endemic to CEE and to Russia. Among the most serious are declining urban air quality—a dilemma detailed in most chapters of this book. Also, CEE countries that are members of the OECD are important contributors to a problem that many experts consider most worrisome of all: global climate change.

The Kyoto Protocol requires most OECD nations to reduce their greenhouse gas emissions by approximately 5 percent below 1990 levels by 2008 to 2012. Nevertheless, the OECD expects its member states' emissions to rise by another 33 percent through 2020 (OECD, 2001: 19). More cars and trucks traveling more miles will account for a large portion of these new emissions. Motor vehicles in OECD countries will travel 40 percent more kilometers in 2020 versus 1997; air kilometers per passenger will triple during this same period (OECD, 2001: 19).

Despite these worrisome forecasts, an enlarged EU will not necessarily lead the way to global climate ruin. Most European countries, after all, are bound to the Kyoto Protocol, whereas the world's largest aggregate greenhouse gas emitter, the United States, remains on the sideline as this book goes to press.

But it is not just Kyoto obligations that provide a glimmer of hope for Europe and the rest of the world. In 2002, California's governor signed a bill mandating strict cuts in carbon dioxide emissions beginning with 2008 model year automobiles (Hakim, 2002: A3). California leads all other American states in promulgating stiff prohibitions on tailpipe emissions; it has done so for decades. Its tough laws impress environmental authorities in Europe so much so that some EU countries model their own rules after California's. Peter Sand calls this practice "model diffusion," whereby countries voluntarily adopt foreign regulatory schemes (Sand, 1991: 261). If in the future the EU is too proud to merely diffuse California's environmental standards, Europe could challenge the Golden State to a contest of environmentally progressive rule making. Such a competition might short circuit the OECD's gloomy projection for markedly higher greenhouse gas emissions.

Enrolling CEE countries and even Russia in a prospective regional contest for enlightened environmental leadership is not as unrealistic as skeptics might imagine. Many CEE countries' environmental protection efforts paid off during the 1990s. As authors in this volume attest, and as reaffirmed by others (see, e.g., Carter and Turnock, 2002, and Pavlínek and Pickles, 2000), these achievements were neither temporary nor illusory: particularly in the mid-to-late 1990s, steep declines in air pollutants such as sulfur dioxide and certain particulates resulted from policy reforms, environmental investments by industry, and the emergence of less-polluting leading economic sectors. Revived economic growth was not accompanied by increased loadings of these contaminants; pessimists had predicted the opposite. Policy interventions were instrumental in achieving lasting relief from pollution pressures.

Moreover, most environmental institutions in CEE (and to a lesser extent in Russia) are more capable today of administering environmental rules and regulations than at any time during the Communist era. This is not to say that these institutions function optimally. Charges and penalties on pollution are generally too low or are poorly enforced; environmental inspectorates are understaffed; illegal logging continues apace; regulators are scrambling to make good on recently transposed EU environmental directives; and many other challenges and constraints confound the region's environmental authorities. Nevertheless, in the twenty-first century, parliaments in countries like Poland, the Czech Republic, Hungary, Slovenia, and Estonia pass laws that are *actually* enforced. This is a dramatic change from pre-1989. Moreover, enforcement is at times both consistent and rigorous. For the purposes of comparison, it should be recognized that authorities in the wealthiest of OECD countries are occasionally accused of lax and inconsistent environmental regulatory enforcement.[4]

The passage of new laws and regulations in CEE stimulate other institutional activities, such as professional personnel recruitment (consider, for example, the great influxes of environmental lawyers to environmental ministries during the EU approximation process). New laws also cause polluters to at least contemplate environmental trade-offs, spurring plant managers to ask, for example, "Should I pay the charge? Or should I invest in pollution control equipment?" More often than not, the charge is too low for the second alternative to be selected. Nevertheless, during the Communist era, neither alternative would be considered, as the state would address the matter through budgetary sleight of hand and symbolic enforcement.

It is heartening to observe progress in the development of CEE countries' environmental institutional capacities. But these observations do not allay a concern raised toward the beginning of this section, namely, whether institutional rules and procedures adopted by the world's most advanced economies—and now, by EU accession countries—are adequate for promoting lasting environmental quality.

Some experts doubt whether Western-style environmental laws and policies promote long-term planetary survival. McDonough and Braungart (1998), for example, contend that North American and European countries' preferences for pollution prevention and clean production do not foster genuine sustainable development, but merely slow down the inexorable process of depleting the earth's natural resources. The skeptics might deem today's relatively more capable CEE environmental authorities as dupes who administer incomplete and inevitably futile policy remedies.

Closing Remarks

Ironically, citizens of Russia and of CEE may be closer than their wealthier Western European counterparts to understanding what long-term environmental protection ultimately entails, at least at the household level. During the Communist era, energy-profligate, pollution-prone industries exacted a huge toll on the environments of the planned economies, but citizens' own private rates of consumption generally did not. This is not to celebrate nor romanticize the privations that generations of Russians, Poles, Romanians, and other European peoples endured at the hands of totalitarian governments. But I have met more than one CEE citizen or Russian who mused about a simpler time when the finest afternoons were spent enjoying the outdoors, rather than working a second job to pay for a bigger car, and before long nights of conversation with family and friends were replaced by home entertainment centers and other material distractions.

CEE citizens certainly do not miss the political oppression and economic hardships that were part and parcel of this more "simple" way of life. Nevertheless, the nostalgic comments and anecdotes that Westerners hear from Eastern contacts suggest that CEE and Russian citizens' quality of life is not necessarily enhanced by gentrifying old neighborhoods and inaugurating new ones, by owning more stuff, or by embracing other trappings of a high throughput society. Moreover, many CEE citizens who are faring well in the post-Communist market economy nevertheless worry about growing disparities between societal haves and have-nots.

So far, the dispensation of knowledge, and the direction of authoritative demands between the EU and CEE have been mostly one way, with CEE countries on the receiving end. But EU politicians and citizens should listen closely for policy advice in the reminiscences of their newest club members. It seems plausible that long-term environmental quality in Europe, and indeed globally, will be assured as much by new inventions and environmentally friendly ways of generating wealth as by peoples' efforts to rediscover older, more temperate ways of living.

Notes

1. Bilateral and multilateral investments in the modernization of St. Petersburg's sanitary infrastructure began paying dividends after 2000. But during the preceding ten years, donors fretted over the slow pace of the projects' implementation and the on-and-off commitments from authorities in both Moscow and St. Petersburg. Much of the aid for these projects was organized under a regional, multistakeholder arrangement to clean up the Baltic Sea, overseen by the Baltic Marine Environment Protection Commission (HELCOM). As late as 1999, a senior official at Finland's Ministry of Environment grumbled, "Personally, I doubt whether the Russian government even knows what HELCOM's aim is. It is possible that none of St. Petersburg's municipal offices knows what HELCOM is" (Iloniemi, 1999: 35). The official also complained, "In Russia, it really still seems as if they couldn't care less about environmental issues, which indeed results in poor funding" (Lindfors, 2000: 41).

2. Even spontaneous and unscripted acts of public environmental defiance are infused with informal rules and rituals, and hence have institutional features. Consider, for example, conventions at play in a typical environmental protest rally. Peaceful, law-abiding protesters, by definition, obey community rules when they abjure violence; the marchers' forward progress inevitably ends at the steps of an important landmark, such as the statehouse or a polluter's headquarters or the margins of the endangered habitat that the marchers endeavor to protect; demonstrators' protests are often voiced in the form of call and response; and so on.

3. In fact (and as mentioned in chapter 6), Russia's harmonization of its environmental laws with that of the EU is a "priority area" in the EU-Russia Partnership and Cooperation Agreement which sets out to create a "common European economic and social space" (Wallstrom, 2001).

4. To illustrate, in 2002, the U.S. Environmental Protection Agency's director of regulatory enforcement (who had been appointed by a past Republican president) quit the agency, charging that the Bush administration willfully failed to take action on lawsuits filed against nine power companies that were blamed for one-fourth of the nation's annual sulfur dioxide emissions (Fiore, 2002: 17).

References

Brunner, Ronald D., and Roberta Klein. 1999. "Harvesting Experience: A Reappraisal of the U.S. Climate Change Action Plan." *Policy Sciences*, vol. 32, no. 2: 133-161.

Carter, F. W., and David Turnock (eds.). 2002. *Environmental Problems of East Central Europe*. London: Routledge.

Fiore, Faye. 2002. "Top EPA Enforcement Official Quits, Blasts Bush Policy." *Los Angeles Times*, 1 March: 17.

Hakim, Danny. 2002. "Detroit and California Rev Their Engines over Emissions." *New York Times*, 28 July: A3.

Iloniemi, E. 1999. "Nordic Dimensio." *Nordicum*, vol. 7: 35.

Lindfors, L. 2000. "The Baltic Sea—A Common Concern." *Nordicum*, vol. 8: 41.

McDonough, William, and Michael Braungart. 1998. "The Next Industrial Revolution." *Atlantic Monthly*, October: 82-86; 88-90; 92.

OECD. 1999. *Environment in the Transition to a Market Economy: Progress in Central and Eastern Europe and the New Independent States.* Paris: OECD.

———. 2001. *OECD Environmental Outlook.* Paris: OECD.

Pavlínek, Petr, and John Pickles. 2000. *Environmental Transitions: Transformation and Ecological Defence in Central and Eastern Europe.* London: Routledge.

Sand, Peter. 1991. "International Cooperation: The Environmental Experience," in J. Tuchman Mathews (ed.), *Preserving the Global Environment: The Challenge of Shared Leadership.* New York: W. W. Norton, 236-279.

Wallstrom, Margot. 2001. "Speech of Mrs. Margot Wallstrom, European Commissioner for the Environment, 'EU-Russia Environmental Challenges'," *Proceedings of the International Seminar on Environmental Aspects of the EU-Russia Northern Dimension*, Moscow, 11 May. Brussels: Commission of the European Communities.

Index

About the Contributors

Joshua E. Abrams has over ten years' experience administering environmental and capacity-building programs in the former Soviet Union, most notably as an environmental educator for the Peace Corps in Kazakhstan, and as regional outreach coordinator for the Eurasia Foundation in Central Asia. He received a master of arts in public administration and master of arts in Russian area studies from Indiana University in 2001.

Matthew R. Auer is associate professor of public and environmental affairs at the School of Public and Environmental Affairs at Indiana University. His research focuses on international forestry policy, comparative industrial and energy policy, and the politics of foreign aid. In recent years, he has authored several articles and book chapters on the performance of bilateral and multilateral environmental aid programs in Central and Eastern Europe and the Baltic Sea region. Dr. Auer is associate editor of the journal *Policy Sciences* and is a policy advisor to the U.S. Forest Service, the U.S. Agency for International Development, and the U.S. Department of Defense. He received a doctorate in forestry and environmental studies from Yale University.

Ruth Greenspan Bell directs IIDEA at Resources for the Future, helping former Soviet bloc as well as Asian countries build a culture of environmental compliance through more effective environmental protection and environmental public participation. Bell was senior advisor to the assistant secretary of state for the Bureau of Oceans and International Environmental and Scientific Affairs, and held management positions in the U.S. Environmental Protection Agency's

Office of General Counsel. She lived in Poland in the early post-Communist transition period and has worked throughout Central Europe. She publishes extensively, including about ways to stimulate better implementation of environmental requirements. She graduated from the University of California at Los Angeles and Boalt Hall School of Law (University of California, Berkeley). Bell is a member of the Council on Foreign Relations and sat on Boalt's National Alumni Board. Further information and publications can be found at www.rff.org/iidea.

Susan Legro currently serves as a regional coordinator for energy and climate change at the United Nations Development Programme, overseeing projects in Eurasia that are funded by the Global Environmental Facility. Prior to joining UNDP, she worked as a research scientist at Battelle Pacific Northwest National Laboratory, where she conducted research on the capacity of economies in transition to mitigate greenhouse gas emissions and managed a project to finance greenhouse gas reductions in Russian municipalities. In the early 1990s, she worked as a program associate for the Energy Efficiency Center, a Czech nongovernmental organization. She holds an undergraduate degree in Soviet Studies from Harvard University and master's degrees in international relations and public health from Columbia University. She speaks Czech and Russian.

M. Cristina Novac was born in Romania. She completed a bachelor's in business administration at the Economic Studies Academy in Bucharest and spent several years in regional health care administration before joining Brasov's School of Economic Sciences as assistant professor of marketing and international business. After earning several grants and scholarships abroad, she completed a master of public affairs in environmental policy and natural resource management at Indiana University. Currently, she works for the Ontario Ministry of the Environment (Canada), while pursuing a doctoral degree in policy analysis from Indiana University.